Judges and the Cities

Judges and the Cities

Interpreting Local Autonomy

Gordon L. Clark

94-19

The University of Chicago Press
Chicago and London

Gordon L. Clark is professor of public policy at the
School of Urban and Public Affairs at Carnegie-Mellon
University.

The University of Chicago Press, Chicago 60637
The University of Chicago Press, Ltd., London

94 93 92 91 90 89 88 87 86 85   54321

Library of Congress Cataloging in Publication Data

Clark, Gordon L.
  Judges and the cities.

  Bibliography: p.
  Includes index.
    1. Social institutions—United States.   2. Autonomy.
3. Local government—United States.   4. Social
structure—United States.   5. Local government—Law and
legislation—United States—Interpretation and
construction.   6. Judicial process—United States.
I. Title.
HN59.2.C57   1985   306'.0973   85-1018
ISBN 0-226-10753-1

For Shirley

Contents

Most terms in ordinary language have many uses, and if we don't notice this and try to correct it in a systematic discourse, we are going to find ourselves left with all the confusions that attend our ordinary thinking.

—Nelson Goodman, *Of Mind and Other Matters*

Preface

The theory and practice of urban public policy is wracked by debate, argument, and dissension. Few principles, if any, seem general enough to garner consensual support, and those that do seem so general as to be indeterminant in specific situations. Not only is there debate over the appropriateness of principles, there is much argument over what these principles mean in different circumstances. I believe that this debate is an inevitable aspect of the texture of our social lives—social and political heterogeneity is riddled with ambiguity and indeterminacy. As a consequence, institutions have a major role to play in our society. While they reflect social heterogeneity, being the representatives of various interests, values, and interpretations, they are at the same time the means of achieving social determinacy. Institutions resolve disputes and manufacture determinant interpretations of principles and policies in situations that require resolution for collective action. Hence, the courts, legislatures, and executive administrations are simultaneously representatives of dispute, the objects of dispute, active participants in dispute, and the final arbitrators of dispute.

Our institutions make and remake society through their interpretative and determinant actions. For instance, the courts, like the legislature, define and interpret interpersonal relationships, structure institutional relationships, including those between themselves and society, and define the relationships between institutions. Accordingly, there is no ready-made integrative social blueprint in my conception of social life. The rules and standards of social conduct are always being made and remade by our institutions. Therefore, we cannot appeal to a final, consensual, moral arbiter that is somehow unaffected by society and its schisms. Indeed, I suggest here that institutions are not only part of society, they are in many ways society itself, providing its form, character, and determinacy. I assume that society has no inherent or complete character and that any understanding of society requires an appreciation of what makes society in particular times and places.

In this book I am not concerned with deriving the necessary or required nature of institutions out of some ideal conception of human life. Rather, my interest is in how institutions structure and interpret social life in contemporary America. Specifically, the focus is on local government autonomy and on its meaning and interpretation in various circumstances. My analysis of contemporary disputes over local government power deals with how the courts adjudicate competing arguments regarding the meaning of local autonomy and how they fashion and manufacture determinant interpretations. At this level, the focus of the book is more on relationships between institutions, less on the necessary role(s) of institutions vis-à-vis liberal democratic society. In this respect, I utilize a state-centered mode of inquiry (introduced previously in Clark and Dear 1984) rather than a more traditional society-centered mode of social analysis.

My reasons for concentrating on local power and autonomy are threefold. First, research and teaching in urban studies and public policy have convinced me that any understanding of urban structure must account for the considerable power and influence of government policy. Of the recent developments in urban theory, none are more important than those concerned with understanding the local state and its role in the structuring of community life. Clearly there are many similarities between countries in how the public sector is spatially organized. These similarities have been the basis of a number of attempts to formulate a general theory of the local public sector. At the same time, and this is the second reason for concentrating on local autonomy, there are major differences between the United States and, for example, the United Kingdom, especially in terms of their attachment to the notion of local government itself. Few countries are so principled in their devotion to local autonomy and decentralized democracy as the United States.

The form of local government proper for some groups, however, is not the form desired by other groups. Unlike those in most other countries, political interest groups and scholars of various political persuasions in America are committed to the ideal of local autonomy. Local control of community resources is a major strategy of American left-wing progressive groups and is promoted to a level unknown in most other countries. Many right-wing groups also desire local autonomy, and while these various groups may not agree on the virtue of specific outcomes conceived by local governments (such as racial segregation), the ideal itself is rarely challenged. It seems to me that the principle of local autonomy is sustained by a variety of values and interpretations. Indeed, I would suggest that the only thing these groups agree on is the principle. The actual dimensions of local autonomy, its revelance in specific circumstances, and its interpretation are subject to continual debate and revision.

In the face of such heterogeneity of values and rationales, it is not surprising that so many issues related to local government power are subject to litigation. But, of course, this is another basic difference between the United States and other countries and is the third reason for my interest in local autonomy. Disputes over the interpretation of local government power, like many other aspects of American society, typically end up in the courts rather than in the legislative system. Social values, like local autonomy, are given determinant readings by the courts: in essence, social meaning is institutionally manufactured. In this respect, the judicial system is the major interpreter of American local autonomy, something unheard of in most other countries. Thus, in attempting to understand local autonomy, we have an opportunity to consider the role of the courts in American society.

This book is about American local government, what it means to different groups, and how determinant interpretations are reached amongst competing interpretations. My goal is to cast a critical light on the moral values that sustain local governments as well as the institutions that adjudicate and make meaning. In doing so, I am concerned with the institutional "interpretation" of local government power. As shall be seen however, institutions are not perfect instruments of social action. Their capacity to deliver unambiguous and defendable interpretations of common social categories is at best a sometime thing. At worst, institutions like the courts face a continual struggle to assert their legitimacy and virtue. In this regard, interpretation is conceived in this book as a highly political act involving disputes over doctrine, interests, and logic. While the courts have a special place in our society, they suffer no less than society itself from the plurality of social values.

Acknowledgments

This book was prompted by my involvement in a comparative study of North American urban land-use policy headed by Dr. Elliot Feldman of Harvard University's Center for International Affairs. We were fortunate to be sponsored by the Lincoln Land Institute of Cambridge, Massachusetts. Thanks to Elliot Feldman and the Lincoln Land Institute, I have been able to trace contemporary land-use issues from specific policies through to the role of our social institutions in adjudicating social conflict. I am pleased to be able to acknowledge their support.

Discussions with Gerry Suttles, Michael Dear, Meric Gertler, Richard Higgott, John Whiteman, and David Kennedy on contemporary social and legal theory also contributed greatly to the enterprise. Their guidance, enthusiasm, and encouragement are gratefully acknowledged. The faculty and staff of the University of Chicago Law School were particularly helpful and generous with their facilities and knowledge. Likewise, access to the resources of the Harvard Law School during the academic year 1982/83 was also very important. The Association of American Geographers kindly allowed me to use portions of my paper published in *Annals* (1984).

Of the many people who helped with the preparation of this book, Brad Hudson, Kathy Patillo, Meric Gertler, Paula Proia, and Diana Valdivia deserve special attention. Brad delved deep into the legal literature on local government power and provided a critical perspective on contemporary legal theory. Kathy interviewed local participants in the Boston jobs controversy and collected the material on the construction industry. Meric did much of the background research on Illinois and Ontario municipal statutes. Paula once again demonstrated her considerabe wordprocessing skills while Diana typed portions of the first draft of this book. Without all their help, this book would not have been completed.

1

Introduction

To understand the basic thrust and assumptions of this book, chapter 1 provides an overview of what is to come in subsequent chapters. At the outset, I should stress that I am interested in the modes of social theory, especially as these modes reflect upon society and what are understood to be its principal properties. The issues of most concern here are (1) how social discourse is structured and (2) how determinant interpretations are reached. With respect to these issues, two basic positions are compared and contrasted: the well-known logical positivist mode of social inquiry, which supposes that an objective and unique truth can be established, is contrasted with the less familiar notion of moral pluralism, which supposes that social knowledge is relative and heterogeneous and thus determinant interpretations must be manufactured.

From that position, I then move to the substantive concern of the book, local autonomy, and how I propose to study the issue. To do so means providing a brief overview of the interpretive problem—what local power means to different groups and individuals—as well as a theoretical frame of reference for tackling various interpretations. The chapter closes with an overview of the contents of the subsequent chapters.

Theory and Society

As students and teachers of social theory, we are conditioned to believe that there must be complete and determinant explanations of the phenomena we study. Similarly, in studying and analyzing public policy, we are accustomed to believe that, as academics, we have a special capacity for discerning the truth—a truth somehow independent of partisan politics. This is, after all, the promise of logical positivism.[1] Moreover, this is the dominant conception of doing "good science," which has been copied from the physical sciences. To the extent we accept logical positivism as the blueprint for social research, we value contributions to the literature by how they add to, complete, and generally advance our knowledge of social processes. According to this paradigm, knowledge building is an incremental process of discovery.[2]

If the positivist position is to be taken at all seriously, we must assume that the conduct of research depends upon two basic premises. First, cooperative scholarship, grounded in shared values of the meaning and intent of scholarship, builds more complete theories. Secondly, since research is conducted *on* society, not *in* society, social theorists have a separate and superior vantage point from which to understand social discourse.

These are the basic tenets of contemporary social science, tenets fostered by the professional academic elite and our institutions of knowledge. Universities and research foundations alike typically justify their actions in promoting particular research programs and rewarding faculty by appealing to these tenets. And ultimately, how our peers judge our intellectual contribution to social theory typically reduces, in this paradigm, to how we add to the store of knowledge. *New* facts, *better* theories, more *complete* descriptions, and *determinant* explanations are the raison d'être of the positivist theory of knowledge.[3]

One of the problems of this kind of theorizing is the arrogant imperialism of its practitioners. As Keat and Urry (1982) argued, the philosophical assumptions of logical positivism are taken for granted as if, for whatever reasons, the claims for logic and positivism are self-evident. Alternative traditions, such as realism and historicism, have fared poorly as datum points for judging various explanations of social phenomena although it is often the case that these traditions have been the rallying points for alternative radical explanations. Not only is logical positivism the *only* mode of inquiry for many, alternative methodological devices are summarily dismissed by perjoratives such as irrational, emotional, and subjective (see Elster 1983 for a more in-depth analysis).[4] This kind of labeling is a well-exercised social practice of the academic establishment, a point that has been noted by Foucault, amongst others. The irony, of course, is that it is rhetoric which is used to legitimate positivists' claims of exclusive knowledge, not undeniable facts; these facts don't exist.

The second, and surely more insidious, problem with the positivist theory of knowledge is its treatment of political debate and public policy. As a mode of inquiry, it presumes that social debate can be uniquely resolved. The assumption of determinacy depends upon the existence of *one* truth—an exclusive interpretation of reality justified by appeal to supposedly neutral facts and expert witness. If debate persists despite expert testimony, such opposing interpretations of reality are wont to be dismissed as irrational or as ideology or both. Indeed, Daniel Bell's famous dictum of the "end of ideology," proclaimed at the end of the

1950s, reflected an unquestioned belief in the power of logical positivism to arrive at complete and determinant truth(s). Social inquiry, according to this model, must be outside society because political debate is inevitably biased.

Generally, positivists suppose that the facts should speak for themselves and moral beliefs should be adjudicated according to the pure flame of empiricism.[5] In this manner, political conflict would be replaced by political consensualism, and ideology would be replaced by the facts. Essentially, democratic pluralism itself would be replaced by a single-minded truth. It is not surprising that this vision of intellectual virtue has been equated with political totalitarianism for, as in Aldous Huxley's *Brave New World*, it denies individuals their separate and sincerely held moral visions of society. Indeed, it challenges the right of people to make decisions against the advice of this model of social discourse, whether or not these decisions are right or wrong.

Not only does logical positivism deny firmly held but diverse moral beliefs, it also suppose a quite rigid framework for the design of public policy. The "new science" of policy analysis proposed by Stokey and Zeckhauser (1978) ignores the substantive ends of policy by focusing on the rationality of the means. It is thought that if the procedures of policymaking are rational or logical or somehow efficient according to some external test of validity, then we need not concern ourselves with outcomes.[6] Furthermore, by concentrating on procedures, all the tools of social science can be brought to bear without being compromised by values. According to this paradigm, public policies must be justified in terms of their coherence and correlation with higher-order procedural principles. Furthermore, it is assumed that these procedures are conceived unambiguously, that is, they have determinate interpretations. And it is assumed that these procedures are neutral and beyond debate. By reference to rationality, logic, and coherence, it is hoped that value judgements (like the proper design of policy) can be circumvented.

Yet social theory and social practice are never so logical, never so unambiguous, and never so complete as we are led to believe. As social theorists, we often disagree over the meaning(s) of social symbols, and the relevance of social contexts in making meaning out of symbols. Similarly, as active social individuals we have to deal with others and their different social experiences.[7] Indeed, we are continually confronted with such an incredible variety of values, morals, and interpretations, that it is difficult just retaining our worldview, let alone integrating others' views with our own. There seems to be no one complete theory of society that is capable of accommodating this diversity, as there seems to be no one complete procedural device which can claim unanimous public support. Inevitably, outcomes matter and are interpreted and valued differently.

Reasons for this social heterogeneity range from the most obvious to the most subtle.

Obviously, as events unfold, any understanding of society and its structure changes. And, as the environment changes, so too does any understanding of our own place vis-à-vis society. Decision rules, rationales, and frameworks are continually revised as new information becomes available. Thus, there is a continual interplay between how we act and what we wish to achieve—ends and means are inextricably tied together and depend upon particular circumstances (Walzer 1983). To assume otherwise would be to isolate human agency from its desires (Sen 1982). Of course, some might argue that the fact that the environment changes doesn't necessarily invalidate the notion of the existence of unique determinancy, and, in fact, it may be entirely consistent with the physical sciences version of good science. That is, more information could mean a more complete social theory and a more determinant social practice. But there are three more subtle problems with this response that are hardly ever acknowledged.

First, if analysis starts with different world views, no new event will ever look quite the same to different people. Events may have no uniform importance for various intepretive frameworks. In this respect, since social heterogeneity of values, morals, and beliefs begins with social position, our interpretive frameworks will vary as well. In this sense, time and place make us what we are, as much as our conscious agency manipulates our context (Williams 1979). Thus, what is inspired to, how events are interpreted as they ought to be, and how meaning is given to everyday life is both a liberating and an intensely political act.

At this point, proponents of the positivist theory of social determinism might still argue that even this *problem* can be resolved. Presumably, if all information were shared, then interpretations could be iteratively revised until common agreement is reached. However, my second point is that not only do interpretations determine actions, individual responses to events are required before all information can be collected. Few, if any of us, have the luxury of being able to sit out changing circumstances. Our social world must be then characterized as a heterogeneous set of overlapping interpretations and actions, with each interpretation being made without complete knowledge or understanding of others' perceptions. Because people live in a world which cannot be ignored, people are required to respond to circumstances. In these circumstances, rationality is circumstantial.

My third point is that knowledge cannot be a neutral resource. We profit from other peoples' limited knowledge and are similarly vulnerable to the relative positions of others vis-à-vis knowledge of changing circumstances. Inevitably, knowledge is a strategic variable that reflects upon our social position, power, and ability to persuade others of the virtue of our own opinions. Cooperative knowledge sharing depends on a prior agreement on the ends and means of social discourse. As such, knowledge sharing presupposes social homogeneity, not heterogenity, as well as the existence of a unique and determinant truth. These assumptions hardly capture the range of contemporary social values and their conflicts.

The implications of this pluralist model of social discourse are far-reaching and will occupy us for much of the book.[8] For instance, social heterogeneity implies a kind of moral relativism rather than moral absolutism. Social values are ordered and arranged in terms of one another, not in the terms of one external truth. However, it is important to recognize that relativism does not have to mean chaos or arbitrariness.[9] As social position structures interpretations, and as circumstances require consistent responses (at least in terms of past actions and values) there may be a wide variety of consistently held opinions. Of course, some kind of social determinacy is still required if society is to act purposefully. What must be also acknowledged, however, is that social decision making is itself caught within this heterogeneous fabric.

To put it most crudely, not only may there be disagreements over specific policies, such as the efficacy of tax credits for the gentrification of inner-city areas, there are likely to be disagreements over principles, such as the virtue of private property. And, to take this argument to its ultimate conclusion, there will not only be disagreements over what is known, there are also likely to be disagreements about how we know; our models of knowledge are part of the debate. Once there is disagreement over how knowledge itself is conceived, we must also recognize that there can be no agnostic, superintegrative framework that can rationalize and reduce competing social visions to one determinant truth. In this respect, social heterogeneity is inevitable and inescapable. While social determinacy is required for social action, such determinacy is always contested and socially manufactured, not found.[10] Following Said (1983a), I believe that this reality and the resistance of contending movements give social discourse its texture.

Local Power and Autonomy

This book is about the heterogeneity of social values and how determinant interpretations are manufactured. I aim to take seriously the notion that moral heterogeneity is an inevitable, perhaps even a desirable, aspect of social life. My goal is to draw out the implications of this presumption for understanding the nature and interpretation of local government autonomy.

Local self-determination is a powerful image in American society, even though its interpretation is hardly unambiguous or, for that matter, universal. All kinds of people use this image and the idea of community as a rationale for action and judgment. For example, Chief Justice Burger of the U.S. Supreme Court has used the idea of community to justify local restrictions on matters as diverse as zoning, pornography, and even racial exclusion.[11] For Burger, community standards are a good test of the reasonableness of government action, although in many respects his particular community standards are often conservative (see Chesler 1983 for an in-depth critique and discussion). At the heart of notions such as community standards and local self-determination is a more general principle, that of local autonomy. Without some kind of autonomy, no community could have standards or even goals. And, a community without autonomy would hardly be distinguishable from the wider social system.

Local autonomy is defined here as the capacity of local governments to act in terms of their interests without fear of having their every decision scrutinized, reviewed, and reversed by higher tiers of the state. A good deal more effort will be spent in coming to more subtle definitions of autonomy in the following chapters. For present purposes, two implied assumptions need to be recognized, for two general principles of autonomy have to be explicated. It is assumed at the outset that local governments reflect and act, in part, in the interests of their constituents. Local governments are, at one level, the collective instruments of social aspirations and thus have a specific role to play in representing their constituents before other agencies and citizens. However I do not assume that local governments need represent all local citizens, or even the majority of citizens. Rather it is assumed that local government legitimacy rests, in part, on the extent to which it fulfills this representative role. It is also assumed that local governments are more than derivative symbols of democratic society; they are bureaucratic organizations with their own agendas of power and continuity (reproduction). Hence, it is assumed that local governments are purposeful actors and agents that interpret statutes, coerce their citizens, and manipulate their legitimacy.

These two assumptions are based on a previous study of the relationships between the state and capitalist society (Clark and Dear 1984). At first glance, this model of institutions may appear structuralist in that it is assumes that the state has a dominant role in arranging the social order.[12] However, I do not wholly subscribe to this view. For example, it is probably exaggeration to assume that the state has the monopoly over coercive powers. Similarly, I would not agree with those who argue that social relations (between classes, and between classes and the state) must be exclusively described in terms of subordination, domination, and reproduction. To assume this to be the case would be to dismiss the varied emancipatory values of society, and to impose an order akin to a ready-made world on society. Moral values have power in the sense that they are individually and collectively consciously desired and actively pursued. It would be hard to argue that statism is such an important value in this context. Nevertheless, it is also apparent that institutions have a wide range of powers including powers of social determination.

Two further dimensions of local autonomy require brief acknowledgment at this point. First, for autonomy to have any meaning, local governments must have a capacity to *initiate* actions over a range of important and trivial issues.[13] Nozick (1981)suggested that this kind of autonomy is crucial for a person's or community's self-definition and feeling of self-worth. Without a doubt, such autonomy refers to the capacity of a community to act in terms of its goals. Second, autonomy can also be understood as the capacity of an institution to act free from the review powers of other institutions. For local autonomy to have any strength, there must be a sphere of local *immunity*. Notice, however, that autonomy in this world is more a matter of degree than an absolute virtue. More will be made of these dimensions of autonomy is subsequent chapters. For present purposes, local autonomy is best understood as the capacity of local governments to act in such a way as to affirm (even transform) local or community goals.

Despite these definitions and assumptions, it should be quite evident that no single, complete, or exclusive definition of local autonomy is being offered in this chapter. This ambiguity is retained for good reason. After all, the meaning of local autonomy, like community, is the subject of many different interpretations. Providing a wide range of possible interpretations is part of the object of this book.

For instance, it could be easily observed that local autonomy is both revered and hated throughout the United States. It is promoted by many different groups, especially those who think that the community is the crucible of democratic life. Writers as diverse as Manuel Castells (1984), a socialist, and Robert Nozick (1974), a libertarian liberal, have contended that local autonomy (sometimes read as community integrity) is a fundamental principle of American democracy. But, of course, they value it for different reasons and interpret it from different standpoints. For Castells, community integrity is a necessary part of human existence. The community, according to Castells, is the locus of social life. For Castells, it is also a means of radically transforming society from the everyday life of local citizens through to the dominating influence on the nation-state. Castells has not always argued in this manner. *The Urban Question* (1977) suggested that there were no urban issues as such, rather class issues situated in space. Local autonomy in this latter kind of context would hardly matter, except perhaps in how specific classes might capture the local state and use it to further their interests. Castells's later writings support this strategy but go further by suggesting that urban life has a structural quality all its own.[14]

In contrast, more conservative writers such as Nozick have argued that local autonomy is a means of protecting individual freedom. In his theory, individuals have life-style preferences reflected in specific community ties, and it is this *derived* collectivity that local governments strive to protect from outside interference. In this manner, local governments protect the values and choices of their citizens through the exercise of their legitimate powers. Here, however, local autonomy may be contingent upon higher principles, particularly individual rights. Even so, local autonomy is a *necessary* component of Nozick's theory of social and individual association. And thus, both Nozick and Castells promote the notion of local autonomy in principle, but interpret its meaning (substantively and instrumentally) quite differently. Their agreements and disagreements are equally revealing.

It is also apparent that local autonomy is hated by many groups in American society. Interestingly enough, it is hated by minorities, by women, and by the disadvantaged in general. With respect to these groups, local autonomy has been interpreted as an exclusive haven for white privilege (Sager 1969), a cultural-spatial prison land-locking the emancipatory aspirations of women (R. Miller 1983), and the site of unattainable opportunity protected by government elites (Smith 1977).[15] Castells and Nozick may even agree with these interpretations in specific instances, but nevertheless understand these conditions quite differently. For instance, when blacks interpret community integrity as spatial exclusionism, a theorist following Nozick's lead may simply interpret exclusion as the legitimate protection of private property rights albeit undesirable as a social policy. Nathan Glazer (1981) has recently argued along these lines and even suggested that racial prejudice, being what it is, is almost impossible to overcome, as are geographical inequalities.

Similarly, when women identify local autonomy as stifling cultural-spatial homogeneity produced through male domination, a theorist following Nozick's lead may simply proclaim the virtues of voluntarily chosen preference communities. And, when the working classes associate economic domination and exploitation in single-employer factory towns with the principle of local autonomy, the Nozickian among us might simply point to the existence of universal mobility rights to justify the principle (if not the practice). In this context, it is obvious that social heterogeneity is a product of social structure or position and also a product of how society is understood theoretically.

There is a certain irony in the circumstances of these groups vis-à-vis the principle of local autonomy. It is as if they are the victims of local autonomy, even though their experiences are probably most consistent with the idealized image of decentralized democracy. That is, many minority groups have tightly bound spatial activity patterns compared with white middle-class males. The lives of the former groups are circumscribed by the walls of ghettos, and their opportunities constrained by a nexus of racial, income, and spatial segregation. On the other hand, white males have extraordinarily wide spatial networks, typically extending across whole metropolitan areas, even intermetropolitan areas. Their communities are temporary and purely residential, job advancement provides tremendous personal rewards but at the same time, requires a high degree of residential mobility.[16] The irony is that for the most successful groups of our society, local autonomy and community identity remain very much of an ideal while, for the disadvantaged, communities are all too enveloping.

One of the most forceful expressions of this type of argument comes from political theorist Carole Pateman (1983). Although dealing with a rather different issue, the virtues of democracy, her argument is much the same—interpretation has a great deal to do with social position. She argued that if you are a woman, democratic and for that matter most social institutions look like cliques or clubs composed and run for the benefit of specific male client groups. She suggested that women are rarely *given* full participation and instead provide auxiliary social services. For those schooled in conventional democratic theory this claim must seem absurd. After all, don't all people have the right to participate? Her point is that whatever the theoretical logic of democracy, its practice is obviously sexist, exclusionary, and discriminatory. Furthermore, she argued that the theory itself is used rhetorically, to legitimate the status quo. Women are thus doubly excluded: from the institution of democracy and from interpreting its meaning. Lest the reader dismiss this idea as fanciful, a similar point has been made by Burns (1983). He argued that the existence of institutions such as the male-only Bohemian Club of San Francisco should be interpreted as denying women their social rights to participate in the social lives of other groups. Accordingly, equality in these instances is a sham, but nevertheless legitimated by a very specific interpretation of the principle.

As was noted in the previous discussion of community identity and local autonomy, social theory is neither neutral nor capable of delivering a determinant, universal interpretation. Social position and social relationships are crucial aspects of any interpretation, as they are in any claim to an exclusive meaning.

This book is about how and why local government autonomy is interpreted as it is in the United States. The issues dealt with include the various meanings attached to local autonomy, how these meanings are conceived, and how their logic is structured by the events and contexts that produce disputes over meaning. Emphasis is on the heterogeneity of interpretation, the values implied, and the values denied by attempts to fashion determinant meanings. My objective is to understand the role of local government through an analysis of the manufacturing of meaning itself.

Overview

There are a number of ways we could go about executing this task. For instance, alternative utopian visions of urban life could be analyzed including feminist, anarchist, and pluralist notions of what local autonomy means. Hayden (1976, 1981), in particular, has done remarkable work along these lines, as has Friedmann (1979), albeit from a quite abstract vantage point. Alternatively, Perin's (1977) lead could be followed by an analysis of the social symbols of urban America for underlying values and dominant views. Whatever their virtues, these types of studies have tended to assume the existence of alternative visions of the local community without ever really asking how *specific* interpretations are attached to *specific* institutional arrangements of local powers. Recognition of the heterogeneity of social values is only the first step; we must also consider how dominant interpretations are arrived at, and how such interpretations are legitimated. Hayden, Friedmann, and others, such as Suttles (1972), have given us crucial insight into the plurality of moral visions of urban society; the question remains, however, how dominant interpretations are arrived at.

My study is based on a series of legal decisions drawn from U.S. federal and state courts as well as the Canadian Ontario provincial court system, which have dealt with the question of local government powers. Not only is the question of local powers of interest in its own right, it is also a vehicle for studying the processes of social interpretation and determination. In this context, the legal apparatus is a most important institution of contemporary North American society. Obviously, the courts provide a forum and means for settling disputes. And in this regard they must occupy a central position in any study of contemporary urban structure and the distribution of institutional powers. But the courts are more than neutral arbitrators; they provide determinant interpretations of urban powers in situations where there is a great deal of dispute over what local autonomy means. How they manufacture meaning, what principles they use to justify their particular interpretations of local powers, and how they understand contemporary society are all crucial issues to be considered.

Part I of this book is concerned with how social categories are interpreted in an institutional context. I follow the logic of my previous study of the capitalist state, which was premised on a state-centered mode of inquiry (Clark and Dear 1984). Rather than deriving the state out of the individual and collective preferences of citizens (the typical liberal strategy), the state is assumed to exist as a separate and relatively autonomous institution, only tenuously connected to capitalist society. It is argued here that judges have a great deal of legitimate and coercive power, as befitting their position in the legal apparatus. They have a major role, however, in the structural sense as well in sustaining social discourse. Generally, this mode of analysis depends on an understanding of the bases of social heterogeneity, in terms of both social theory and social practice.

Chapter 2 considers in depth the liberal and struturalist models of society. It is argued that both are incomplete, but nevertheless offer useful and different insights on the role of social strucuture in social discourse. Their respective inadequacies are, in turn, the advantages of their respective competitors. For instance, the failure of liberals to place individual action in community context is met by the structuralist model, which derives individual action from the community. This argument is extended by considering the various sources of social heterogeneity, including the problem of interpretation. Social and moral heterogeneity, pluralism, is argued to be a basic feature of contemporary North American society, indeed, perhaps all societies. I mean to suggest that there is no overarching superintegrative social theory that can reduce heterogeneous social values to consensual agreement. This argument progresses by suggesting that the common strategy of appealing to neutral facts is implausible, for the facts themselves reflect socially conceived categories. It is also argued that the urban realm, our institutions, and their moral values are products of competing and overlapping visions of the world itself. Any adjudication between competing values must be, by necessity, a political act. Meaning, valuation, and interpretation are, in this vision, socially manufactured.

Chapter 3 then considers the role of the judiciary in sustaining social discourse. Their role does not have to be considered unique; rather they are one of a number of such institutions. Their claims to legitimacy rest upon the rhetoric of the rule of law as much as their roles in creating social determinacy. Even so, in a democratic society such as the United States, there are tensions and conflicts over judicial interpretation, some of which stem from the fact that the judiciary is essentially undemocratic. In this chapter, it is argued that the legal apparatus makes possible social cohesion in a world of conflicting values and differing world views. Thus, this chapter is also about the relationships between law and society, assuming a quite specific social and political context: American liberal democracy. What judges do and how they rationalize their decisions in terms of the social heterogeneity of society are the principle issues of the chapter.

In chapter 4, I introduce a framework for the study of the local autonomy question. This framework uses the twin concepts of *initiative* and *immunity*, both of which can be shown to be derived out of Bentham's theory of judicial powers. A taxonomy of possible interpretations of local autonomy is presented, and it is this taxonomy that serves as a means of organizing substantive disputes over the meaning of the concept. A number of other congruent issues are also considered in chapter 4. In particular, the issues of how autonomy is reflected in local decision making—the extent of local discretion, the power of local officials, and the spatial-hierarchical structure of authority—are all considered.

Each chapter in Part II of this book aims at understanding a particular dispute over the interpretation of local autonomy. Starting with chapter 5, the recent decision of the U.S. Supreme Court to uphold Boston's residential quotas on city-financed construction employment is considered indepth. This case is an example of what we might term the *strong* autonomy position. This chapter is concerned with two interrelated issues. Most generally, we deal with the politics of Boston's resident-preference policy: how it came into being, who supported it, and how it was implemented. But I also argue that the politics and legalities of social discourse are very much related. The legal challenge to Boston's employment policy grew out of a political fight over signing and implementing the policy. This dispute was based on obvious patterns of racial and residential discrimination in local construction unions. Thus, at one level the legal challenge could be interpreted as a stratagem by the unions designed to thwart the objectives of the dominant political interests. Not only did the legal challenge remove the dispute from the local arena, it also transformed it into a different problem, one based on legal precedent and interpretation. Here, a further proposition is suggested: law is more than politics transposed.

In chapter 6 I turn to a more ambiguous definition of local autonomy, one based on a series of disputes between two Ontario cities and the provincewide land-use review board. This example illustrates in dramatic detail the importance of context in fashioning interpretations of local autonomy as well as the overarching rhetorical significance attached to notions such as decentralized democracy. Not only is the logic of liberalism explored with reference to the spatial division of power, local and province-level responsibilities are evaluated in terms of their correlation with liberal doctrine. While the match between theory and practice is not exact, the rhetoric of judicial adjudication depends on the veracity of liberal doctrine to justify decisions. Thus, this chapter seeks to understand local autonomy in the context of doctrinaire liberalism, a language of judicial decision making. The Canadian case is used both to illustrate the relevance of this approach to other countries and to emphasize the structural character of liberal institutional arrangements.

An interpretation of *weak* local autonomy is presented in chapter 7. This example is drawn from the Chicago, Illinois, area and concerns a series of disputes between the City of Des Plaines and the Metropolitan Sanitary District of Greater Chicago over the provision of urban public services. Questions of scale are important here, but so too are questions of responsibility and local authority. This example is a prelude to the next chapter, especially in how the courts resolve jurisdictional disputes while, at the same time, justifying their particular vision of local autonomy.

As a point of comparison and analysis, I also consider the relevance of an alternative mode of decision making, one which is thought by some to be superior to judicial decision making—empirically and theoretically based public finance rules. As applied to urban public facilities, many public finance theorists have argued that public finance theories provide a better way of making decisions regarding the optimal assignment of public services between jurisdictions. By invoking neoclassical positivist conceptions of economic analysis, this school of thought supposes that we can avoid what they identify as the "subjective nature of politics," and the "arbitrariness" of judicial decision. While I would agree with those who argue that judges are inevitably entwined in politics, I also contend in chapter 7 that conventional law and economics solutions are no less flawed.

The final chapter in Part II is concerned with a series of disputes in Colorado over the proper identification of "local matters." I trace the evolution of judicial doctrine beginning with an initial *strong* definition of local autonomy through to a very *weak* definition of local autonomy. The twists and turns in adjudication, the various rationales, and their various circumstances are given emphasis, as are the changing interpretations of local autonomy itself.

It is argued in chapter 8 that the doctrine of local matters is incredibly fragile. While often invoked as a defense of local autonomy, even as a blueprint for public administration, it has proved to be very unstable in changing circumstances, encouraging pragmatism, not firm rules of adjudication. Its American origins can be traced at least as far back as de

Tocqueville and his romantic conception of seventeenth-century New England life.[17] I suggest that de Tocqueville's conception of local autonomy is embodied in more recent theories of local public finance and local government legitimacy. As such, the doctrine of local matters promotes an idealized image of community life more than it does stable principles of how to organize governmental responsibilities efficiently. In this context, the doctrine of local matters is interpreted as a rhetorical device used to justify judicial discretion.

The final part of this book seeks to place these arguments and examples in a more substantive theoretical context. Chapter 9 is concerned in part with recent arguments made by Castells (1984), Paris (1983), Saunders (1983), and others regarding the urban basis of social conflict. It is suggested that contemporary social theory, whether structuralist or liberal, is fundamentally inadequate and that we need a new theory of personality and place. The various arguments and examples of this book are used to expand upon these issues. In doing so, the final chapter draws together the themes of the book and reconsiders the notion of interpretation itself. Here, I focus upon the importance of social and spatial position in interpreting society. The final issue considered is the limits of judicial authority in social discourse.

This study has two overriding goals. First, I wish to demonstrate the heterogeneity of social values as found in contemporary interpretations of local autonomy. Second, I wish to demonstrate that exclusive interpretations are socially manufactured, not somehow naturally found. In this regard I seek to go beyond the methodological prism (some might also say, prison) of logical positivism by directly embracing the relativism inherent in social life. New absolute knowledge is not the primary, or even secondary, goal of this study. Rather, I hope at the end of this book we will better understand how social categories are interpreted and how social meaning is institutionally structured.

I

Interpreting Social Categories

Following a rule is analogous to obeying an order.
We are trained to do so; we react to an order in a
particular way. But what if one person reacts in one
way and another in another to the order and training? Which one is right?

—Ludwig Wittgenstein, *Philosophical Investigations*

2

Public and Private Space

To begin analysis of the social interpretation of the urban landscape, we begin with the basic argument of this book, that is, that decentralized democratic government is legitimized and valued from a variety of moral perspectives. Indeed, the impression that social and moral heterogeneity buttress claims for significant local autonomy and power is overwhelming. The rationales and ideologies that promote local government autonomy intersect with one another, but are at the same time their own critiques. For instance, American liberalism values localities for their instrumental efficacy in sustaining individual sociability. In this manner, decentralized government is thought both to guarantee individual freedom and to socialize isolated individuals.[1]

At the same time, locales are at the core of the structuralist vision of community association. For structuralists, locales are the crucibles of social life. Indeed, individuals are conceived only in and through their community relationships, through their past and present in specific places.[2] Thus local governments are not only of instrumental importance, they are also thought of as the institutional representations of social structure and social identity. Notice, though, that liberals often argue that structuralism is overly deterministic and denies human agency.[3] On the other hand, structuralists insist that liberalism itself is fundamentally flawed by its failure to deal adequately with the conditioning of individual behavior by history and spatial position.[4] Yet both find virtue (as well as danger) in local autonomy.

The problem here is to understand not only how competing visions of social structure coexist, but also how they invest social institutions like local government with parallel virtues. More broadly, the problem is to understand the heterogeneity of social values as well as the processes of interpretation which apply meanings to our social structure. This issue is undeniably complex and, unlike most studies of urban form, takes as the object of study the very categories (in this case local autonomy and decentralized democracy) used by empiricists to describe reality.[5]

17

The argument of this chapter is twofold: First, society's institutions are normatively conceived, and, second, a continual tension exists between alternative visions and alternative interpretations of institutions. Social and moral heterogeneity is argued to be a basic feature of contemporary North American capitalism, indeed perhaps all societies (Goodman 1978). I mean to suggest that there is no overarching and superintegrative social theory that can reduce the heterogeneous social values to consensual agreement (Sen and Williams 1982). This argument is based upon a number of suppositions, all of which will require further explanation and justification as the chapter progresses. Generally, it is argued that the common strategy of appealing to neutral facts is implausible since the facts themselves reflect socially conceived normative categories. It is also argued that the urban realm, institutions, and their moral values are a product of competing and overlapping visions of the world itself. Any resolution or adjudication between competing images must be necessarily understood as a political act. Meaning, valuation, and interpretation are, in this view, socially manufactured.

Virtues of Local Autonomy

In a recent book, Manuel Castells (1984) proclaimed the virtues of American decentralized democracy, emphasizing in particular its potential for radical social transformation. By taking control of community institutions, Castells argued that social activists could improve local circumstances and foster a more "socially conscious" environment. His argument was made against the sweeping winds of conservatism at the national and even international levels. Nevertheless, his conception of the role of the community, its institutions, and its potential for radical change are found throughout the radical intellectual elite. For example, writing in this tradition, Mansbridge (1980) not only proclaimed the virtues of local democracy, she also provided in-depth case studies of local decision making in action. Her study of a set of New England town meetings was based upon a claim that local government offers people a chance to control their own destiny, a chance that is very rare in today's society. Her study attempted to go beyond the current climate of adversarial democracy (found in radical and more mainstream organizations alike) by demonstrating the possibilities of social cohesion and community solidarity at the local level.[6]

It would be easy to dismiss both Castells and Mansbridge as idealists, even romantics. They could more easily be accused of reinventing older utopian community ideals more often associated with Sir Thomas More and others (Davis 1981) than of providing a new blueprint for social discourse. Even so, it is now fashionable for radicals on both sides of the

Atlantic Ocean to propose grass-roots strategies for social change. In the United States, it has been suggested by writers such as Mansbridge that one of the lessons of the 1960s civil rights movement was that change can only be won by gaining the "hearts and minds" of ordinary people situated in particular locales. Although I would not wish to deny this vision its place in history as well as its place among several possible strategies, there remain many reasons for questioning the realistic chances of such an approach. For a start, its idealization of community and local struggle ignores the institutional limits placed on local governments by higher tiers of the state apparatus. It is one thing to capture the local state through democratic activism; it is an entirely different matter to use the apparatus of the local state against the wider social structure and its higher bureaucratic tiers. The limits placed on local autonomy by higher tiers are so well known that we could be excused for dismissing the radical grass-roots change strategy out of hand (Clark 1984). Even more difficult is their underlying conception of community. They seem to assume communities to be cooperative, socially integrated cultures, a vision that has more in common with liberal visions of homogeneous preference communities than radical conceptions of class antagonisms.

This radical vision of American local democracy is a mix of ideal conceptions of society and more pragmatic considerations of the best political strategy. The idealism embodied in this image has its roots in traditional communitarian conceptions of the proper social life of individuals. And in this mode of inquiry, utilitarianism has been identified as a major evil because of its denial of the necessity of social relations. The communitarian vision, in contrast, seeks to analyze people as human beings *only* in their social relations. That the community should be the sociogeographical focus of this conception reflects a particular history of American social organization as well as the recognition of the realities of people's everyday lives. Thus, the pragmatic need to mount an effective campaign for social change presumes that whatever change is envisaged must be relevant to the institutions that directly affect peoples' local lives. To be crude about it, Leninist centralism is eschewed in favor of Maoist decentralization. The model of the committed revolutionary leader rallying the masses through bold acts of courage is replaced by a model of the grass-roots local activist who patiently seeks to mobilize local communities around issues of direct concern.

Not only is this spatial model of social revolution important in the United States, it has had a profound impact on British left-wing intellectuals. David Miller (1983), writing on the current crisis of British democracy, promoted local democracy as a way out of the current impasse. He suggested that Britain should keep the national competitive party model but, at the same time, ensure maximum local democracy in government structure. His argument reflects a more general strategy of grass-roots activism undertaken by the leftwing of the British Labour party: that of local activism through the various borough councils. His analysis of the virtues of local democracy sounds strangely familiar. He sounds, in fact, just like an American liberal (such as Downs [1957]), even though he makes an attempt to distance himself from such logic.

More troublesome is the fact that Nozick's (1974) argument for local democracy as a means of enabling individuals to find their optimal preference community has many of the same implications of Miller, Mansbridge, and even Castells. For instance, all would agree that local democracy enables change, promotes social cohesion, and provides a way of facilitating the voice of the people. To say so is, of course, to risk labelling these writers as revisionists or as theorists only interested in the surface reflections of capitalist society. And we should acknowledge that their conceptions of society are *radically* different from Nozick. Nevertheless, the substantive outcome is much the same: local autonomy and decentralized democracy are *good* from many different perspectives.

A second example which illustrates both the virtues of local autonomy and the heterogeneity of the social values supporting the notion comes from the Reagan administration's recent attempts to construct a new federalism. Of course, Reagan's policies were not new in this regard. The history of American federalism is replete with new beginnings and old failures. Almost every president since the Revolution has promised a new way of allocating functions and responsibilities between the various spatial tiers of government. President Reagan's plans were not so different in this respect from his immediate predecessors: Presidents Carter, Ford, Nixon and others.[7] Essentially, they have all contributed to a debate that had its origins with Jefferson, Madison, Hamilton, and *The Federalist* papers at the end of the eighteenth century (Krouse 1983).

As an abstract concept, decentralized government seems to find favor among many different social groups. The functions, responsibilities, and powers of local government can be suitably legitimated by appeal to the most abstract principles. For example, the notion that governments should be responsible to the needs of the constituents is promoted by all kinds of groups—radicals, liberals, and conservatives alike. Not only does it find favor with political groups, academic theorists like Bennett (1980) promote it as an organizing principle for local public finance theory and policy. From this position, it is only a short step to the argument that local governments are the most responsive branch of government, therefore the best level at which to implement policy.[8]

Yet for all its abstract virtues, the practice of decentralized federalism is a very contentious issue. For example, civil rights groups, including the National Association for the Advancement of Colored People

(NAACP), have argued that state and local governments cannot be trusted to carry out fair elections. Barriers to voter registration and ballot box intimidation, as well as open terror and persecution, some have all conspired to make free elections in localities a hollow and cynical ideal. Whatever the virtues of local democracy in principle, in practice federal intervention in local affairs has been needed to ensure the veracity of the principle. As President Reagan has invoked *local responsiveness* to justify his attempts to strip the federal Justice Department of their powers in civil rights cases, civil rights groups have protested, claiming *local responsiveness* is biased and untrustworthy. Notice none of these groups deny the ideal, rather it is an argument over policy in particular instances. Other government functions could be similarly analyzed, including fire and police protection, public health care provision, and even sewerage disposal—the list could be extended indefinitely.[9]

As was mentioned above, a quite contentious issue in recent years has been the proper definition of local governments' role vis-à-vis local economic development policy. Few citizens disagree with the principle that local governments must concern themselves with the welfare of their constituents. Again representatives from the left and the right can be found to illustrate this argument. For example, Bowles, Gordon and Weisskopf (1983), writing on American national economic trends, have promoted local democracy in economic policy as the only alternative to a monolithic and domineering national corporatist state. Like Bluestone and Harrison (1982), they believe local decision making in corporate policy to be a crucial requirement for an effective local economic development strategy. All these authors invoke a Castells-type grass-roots democracy argument, implying that at higher tiers of the state, policies and practices are insensitive to local concerns. On the conservative side, even President Reagan has promoted local involvement in economic development policy, albeit of a rather different type than the radicals noted above. Reagan argued that local welfare is best ensured by local government policies that maintain an adequate business climate (U.S. Department of Housing and Urban Development 1982).

Obviously, radical notions of local development policy are anathema to the conservative model of economic federalism. Policies of direct local intervention in corporate decision making are viewed by conservatives as an unwarranted invasion of private property rights (McKenzie 1981). The public (local government) role according to conservatives should be to facilitate growth, not direct it or control it.[10] Thus, for example, plant closing legislation, community reinvestment policies, and job rights legislation are all attacked for being antibusiness, or antigrowth, etc. Notice again, however, that the principle of local decision making itself is rarely attacked by conservative critics. The principle is upeld, but the policies criticized. Again, we have a situation in which the virtues of local autonomy are promoted from a variety of ideological perspectives. Agreement in principle is, of course, the only real point of intersection. Not only do the roots of alternative interpretations of the "goodness" of local autonomy differ, how it is to be implemented in practice seems subject to wide and irreconcilable disagreement.

It is tempting in these situations to concentrate only on the points of disagreement. Indeed, the basic premise of the principal public policy paradigm (see Stokey and Zeckhauser 1978) is that these types of disagreements can be reconciled and ordered in terms of their efficacy through social science research.[11] Although it is important to study these types of disagreements in depth, we must also step back and consider the more substantive puzzle: why radicals, liberals, and conservatives agree with the principle of local autonomy even though their theories of society are markedly different. From an understanding of this issue we could move to analyze disagreements over policy and how various schools of thought interpret local autonomy itself. This methodological task (and its implied order of significance emphasizing theory and practice, principle and policy), is large and deals with the substantive basis of social inquiry; it will occupy us for the entire book. To understand the heterogeneity of values and the problem of arriving at determinant interpretations and meanings, we must look below the surface of contemporary rhetoric—beyond agreements in principle to how the principles themselves are conceived.

The Private City

Perhaps the best (albeit critical) representation of the liberal vision of urban America is to be found in Sam Bass Warner's (1968) study of the growth of the City of Philadelphia. He identified "the culture of privatism" as the principal normative conception guiding social behavior throughout his study period. Warner argued that this culture was both a moral image and an historical fact. That is, he suggested that privatism described how people perceived their proper social role and that people actually behaved as if they believed in the culture. According to Warner, this political culture provided political elites with a rationale for separating the public and private spheres, thereby defining the proper role of government itself, albeit somewhat by default (what is not private is public). While it is doubtful that the "culture of privatism" was ever so important that it was wholeheartedly accepted by the lower classes, it nevertheless represented a pervasive and *powerful* moral conception of proper individual and community relationships.

This conception still has considerable force even today. For example, it is now fashionable to design urban economic development plans around what are termed public-private partnerships. Private business acumen, when coupled with public sector resources, is thought by many development practitioners to be the most productive means of achieving social goals.[12] Expressed more crudely, we could describe such partnerships as a combination of private self-interest (profit) coupled with public responsibility (costs). Warner's description of privatism and more recent notions of public-private partnerships are, essentially, liberal interpretations of urban society. Both conceptions start with the individual as the primary unit of society.

Warner defined privatism in the following terms. Fundamentally, "its essence lay in its concentration upon the individual's search for wealth" (1968, p. 3). This definition is based on a utilitarian belief in the subjective, rational, utility-maximizing behavior of individuals. And, it owes a great deal to John Locke, and even Jeremy Bentham, although the latter writer was not, according to Hart (1982), such an important contemporary influence on eighteenth- and nineteenth- century American intellectual thought. Warner went on in his book to identify three dimensions of privatism: psychological privatism (individuals maximize their happiness through their drive for wealth, social privatism (individuals' social ties are assumed to lie with their immediate families and extend to include the community of like individuals), and political privatism (the community strives to ensure the economic and social freedom of its members).

It should be readily recognized that this conception of privatism is closely allied with the more general principles and philosophy of political liberalism. Indeed, Gutmann (1980) defined liberalism in a similar way, beginning with individuals, their interests, and their motivations, and moving on to their relationships with society.[13] Although she expressed social relationships somewhat differently from Warner (focusing primarily upon the state), Gutmann presumed that the state ensures the economic and political freedom of its citizens, thereby ensuring the satisfaction of individual desires. The only limit on this equivalence of the public good with private desires is that the state must ensure that all individuals' rights are protected. This may mean that the state has to limit the behavior of some individuals if the majority's interests are to be preserved. In this respect, Warner's description of privatism is virtually the same as Gutmann's definition of political liberalism.

Liberal theory assumes the state to be equivalent to the community. As such, it is hardly an institution with its own goals and agendas. Actually, it is even difficult to imagine the liberal state as an organization with internal social networks and role-related power relationships. The liberal state is simply a derivative social symbol of community interests. The liberal state is also the means by which the collective good is sustained.

Notice, of course, that the collective good can only be derived from local individuals, and cannot be imposed or defined by the state. The equivalence made by liberals of community and state is intentional and designed, in part, to be a check on the power of the state. For liberals who are concerned with sustaining maximum individual freedom, the implication is obvious: locate the state functionally and spatially so as to maximize its responsiveness to local needs.[14]

At this point it should also be acknowledged that liberalism has quite specific moral and methodological implications. The moral implication is most obvious: individuals are (properly) the principal units of society; their happiness and the protection of their rights are the basic requirements for the community good. The primacy accorded to the individual means that *in principle* the local state must ensure that community interests come second to individual freedom. Of course, there may be instances where the majority would best be served by limiting individual freedom but even so, such a policy could only be justified in terms of the higher-order principle. Notice that the primacy accorded to individuals implies that individual happiness can only be defined in terms of each person's desires. This also means, however, that individual happiness is a subjective and uniquely emotional category. Thus, the state or community can hardly legislate happiness nor provide happiness; the state can only provide the conditions necessary for individuals to find their true happiness in accordance with their own interests.[15]

The liberal notion of privatism carries with it quite distinct moral images of the good urban society. But there are other methodological issues as well to be recognized that are based on liberal principles which structure the practice of social theorizing itself.

To begin, the practice of starting with individuals as the primary unit of society presupposes that individual preferences are noncontextual. That is, individuals' desires are assumed to be conceived outside the immediate social context in which they reside. Otherwise, if individuals' preferences derived from their position in society, communities could purposefully change individual desires by changing the social structure. This policy would reverse the logic of liberalism—instead of starting with individuals and then aggregating to create communities, we would start with communities and then derive individuals (Fried 1983). There have been various attempts to retain the logic of liberalism while at the same time providing a basis for noncontextual individual desires. A favorite option is to imagine an original position, such as Rawls' (1971) more self-conscious version of Hobbes's and Locke's state of nature.

In the hands of Rawls (1971) and Nozick (1974), the original position allows individuals to define their own best interests and establish a set of rules that allows for maximum freedom. Rawls uses social structure as a means of representing life changes or possibilities. Individuals do not know their ultimate social position and thus seek to cover their down-side risks while at the same time allowing for opportunities. These types of social contracts are devices designed to avoid the problems of defining individual preferences and consciousness without social context. Even so, to utilize these devices fully requires some extraordinary leaps of faith. For instance, we must assume that individual rationality is invariant over time, that individuals would use the same logic to analyze their life chances in ancient, feudal, and contemporary times. Such universal claims of rational self-interest seem difficult to believe even if we accept for the moment the idea that individuals have a basic emotional character.

A second methodological point has to do with the distinction made by liberals between means and ends, decision rules and outcomes, procedures and substance. As we noted above, liberalism denies the legitimacy of state-mandated standards of happiness. According to liberalism, the imposition of such standards would deny the freedom of individuals to follow their own best interests. Indeed, liberal theory is generally uncomfortable with the subject of outcomes because it is really a public measure of happiness which would deny private desires. Not only may individuals disagree with the relative virtues of community standards, they may not even be able to articulate their preferences in terms that others can understand. Subjectivism is used by liberals to describe a solitary process whereby individuals separately decide on their on best interests.[16]

In these terms, outcomes are thought by liberals either to deny individual freedom through the use of state power or to be irrelevant given the unique mix of individuals' preferences. One way or another, outcomes are the enemy of the procedural liberal theorist. Not surprisingly, social theorists who depend on this logic have difficulty in "creating" societies (e.g., Olson 1965). They often resort to such schemas as preference relevation, derivation, and consensual accommodation to achieve collectivity. This methodological feature of liberalism is reflected in empirical studies of diverse social practices such as voting, adjudicating conflicts, compensating individuals whose freedom is denied, and, especially, local government functions.[17]

Nozick's (1974) theory of preference communities is especially important in this respect because it provides the most complete liberal rationale to date for decentralized democracy and local autonomy. In Nozick's model, as implied in Warner's discussion and critique of privatism, local government legitimacy is derived from the private consent of its citizens. Although there may be any number of ways of facilitating expressions of consent and of disagreement with the actions of the state, Nozick argued that it is decentralized government that best provides democratic access and responsiveness. While the extent of decentralization, once agreed upon, may be practically conditioned by the types of functions which can be efficiently carried out locally, the most important principle for Nozick is the decentralized structure of the state and, from there, the facilitation of individual expression and choice.

In these terms it is the consent of the citizens that determines the legitimacy of the state. But here other problems arise. For instance, the key issue for liberal political theorists is to show how consent is demonstrated. That is, it is necessary to be able to distinguish between consent and imprisonment, choice and being held hostage. Obviously direct polling, voting (voice), and direct representation are the most common ways of establishing consent. However, in many instances these strategies are too clumsy and/or complex given the myriad issues to be evaluated. At the local level, a common solution invoked is tacit consent—consent that is demonstrated through the residency of an individual in a jurisdiction. Residence as tacit consent depends upon two conditions: first, there must be a choice of localities available for potential residence. After all, we can only imply consent if there is a plausible alternative place to live. But it is not enough that there be a choice between places of similar characteristics. Having a locational choice implies differentiation and heterogeneity particularly with respect to the collective (state) actions and regulations of a given locality. Second, there must also be free mobility between communities. Otherwise, exit would not be possible even though the first condition of plausible choice may be met. The extent to which there is exclusion and barriers to mobility, tacit consent will be fundamentally compromised. Because rights are centered upon individuals, it is encumbent upon the state to ensure that all options (exit, voice, and loyalty) are available for all individuals according to their desires.[18]

Notice that in all these assumptions there is a presumption that the "rules of the game," the procedures whereby choices are made, are uniform between jurisdictions. People can hardly migrate between two places if the destination requires an entry fee. Or, to take another example, potential choices must be capable of being evaluated on a common basis; otherwise individual choice would be impossible. The implication of this requirement is far-reaching. It presupposes universal agreement on the rules of choice and the penalties for restricting choice. Inevitably, these rules and obligations must reside with the state as the ultimate policing agent. Even so, their ultimate rationale, their purpose for being, must be in terms of the higher-order principle. Otherwise, the very structure of society would be subject to arbitrary political power.

So as to maintain intercommunity comparability, the procedures of choice and of mobility, Nozick (1974) invoked a higher-level state. Implicitly, this means that local state legitimacy is conditional. Not only must local states have at least the tacit consent of their residents, they must also conform to a wider set of procedures. This is a fundamental result of Nozick's model (and liberal theory in general) because it defines the relationship between local state and national state interests. Moreover, it provides evidence of a hierarchy of legitimacy, with respect to the proper spatial distribution of state powers. Local governments, according to this theory, maintain their legitimacy up to the point where they lose either the tacit loyalty of their residents or the protection of the national state.

The obvious question is then: Where does the national state draw its legitimacy from? Exit is clearly less practical and, with exceptions, less realistic at this level. Voice remains a crucial means of indicating consent, but at the national level this option is obviously more problematic. The size and complexity of the nation are issues long recognized by liberal theorists (Dahl 1956). But so too are the competing visions of society embodied in constituent communities. Loyalty is even more difficult to evaluate. With fewer real exit options, there is a greater potential for mistaking indifference for loyalty and real dissatisfaction for indifference. Liberal political philosophy attempts to solve these problems by arguing that since rights reside with individuals, regardless of residence, the protection and facilitation of these rights will guarantee loyalty and consent from all citizens regardless of community affiliation. Notice that this solution retains obliquely social heterogeneity by declaring any state intervention in moral debate to be illegitimate. It presumes that competing social visions as emodied in local communities can coexist as long as they do not impinge upon individual freedom, or one another.[19]

The Public City

Set against the liberal vision of individual preference communities and local government autonomy is another vision more socially conceived. Peterson (1981) termed it the structuralist view, for its emphasis is on the structural imperatives of the mode of production. I would concur with this description, although it should be acknowledged that it is only broadly related to the French school of structuralism.

This vision owes much less to Althusser (1971) than to Foucault (1977) and Habermas (1979). As such it is more concerned with deriving the social roles of individuals than detailing the grand scheme of capitalism per se. I describe it here in terms of the public city because the title indicates its fundamental difference, yet inverse relationship to liberal theory. Elsewhere, Michael Dear (1981) has described the public city as an ensemble of public services located in particular areas, servicing and maintaining a dependent client class. While the concept has been used to describe urban structure and social stratification (see, for example, Wolch 1979 and Kirby 1983), underneath these descriptions is a more telling theoretical point. Essentially, all individual life is public in the structuralist world; the public-private distinction is meaningless because the private itself is constituted in the public domain. Whatever the explicit policies of the local state, its role is part of an overarching social structure which at once defines both the individual's place in society and relationship to the state.

To understand this argument, let us return to the liberal argument reviewed immediately above. We noted that the primacy associated with individual choice and the necessarily subservient role of the state in fostering the community good arises directly out of liberal theory itself. Nozick's theory of the role of individuals and institutions is, again, particularly instructive on this point. His assertion that society only has a character after an agreement has been reached among free individuals over what they desire is an essential methodological point which then allows for the creation of preference communities. Logically, individuals come first, then society.

This is the key problem with liberal theories of society—their separation of individuals from society. It is not simply that such a notion is unrealistic; the issue is deeper and essentially philosophical. How is it possible to have individuals as human beings separate and created prior to the social relations that constitute them as socially calculating and emotional actors? The structuralist position is that such separation is inconceivable. Accordingly, individuals have meaning as human beings only to the extent of their relationships with the community. Individuals do not choose to belong to community; in point of fact there is no choice because it is the social relations which define the individual, not a collection of individuals defining the community.[20]

In the structuralist world, interdependence rather than independence is the key building block of what we term the community. This argument can be distinguished from utilitarian and social contract theories of individual and community association because it conceives of the relationship of individuals to the community in terms of their mutual and related obligations. These obligations are born out of social relationships.

Hence the possibilities of choice with respect to an individual's social affiliation cannot be the crucial issue. Since social relations are assumed to be inherent in the human experience, it is inconceivable that individuals should have any choice that is independent of their social experience and social identity. I do not mean to imply, however, that interdependence in any way limits the extent and existence of conflict over the moral principles that may guide social policy. There is, and must be in the structuralist world, continual conflict over what constitutes the community good, individual claims regarding needs and desires, and their relative social positions vis-à-vis community resources. Duncan Kennedy (1979) has summarized this notion in terms of the "fundamental liberal contradiction." However, rather than following the utilitarian tack of analyzing what the individual has to give up for social association, Kennedy argued that complete individual freedom is impossible because we are constituted through our relationships with others—their preferences, wishes, and intimate contact.

Structuralism analyzes individuals in terms of their social character. Inherent in this approach is a methodological emphasis on the social obligations of individuals and the social roots of these obligations in society. This kind of analysis focuses upon moral conflict and social aspirations. At the first level of appearance (defined as being the realm of moral values), we have expectations of ourselves and our fellow citizens summarized in the notion of community. Moral expectations are also social obligations, which must be observed and maintained for the reproduction of the entire ensemble of social relations. Thus, the rights accorded individuals in this world are defined contextually—defined in terms of social relations and expectations of moral conduct derived out of a particular social context.

One consequence of this argument is that any coercion of particular individuals by the community can be legitimized in the name of the interdependence inherent in human relations. Obviously such policies will require some degree of consent, if not unanimity. And it is obvious that community-related social obligations can fall more heavily on one group than another. As long as the ends of the community (as opposed to any individual) are agreed upon, personal sacrifices can be made, indeed enforced. Rather than assuming individual rights and the community good to be antithetical, the structuralist position is that individual rights themselves can only be derived from the circumstances of particular communities. This does not necessarily mean that communities are protected from the adverse effects of specific individual actions. In point of fact, the existence of such adverse effects is readily acknowledged but nevertheless related to the social structure of power which *allows* certain outcomes.

At this point it is often protested by liberals that definitions of rights as contextual obligations are simply extensions of positivistic empiricism. Because rights are contextual they can only be defined in particular instances; there can be no external moral arbiters of right or wrong. According to the logic of structuralism, there are no original positions independent of social life.

This objection has some virtue. However, we should also note that social obligations have significant moral imperatives. Further, the logic of rights as social obligations implies that not only are we concerned with how people act, obligations also embody normative values: implicit or explicit expectations of how individuals ought to act and how the community good ought to be defined. This aspect is missing from positivistic theories of rights and their related interpretations of legal discourse (Hart 1961). Notice that the contextual rights model does not allow for the existence of rights and their associated social values outside of the community. Consequently, the principles that guide and sustain social life are endogenously determined. The structuralist vision denies the possibility of natural definitions of justice and the liberal vision of individuals' rights being constituted separately from the fabric of society.

One implication is that hard cases, where values conflict, or where outcomes are ambiguous, cannot be adjudicated by an appeal to higher values, as liberals commonly suppose. The political structure of society is explicitly recognized and inevitably involved in any process of adjudication. To repeat, so as to indicate the differences between liberals and structuralists, the former theorists are often natural rights advocates while the latter suppose that individual rights are evidenced in the social and political obligations which structure any community.[21] And, instead of ignoring the question of competing values by invoking separate, non-overlapping preference communities (as liberals do), structuralists assume that values are adjudicated in the political arena.

The role of the state in the structuralist world is complex and intimately connected to the social structure. Inevitably, it has a crucial role in adjudicating competing values, competing interpretations, and competing outcomes. Since there is no single transcendent value such as individual freedom to order various competing values hierarchically, the state is fundamentally involved in the structure of outcomes as well as the basis of conflict resolution. As events and situations change and as social obligations vary in response, the state must similarly respond. In this kind of world, local government must be much more than a derivative symbol of homogeneous preference communities. It must have a tremendous responsibility for resolving conflicting interpretations but, at the same time, have a great deal of power in terms of fostering particular social relationships. Indeed, the local state could easily control the moral destiny of a community by virtue of its adjudicatory and initiative powers. Moreover, there is no neat and ready solution to the problem of defining local powers relative to higher-tier powers as in liberal theory. Again, these issues are intrinsically political.

To understand the implications of this kind of social theory we need to consider more specific circumstances. Imagine, for example, economic inequality based upon restricted ownership of the means of production.

How would we understand the role of the state in this context? With an unequal distribution of economic power, the process of defining social obligations is inevitably biased in favor of the more powerful groups. This occurs even if there is equal access to state decision-making mechanisms. Yet it must also be acknowledged that economic inequality implies dependence as well as interdependence.[22] For example, workers need employers for their livelihood as employers need workers for production. The relative levels of dependency can be thought of as key variables in determining outcomes on at least two fronts. First, the state is likely to be caught in the web of inequality unless it has another separate means of existence. In the absence of resource autonomy, the state is intimately implicated in the distribution of outcomes. Second, if all groups recognize their relative dependency, the actual rights of individuals are likely to be defined in terms of the interests of those classes least dependent (capitalists, for example). The definition of class interests in this regard is related to outcomes. Procedures for ensuring the observance of universal rights are not the crucial factors here, because it is the distributive consequences of social obligations that order their initial specification (Calabresi and Melamed 1972).

Moral rights, according to the structuralist theory, can hardly be separated from the community's economic and political structure no matter how universal their appearance. As Scanlon (1976) noted, in arguing against Nozick, the structure and enforcement of rights are intimately related to their distributive consequences. Again, contrasts with Nozick's analysis of the role of the local state in this respect are a useful means of illustrating the argument. In his model, association is based upon preference and choice. Individuals are *in*dependent rather than *inter*dependent (economically and socially). The nation-state equally enforces basic rights because it depends upon all members and communities for support. Of course, this is only plausible if there is no structural arrangement of social and economic inequality. If the state were to depend on one group more than another, its neutrality with respect to the definition and enforcement of rights would then collapse.

Thus, how we understand society, the processes of adjudicating between values, and, more specifically, the meaning of local autonomy—all collapse into a choice between different theories of society itself. To understand local autonomy, we must first choose a theory of society. That choice is inevitably political. Whether or not one agrees with liberal utilitarian theory depends upon prior acceptance of particular philosophical values. The structuralist position is that individuals only gain meaning as human beings by community association; separation of the individual from social relations is inconceivable in this particular mode of social inquiry. Likewise, individuals' rights only have meaning as social obligations—between individuals set within a particular arrangement of community economic and political relationships. When coupled with institutional collusion, this theory also implies that moral values, outcomes, social structure, and power cannot be separated.

A Plurality of Values

Whatever the separate advantages of the liberal and structuralist interpretations of society, they are both vulnerable to criticism. Indeed, they are one another's critique. Discussion of the structuralist position immediately above indicated that the liberal vision is vulnerable on at least two grounds. First, the liberal model is unable to deliver an adequate explanation of the role of individuals vis-à-vis society. An overwhelming emphasis on individual choice strips liberal theory of any chance of integrating social values with individual action.[23] Relatively speaking, social context does not matter for the liberal theorist except in situations where context limits individual freedom. Second, it is also apparent that liberalism has only a weak and formalized theory of local government powers and the state in general. Methodologically speaking, liberal theory is uncomfortable with adjudicating outcomes; it locates social values in homogeneous and exclusive communities, thereby avoiding the issue almost entirely.

On the other hand, the structuralist vision can be readily criticized from the liberal perspective. Structuralism has very little to say about human agency. It is all very well to be scornful of such notions as individual choice, but it is an entirely different matter to ignore the issue altogether. Instead of communities being the derivative symbols of individual preferences, as in liberal theory, it is individuals who are the derivative symbols of social structure in structuralism. The difficulty with this approach is that it is hard to see how social change occurs, how social aspirations evolve, and how moral values are altered. Actually, this is quite ironic because it is radical structuralists who promote change and radicals who have been the principal boosters for grass-roots activism. For change to occur, individuals have to receive either divine inspiration or be led by others (who are presumably more knowing) to a new world. Otherwise, we have to assume that individuals are hoodwinked or duped into playing social roles in which they have no objective interest.[24] Neither rationalization seems entirely appealing.

A second problem with the structuralist vision is that by making everything relative to social position, it seems to suggest that there can be no consistency in adjudicating right and wrong. Indeed, one could easily be led into the nihilist trap: because nothing is judged right or wrong, nothing is then desirable or worth doing. At least the liberals have an overriding good, individual freedom, even if they are stymied once they have to deal with reality. I have, of course, argued that moral values are part of the structuralist vision; that is, there is a great deal of scope for socially conceived normative ideals. Even so, it must be remembered that these ideals are derived from particular contexts. Does this mean that once achieved, these ideals would lose their value? Would there be another ideal to take its place? Surely the answer to both questions would be in the affirmative, but it also means that interpretive consistency may be unattainable as events and situations change.

We could go on criticizing liberalism from the structuralist position, and structuralism from the liberal perspective, but to do so would be largely futile. We might gain greater precision in terms of their respective key elements, but this would hardly get us closer to any reconciliation between these theories. What one theory ignores, the other takes as its central analytical task. What one theory proclaims to be the overriding moral value, the other theory dismisses with hardly the wave of a hand. Put more concretely, liberalism ignores social structure, whereas structuralism argues social structure to be the crucial determinant. Liberalism proclaims the fundamental value of individual freedom, whereas structuralism trivializes it. There seems to be little in the way of overlap that could allow us to adjudicate their relative virtues. It is more useful to recognize that both are partial and are related to one another only in terms of their weaknesses and strengths. They are like two parallel languages rather than overlapping transparencies designed to highlight different aspects of a constant world. What remains is only a superficial agreement on the value of local autonomy.

For those readers schooled in contemporary social sciences, this argument must seem scandalous. By refusing to take a stand on the goodness-of-fit of each theory vis-à-vis reality, I have abandoned one of the basic principles of scientific inquiry: empirical relevance.[25] And, by arguing that theories of society coexist rather than reduce to one single complete explanation, I have abandoned a second principle, that of determinacy. These principles for doing good science are so pervasive that virtually all major factions hold to these principles as a matter of course. The result is a war of words, evidence, and assertions, each faction declaring the battle won with the introduction of each new piece of evidence. Marxists hold to the notion of objective science as strongly as conservatives, and competing interpretations are often ridiculed, left and right, for being merely words, unsupported by solid evidence. The war is played out on a terrain occupied by rigorous theorists, objective scientists, and uncompromising empiricists (Fincher 1983).

But for all the rhetoric surrounding the scientific mode of inquiry, there are strong reasons for doubting its claims of seeing truth. These doubts bear directly on the problem of social interpretation.

One of the more arrogant claims of scientific theorists is the one that proclaims a single and exclusive truth. Implied in such claims are at least the following suppositions. First, that their procedures for discovering truth are neutral and objective. This supposition is quite extraordinary once we recognize that the categories of empirical analysis are themselves derived from specific normative visions. For example, the category of local government power has at least two contending interpretations—interpretations which, nevertheless, appear irreconcilable. When scientific theorists proclaim the efficiency of providing public facilities at the local level, what moral theory do they depend on for the category itself? If the study is within the liberal tradition, this would in no way deny the veracity of the structuralist position. Yet, this is precisely the exclusivity of truth proclaimed by methodological empiricists. The only other option for scientific theorists is to claim that social categories are somehow naturally received and are invariant of the context in which they are analyzed. Yet, any appeal to neutral facts seems as impossible as the notion of a natural objective world (Cavell 1979).

The second problem with claims of exclusive truth is that such claims seem to deny the basic characteristic of social values, in particular their normative nature. Moral arguments for local government are not simply statements of fact; indeed, quite the contrary, they are ascriptive statements of worth and have, as a consequence, powerful normative appeal. Unfortunately, many empiricists ignore the inherent rhetorical appeal of moral language, preferring instead to believe that language itself is neutral and/or that language can be stripped down to an essential meaning.[26] Such notions seem quite implausible once we recognize that phrases such as "individual rights and the community good" can only be interpreted in the context of a quite specific social theory. For instance, based on the previous discussion of liberalism, it is more than plausible that liberals mean by this phrase that individual rights must come before claims of the community good. After all, this is the underlying logic of liberal theory. A completely different interpretation could be offered by structuralists in the rhetorical question: "doesn't the community assign rights?" Rhetoric is interpretation.

A more subtle issue related to these claims of exclusive meaning has to do with the position of the researcher vis-à-vis society. Gregory (1978) has noted that empiricists by and large work *on* society, not *in* society. By that, he means (I think) that empiricists attempt to step outside of society, for reasons of objectivity and the like noted above, and conduct their analysis as if they were the final arbiters of reality, right and wrong.

Not only is this practice undemocratic and elitist, it ignores the very real claims of others for their own interpretations. Empiricists want a complete determinant and exclusive truth. They would sacrifice others' interpretations and aspirations to a single and essentially vacant interpretation. As Williams (1981) suggested, this strategy denies the essential virtues of moral beliefs: their emancipatory and idealistic character. This kind of reductionism is a threat to liberals and structuralists alike and reduces democracy to a simple empirical calculation. This kind of reductionism is at the heart of George Orwell's *Animal Farm*.

The counterfactual to truth, for positivists, is false. The methodological structure of positivism requires a binary classification of propositions into one or the other position. By this process, it is hoped that a single truth, or set of sequentially dependent truths, will be revealed. The true-false dichotomy is a device for sorting and arranging propositions about the world. Unfortunately for positivists, it is a quite crude and absolute means of categorizing observations. Relative truth—that is, propositions dependent on circumstances and interpretation for their applicability—does not fit easily within the positivist framework. Moreover, the possibility that two contending interpretations could "fit the facts" is equally disturbing for positivistic theorists. Relative truth is a threat to the positivist framework because it implies a necessity for value judgment—if you like, moral judgment about relative worth. And even here, relative standards of worth are applied, not absolute measures of true and false. Once standards are the issue, then adjudication of meaning depends upon ordering, in a cardinal sense, better and less better truths. This is just not possible unless we use some kind of moral framework, that is, a theory of society itself.

Equally plausible interpretations are similarly very difficult to fit within the positivists' rubric. Given that decentralized democracy and local power are desired by both the left and the right for fundamentally different reasons, how might we distinguish between their veracity? The question is absurd because there is no basis for judgment other than a return to valuing the moral arguments. The only other strategies open are to invoke specific contexts, thereby denying positivists' claims for universal determinant explanations (and, incidentally, compromising liberal theory as well), and to appeal to yet another more rigorous test. Putnam (1983a, pp. 226-27) noted, in these terms, that "the scientific method seems to me to be chimeric." Indeed, Putnam's implication is that the scientific method is itself indeterminant, especially in terms of its datum points of adjudication. Attempts to define rigorous empirical tests which can discriminate between contending interpretations seem open to exactly the same charges made against moral relativists: these tests can only be arbitrary, contextual, and historically specific.

At this point in the argument, a counterclaim could be launched by positivist truth seekers to the effect that the goal of determinacy is just that—a methodological goal that can be only approximated, not completely attained. Thus, we should interpret positivism as a desirable procedure even though we are, as yet, unable to deliver the goods. Here, two related concessions might be made by the positivist theorist (see Berlin 1978 for an extended critique of this position); the world is full of incomplete information, distorted signals, and false consciousness. Essentially, people do not say what they believe or, worse, are unable to make unambiguous judgments because of the fragmentary nature of social life. The implication is that in a perfect world, all would be revealed.

The most problematic part of this counterargument is its conception of consciousness and rationality. It depends on a utilitarian notion that once an individual recognizes his or her true interests, then a complete deterministic solution will be produced. Not only does this presuppose an underlying normative conception of how individual decisions ought to be made given the circumstances, the whole notion of procedural determinacy can only be justified by some other moral value like "rationality is a good thing."

Furthermore, if any individual is capable of calculating his or her interests, there is nothing to stop recalculation of interests given that a person could recognize that another person may also be recalculating given knowledge of another's interest. Sequential recalculation, game-playing, and ultimately power plays would make any stable known world a pure fantasy.[27] This is a fundamental issue—achieving determinacy in an ever changing world filled with partial and intersecting interpretations of events and institutions must always be implausible. This is not the result of less-than-perfect information, irrationality, or false consciousness, but rather the product of sincerely held moral beliefs about how the world ought to be structured as well as about the interdependence of social position and power.

As Goodman (1978) says, we should give up the idea of one world, one truth, and one explanation. We make and interpret reality as many worlds, all based on how we understand our social position and what we would aspire to. Even understanding our social position is itself founded upon moral beliefs, a theory of society in general. There is, then, a never ending spiral of values, judgments, and conditional statements about "goodness" in specific circumstances.

Values and Rationality

It would be a mistake at this point for the reader to conclude that my argument for a plurality of values is nihilistic or a form of virtuous irrationality. Rosen (1969) defined nihilism in the following terms: If there are many values, all with their own virtues and no order of relative merit, then any one value must be equal to the others. From this point, Rosen went on to argue that if all values are equally virtuous, then no value is transcendent. Consequently, no one value is worth pursuing. The nihilist world is one in which people are unable to reach good judgments. I think it would be very difficult to sustain any argument to the effect that we inhabit such a world. Although there is a good deal of conflict over the relative worth of contending values, our social institutions do not seem unable to make decisions. A more plausible description of current social practice would emphasize the practical necessity for making decisions regarding the relative worth of contending values.

A world without a means of social interpretation would be paralyzed and chaotic. Policies could not be conceived, let alone implemented. Nor would it be possible to use social institutions to achieve certain goals. In a world of interdeterminacy, no decisions could be made regarding the present or the future of our society. Indeed, we would have no past! As a practical matter, outcomes need to be defined and conflicts over solutions—interpretation—reached. For instance, we need a final reading of local power if we are to know if we should provide public services to communities that express a desire for certain kinds of services. If we accept the liberal notion that local government should be responsive to citizens' preferences, then the implication for public policy is clear. On the other hand, if we argue that such preferences are irrelevant and that social standards of welfare are the crucial indicators of local need, then, again, the implication for public policy is also obvious. In the first instance, it would be right for local governments to respond with public services; in the second instance, it would depend on the play of power and the specific situation. Such interpretations are necessarily unavoidable and required for public policy. They cannot be ignored. Not only do we have to deal with the exigencies of situations, we also have to deal with the historical legacy of past interpretation and meaning.

Clearly, my position is not one of nihilism; at the very minimum, I believe that interpretations have to be made, and are made. How does this square with the previous argument regarding the plurality of values? My answer to this question is premised upon two suppositions: First, just because there is a plurality of values does not mean that any one person has no opinion. In point of fact, opinions are firmly held and promoted as part of the political life of any society. Second, the notion of interpretation is itself inevitably relative—relative, that is, to the events, contexts, and balance of power between contending social groups. Thus, I assume plurality to mean that there exist contending values and claims for their respective virtues.

Notice that this argument does not deny rationality or even logic. But it is also the case that rationality is contextual rather than an ahistorical method of divining a universal truth.[28] There can be logic and order in any interpretation, and it is clear that many citizens value such characteristics for their own sake. Even so, we should be wary of equating such characteristics with methodological (positivist) truth-seeking. It is one thing to value rationality, it is an entirely different matter to hold that rationality is the means of finding a determinant truth.

3

Making Law and Interpreting Law

In the two preceding chapters I suggested that social determinacy is manufactured out of social heterogeneity. According to my argument, there are no transcendent external values and no ready formulas for ordering competing claims. Determinacy is an on-going project but nevertheless a politically sensitive issue, created and recreated by our institutions and political leaders as situations require. But simple acknowledgment of this reality is not enough. We have to go further and develop an understanding of how determinacy is manufactured in specific situations by specific institutions. This is the object of this book, to focus in particular on the issue of local autonomy and the role of the courts in creating determinacy. The courts are a principal agent of social determinacy in America although they are not alone in this role. Other institutions and groups also perform this role; the state in general has a crucial role to play in reproducing society itself (Clark and Dear 1984). Even so, it is readily apparent that the courts have a special place in American political culture.[1]

For a start, law has a special place in contemporary American liberal philosophy. For many political groups and intellectuals, law is (or should be) above society and the cut and thrust of normal politics.[2] The "rule of law" for these groups is an ideal that promises suprarational objectivity not found in the political arena (for an extended discussion and critique, see Horwitz 1975). As law is objectified, even deified by writers such as Berger (1977), partisan politics is similarly scornfully dismissed as being irrational, exploitive, and dominated by self-interest. American liberals and conservatives alike have sought refuge in the judicial system from pressure groups, special-interest coalitions, and the like (see Perry 1982).

This popular image of the virtues of law is shared by many academics, particularly those who imagine judges to be superhuman, all-knowing seers of the right and true. A contemporary American instance of this kind of belief is to be found in the attempts by Richards (1979) and others to elevate the late Justice Cardozo to what amounts to sainthood. Even Dworkin (1978) has a very similar type of judge, Hercules. Justification

39

of this belief in the superobjective power of the judiciary typically depends upon such assertions as judges know more because they are supposedly more objective and therefore more capable of making decisions, which will promote the long-run greater good of society than the common political caucus (Posner 1981*b*). As a consequence, the political system is limited in its legitimate role of making the hard decisions of which priorities, principles, and policies ought to be followed in specific instances. Paternalism, and a formal (if not real) separation between law and society, are two consequences of this unwillingness to trust the political system. The rule of law is a rhetorical slogan that both limits the political power of the legislature and legitimates the judiciary. This slogan can be traced back at least to Edmund Burke and Thomas Hobbes.[3]

There are, of course, other more radical arguments which suppose that judges cannot be trusted because of their privileged class background (Thompson 1975). Moreover, there are even conservative arguments which suppose that judges should be limited to deciding on the principled coherence of legislation, rather than actually making law through adjudication and interpretation (see Berger 1977). One way or another, all these issues are about law and society, the role of judges in relation to democracy, how they adjudicate cases, and their limits as lawmakers and interpreters.[4]

In this chapter I argue that the legal apparatus is a crucial, socially conceived intepreter of society and a principal American agent of manufacturing social determinacy. Whether or not the courts should have these roles is hardly at issue. In point of fact, it is the legal apparatus that makes possible social cohesion in a world of conflicting values and differing world views. Therefore, I am concerned in this chapter with what judges do and how they rationalize their decisions in terms of the heterogeneity of society.

Relative Autonomy of the Judiciary

A number of preliminary methodological problems need to be addressed before we can turn to the relationships between law and American society. These methodological points bear directly upon how to analyze this issue, so it is important that we acknowledge them directly. To begin with, I wish to make a distinction between the practice of law and the position of the judiciary in relation to the social structure. Conventionally, the practice of law is best described in terms of legal formalism—the notion that law is a set of logically related, noncontextual, uniform rules of adjudication. Legal formalism is closely related to logical positivism, and although the judiciary derives a great deal of power through its use of the tools of formalism, I would argue that how we understand formalism depends on considering first the role of the judiciary vis-à-vis capitalist society.[5]

Most abstractly, capitalism, and perhaps all other metasocial structures, can be described by four first-order conditions. First, property rights are protected by the judiciary and enforced by the state. Second, while there are no legal rights to *equal* ownership of property, there is a universal right to buy, sell, and hold property if one is wealthy enough. Third, owners of the means of production own what is produced and have the right to decide how goods are to be produced and sold. And fourth, capitalists produce goods and services to be exchanged at money values in the marketplace. Capitalists have a unilateral right, protected by the judiciary, to "hire and fire at will" (Clark 1983*b*). While capitalism is described here in terms of capitalist labor markets, more general principles apply, especially as regards the overall structure or rules of society.[6]

These first-order conditions are illustrative of what Calabresi and Melamed (1972) have termed the essential entitlements and obligations of society's citizens. In this context, my description has some elements in common with Hart's (1961) notion of legal structure. For instance, first-order conditions could be thought of as being equivalent to Hart's primary rules. And thus derivative procedures, in their technical sense, should be considered equivalent to his secondary rules.[7] Unlike Hart, however, I would argue that first-order conditions derive from social relations in a continuous spiral of design, interpretation, and structure, as well as implementation. Hart only assumed these structures exist; he could not explain their origin.

These first-order conditions are social structures and are concretely expressed in unilateral rights (wherein no person can force another to give up their entitlements unless they consent to do so).[8] Again, in the example of capitalist labor market, firms, being personified agents in American law, have the unilateral right to produce whatever they want, using whatever technology they decide appropriate, and with workers hired for that particular task (Clark 1983*b*). Of course, unilateral rights may not be absolute; the state may enact, for example, equal opportunity laws, which limit the applicability of unilateral rights. Yet, even in this instance property rights themselves are protected by the judiciary; public policies are only capable of compensating for undesirable results.

The first two conditions are crucial descriptors of capitalism, the latter two conditions derive from the structure of property rights. And, in this respect, the state is intimately involved in the *definition* of society. Only through the specification of such entitlements, their interpretation, and their judicial protection does capitalism itself exist. Consequently capitalism, like any other mode of production, is as much a political system as a

purely economic arrangement of production (Ryan 1982). This proposition depends on a relatively autonomous judiciary and, in the lexicon of
Marxist theory, an integration of the base and superstructure categories
of conventional theories of the state.[9]

This argument is not common, however, in the Marxist literature.
Some theorists, notably Poulantzas (1978), have argued that there is little
substance to the question of legal authority because the judiciary is
assumed to be part of an all-enveloping structural arrangement of state
power that is ultimately derived from the capitalist mode of production.
If this is the case, the judiciary could hardly have any independent
agency; it could hardly cause significant social change if it is created and
structured by higher-order economic imperatives.

The reader should recognize that this conception of social power and
social structure is a variant of the structuralist argument reviewed in the
preceding chapter. One consequence of this argument is the conclusion
that law is only ideology. This is very much the message to be drawn from
the comments of Eric Sheppard (1981) on a previous argument of mine
(Clark 1981b). He argued that local governments are used by the judiciary (among other state institutions), under the guise of the dominant
ideology, to enforce social inequality and racial exclusion. For Sheppard
(1981) and others, legal formalism is simply an ideology blocking our
appreciation of the more fundamental mechanisms of geographical and
social stratification. While not denying that ideology can be so used by
those legitimating their power, I do suggest that this is not enough,
because the interpretation given to social values and legal rights can
restructure society itself. That is, interpretation can make and remake the
underlying first-order conditions of society.

It is also simplistic to assume law to be the instrument of ruling classes
or some dominant elite; to do so would be to assume that people are
easily duped or somehow confused. I would tend to agree with Thompson
(1975, p. 262), who argued that people "will not be mystified by the first
man who puts on a wig." Of course, there is continual struggle over the
interpretation of social values, their legal representation, and the structure of decisions. And it is obvious that the conservative nature of the
legal profession encourages interpretations that sustain the status quo.[10]
However, the judiciary does have a great deal of power which goes
beyond its simple ideological hegemony in structuring society. Thus, as
Thompson (1975, p. 263) argued "law may be rhetoric, but it need not be
empty rhetoric."

In a number of fields of social theory it has become fashionable to
eschew all notions of causality in favor of the "totality of structure"
argument (compare Scott's 1983 editorial with Clark 1983b). For some
everything is so intertwined that it is impossible to identify distinct lines of
social causality. As Putnam (1983b) has noted, there has been a great

deal of reluctance on the part of radical philosophers to take Humean causality seriously, despite their dependence on his skeptical reasoning. Here my intention is certainly not to derive universal laws of causality; after all, the thrust of chapters 1 and 2 was to suppose such universality to be quite implausible. Nevertheless, I also argued that social structure is not complete or capable of autonomous determination and reproduction.[11]

Poulantzas's (1978) position not only denies social heterogeneity, it also reduces the relationships between the judiciary and society to simple association. Causality in Poulantzas's world is of little importance because the world is so fully determined and made that radical control of the legal apparatus would be futile. This position seems problematic on at least two grounds. First, it denies the obvious and tremendous changes wrought by the Supreme Court on American society during the 1960s. We have to assume that these changes, especially in race relations, were unimportant or purely surface reflections, or somehow darkly beneficial to the established elites. Second, Poulantzas's position is at odds with my more substantive theoretical argument that society itself is not a ready-made logically ordered world. Society is continually ordered and re-ordered in the face of heterogeneous and conflicting values. Poulantzas supposed a structural capitalist hegemony and clarity which is hardly conceivable.

Of course, to assume that the judiciary has some institutional power and authority not immediately derived from the mode of production is to assume a degree of autonomy at odds with conventional Marxist theory. Even so, there are good practical reasons for believing this to be the case. For a start, it is difficult to sustain any argument to the effect that the state is solely a creature of capitalism. Its functions, size, complexity, and power go far beyond those dimensions solely necessary for the reproduction of the capitalist system. Moreover, the political separation of the state from the economic system introduces a degree of discretion not captured by simple one-to-one accounting of the base-superstructure conceptualization of traditional Marxian theory. Indeed, to believe this general theorem would be to miss the major point of dispute in contemporary American society: the independence of the judiciary from the democratic caucus. Thus, we need to go beyond simple accounting frameworks of social power and seek an understanding of the judiciary's position vis-à-vis democratic society.

Law and American Society

In general judges have a quite ambiguous social position in North American society. On the one hand, they are drawn from society and directed (albeit subtly) to act in the interests of society (however defined). On the other hand, they come from privileged backgrounds, are trained at elite colleges, and live in situations quite different from those of their fellow citizens' everyday lives. As judges and citizens, they are located at the very top of the social hierarchy in professions which are hardly ever open to scrutiny and are typically tenured for life (or for a duration of their own choosing).[12] They are the active instruments of the state apparatus, performing crucial roles in American democracy, as interpreters of statutes, laws, and policies, as adjudicators of disputes, and as the ultimate makers of determinacy. However, these roles are not exclusive to the legal apparatus. Other congressional, bureaucratic, and administrative groups of the state perform these functions as well, although at times in relative obscurity (Clark and Dear 1984). Thus, we need not idealize or overemphasize the significance of the legal system in this regard. Nevertheless, its crucial determinant powers make the judicial apparatus fundamentally important.

A variety of rationales have been offered for the ambiguous position of judges in the American political system. Most writers on this issue have been concerned as well with the interrelationships between the judiciary and democracy in general. The problem for many, like Huntington (1981), is to justify the essentially extrademocratic role of the courts. Conservatively speaking, the most recent defense of the non-democratic review powers of the Supreme Court has come from Choper (1980). He argued that the courts perform necessary interpretive functions as well as necessary protective functions and these functions require judicial independence from the legislative arena. Choper argued that, given basic principles, the Supreme Court's role is to maintain the veracity of received moral principles by ensuring their consistent interpretation and application. For Choper, the real problem is actually with legislative actions being susceptible to powerful majority interests, which ignore, repress, even deny minorities' rights.[13] The conservative solution is to isolate the judiciary from direct democratic control. According to Choper, this is a necessary functional solution to the imperfections of human nature.

Notice that Choper's analysis is a little different from the conventional liberal theories of society reviewed at length in the preceding chapter. Individual interests are assumed to have primacy, being the basic rationale for individual action. Further, it is assumed that their protection enhances human fulfillment as well as, in sum, a better society. But because of individuals' selfish interests, preference groups cannot be trusted to observe the rights of other groups or the fundamental integrity of their separate interests. For Choper, these facts are an unavoidable part of the human experience. For us, of course, these "facts" are not so automatic, but rather the necessary result of a particular mode of social theorizing. Judges, in Choper's world, are isolated from democratic society because any involvement would directly compromise their independence and objectivity. The lessons of this kind of social analysis are twofold: First, collectively, individuals are not to be trusted, and second, the virtue of an independent and authoritarian elite is their general concern for sustaining principle.

Yet, not all conservatives trust judges. For instance, Berger (1977) has argued that the Warren Court in particular went far beyond protecting principles when it (radically) reinterpreted the meaning of the Fourteenth Amendment. According to Berger, the Warren Court radically reconstructed society. And there is little doubt that Berger was substantially correct. The Warren Court was the principle force behind racial desegregation. By legitimizing the concerns of grass-roots activists the Court forced the democratic political system to redefine racial equality, leading to a radically new federal program of social policies. Those who deny this achievement not only deny the judiciary a place in social structuration, they also deny the tremendous social forces at work in America during the late 1950s and early 1960s.[14]

Of course, whereas some might consider this an achievement, Berger righteously argued that the judiciary went far beyond its legitimate role. And he had a point in a way, because his arguments are as relevant now for leftists in arguing against the conservative nature of the current court as they were relevant for Berger in arguing against the progressive Warren Court. Indeed, it has been noted elsewhere (Clark and Dear 1984) that there is a close relationship between left- and right-wing arguments against the extrademocratic power of the judiciary. In both cases it is argued that judges impose values as much as they protect principles and protect elite interests as much as they protect against majority tyranny.

Choper's argument was for a conservative and independent Court, concerned with principles, not policies. Yet for this argument to work, we must assume a paternalistic elite who take as given the underlying principles of human life and who would ignore the substantive basis of existing power relations. Principles, in this vision, could not and should not be altered through reinterpretation, rather social positions should be maintained and legitimated. Any change in social structure should come from society, not the judiciary, even though the judiciary would have the right to review such changes for their conformity with principles. In these terms, Choper's model is both idealistic and static. It is idealistic because it asserts a proper role for the judiciary despite his claims of relevance vis-à-vis human nature. It is static because it presumes that the principles of society cannot change, that society is bound by naturally derived laws of moral right and wrong. Whatever his apparent claims to a functional (or realist) theory of judicial powers, his model reduces to an idealized utilitarian conception of human nature. Again the structuralist critique applies with savage force, and in terms of democratic practice, we must give up any claims we may have to alter the rules of society radically.

While Berger railed against judges who, he believed, imposed their values through adjudication, Choper basically ignored the issue or assumed that judges would do the right thing (however defined). Both accepted that values do figure in adjudication, although Berger wanted somehow to minimize their influence and Choper evoked a kind of natural order to justify the primacy of his values.

Not all commentators on law and democracy are so perplexed as these two writers when it comes to rationalizing the values question. Indeed, a common approach is to argue that the values imposed are actually consensual and/or consistent with more general social principles of the good society (Posner 1981b, Ely 1980, Dworkin 1980a). Essentially, the imposition issue is avoided by arguing in effect that judges' values are less personal and more socially derived. One characteristic of these rationales, however, is that they depend on an assumption that there are higher-order principles which all society would agree upon. But as we shall see in detail, those who propose these principles have to believe that they are unambiguous and consenual. At this highest level, they have to assume moral homogeneity as opposed to heterogeneity.

For Posner (1981b), judges act to ensure economic efficiency. He argued that even though some may be unaware of the economic implications of their decisions, the history of adjudication is best understood in these terms. Economic efficiency means, for Posner, maximum national wealth given existing resources and other constraints. In earlier writings, Posner suggested that his notion that judges promote economic efficiency was a matter of fact: no normative intent need be implied. This position was consistent with Posner's more general interest in applying neoclassical economic theory to legal issues, as well as his distinction between positive (objective, value free) and normative science. There is evidence that judges do, in fact, take into account economic issues, even efficiency, when dealing with questions of adjudication. For instance, I have argued elsewhere that the spatial integration of the United States over the past two hundred years could be interpreted as a conscious and on-going policy of the Supreme Court to foster national economic growth and development (Clark 1981b and compare Easterbrook 1983). Many judgments of the courts make explicit this goal and have denied local and state interests in the name of a principle much like efficiency: maximum national growth.

These examples could be multiplied with reference to tort liabilities, contract law, and individual mobility rights (just to name a few areas).[15]

Both conservative and more critical legal scholars have agreed that economic issues are important in any understanding of judicial decision making (see, for example, Horwitz 1977 on contracts, Kennedy 1979 on Blackstone's *Commentaries*, and Coase 1960 on the assignment of liabilities). Yet, there remains wide disagreement with Posner's argument because he maintained that economic efficiency is the one and only datum point with which to evaluate judicial decisions. Dworkin (1980*a*,*b*) in particular, has been a trenchant critic. Dworkin's critique has been so effective that Posner has had to concede some ground reluctantly (Posner 1981*a*). In the beginning, their debate centered on whether or not economic efficiency was the fundamental principle Posner claimed it was. Dworkin argued that there is no a priori positivistic logic that could justify the primacy accorded by Posner to economic efficiency. Indeed, Dworkin argued that it only makes sense as something of value if it is in fact a normative ideal. Posner (1980) initially resisted the idea but had to concede that efficiency is itself a normative or desirable value.

But from this position, Posner went on to argue that in any event economic efficiency is a universally desirable goal, a higher-order consensual value which has no equal. When equated with maximum national wealth, economic efficiency, according to Posner, was a value judges should and actually do pursue. The argument did not end here, because Dworkin (1980*a*) then argued that economic efficiency as maximum national economic growth was unintelligible as a value standing on its own. He argued that it can only be interpreted as a means to some other substantive end. For example, efficiency might be interpreted as a means of ensuring that everyone is made better-off. Or economic efficiency could mean that greater inequality is necessary for the overall good of society. Indeed, like equality, efficiency has a myriad of meanings associated with the concept (see Rae et al. 1981). Dworkin's point was essentially twofold: First, to understand efficiency, it must be linked to some desirable end, but second, there is an incredible diversity of ends as well as values attached to those ends. Thus, not only does economic efficiency dissolve into an argument over relative values, it can no longer be claimed to have universal and unambiguous support. To give economic efficiency substantive meaning, social values need to be introduced.[16]

Without doubt, Dworkin's analysis of the ends of efficiency thoroughly discredits Posner's claims of universality. Notice that it is plausible that economic efficiency is a valid rationale for judicial decision making. It cannot, however, be interpreted unambiguously, nor can it be thought to be independent of its consequences. Indeed, its meaning very much depends on what would be accomplished in any situation by following its claims. Consequently, judges cannot avoid social heterogeneity, even in situations that are at first sight thought more technical than substantive.

For these reasons, it is obvious that any claim that judges foster the general good is bound to be inadequate as a defense of their isolation from society. To give meaning to the general good we need to introduce a specific context, and yet in doing so, we also introduce social heterogeneity.

Another universal integrative principle that has been proposed is that of maximizing citizen participation. Ely (1980) argued that since judges do impose values, it is important to ensure that there is political diversity. One way to sustain diversity would be to ensure that judges sustain political participation and thus leave substantive outcomes alone. Ely's (1980) argument has some merit, which has been overlooked by those rushing to criticize his procedural solution to judicial decision making (see Tribe 1980 and Tushnet 1980). If it is accepted that judges can't be trusted and are located, so as to speak, extrademocratically, then one way to make judges responsive to democratic diversity is to make them policemen of democratic practice. For Ely, this is a way of making the judiciary responsible to the democratic arena without involving them in substantive disputes. Another merit of his approach is that it recognizes social heterogeneity as a valuable dimension of society. But even so, his own fascination with universal rules of adjudication led him to ignore the substantive content of what he proposed. Just what is maximum political participation? Dworkin's critique of Posner applies to Ely: substantive social values are hidden from view by touting the universal significance of participation.[17]

There is just no satisfactory way to rationalize the extrademocratic role of the American judiciary. Judges impose values and represent elite interests. It is impossible to justify their position by invoking universally accepted social values. What we are left with is a recognition that their political position is vulnerable to criticism both in terms of the language of democracy and the practices of democratic decision making. At the same time, judges provide a valuable, if not exclusive, function: making determinacy out of social heterogeneity. For these reasons, Calabresi's (1982) treatment of statute interpretation deserves special mention. He argued that a basic objective of law, and even of our language, is to "preserve our conflicting ideals."

The Power of Rules

If the courts cannot claim an exclusive truth or an ultimate principle to justify their relative autonomy and if, in consequence, their power is continually threatened, how can we explain the apparent strength of the judiciary in American society? One obvious answer, given the preceding discussion of social heterogeneity, is that the judicial function of manufacturing determinacy is valued by society, indeed is necessary for society, to the extent that other institutions cannot provide similar functions. Yet another, more subtle answer, however, has to do with the nature of law itself, the nature of rules, and the discretion embodied in operating and structuring a framework of rules.

I defined "law as rules" as legal formalism in the beginning of this chapter because I wished to indicate that this conception can be understood as being quite distinct from the more popular notion of common law. The historical importance of legal formalism in American law was linked by Horwitz (1977) to the rise of the merchant class in the pre-Revolutionary era. He argued that establishment of universal rules of obligation and entitlement during this period was a necessary political act—necessary, that is, to ensure wide consensual support for the new post-Revolutionary merchant elite leadership. By making law appear universal and nonarbitrary, the judiciary was to be more responsible than the English system. While Horwitz's (1977) thesis has been the subject of sharp criticism, especially with regard to the application of his ideas to contract theory, it is indeed clear that American legal formalism has come to dominate the inherited English common law tradition.

Law as a system of noncontextual, neutral rules of social adjudication is not only a social practice, it is also an important theoretical doctrine. Based on Austin, Hart, and others, the doctrine of law and rules has come to be interpreted as a positive theory of law. In the hands of H. L. A. Hart (1961), legal formalism has come to be the dominant means of theoretically rationalizing the practice of American judicial decision making. Three general propositions can be identified as the organizing framework of legal formalism (Dworkin 1972). First, the law of any society is a set of rules that purposely direct social behavior. Second, although these rules are designed to cover possible contingencies, they may, nevertheless, be indeterminant, especially in terms of which rules cover specific cases. The roles of judges in this system is to apply rules and decide which rules are relevant and which rules are not. Third, the courts have legitimate coercive powers to force people to carry out the obligations implied or expressly defined in this system of rules. These propositions describe what positivists believe to be the major dimensions of the "law as rules" conception of judicial practice.

Hart's *Concept of Law* (1961) is very much based upon these notions, although he introduced a number of added complexities. For instance, Hart made a distinction between primary and secondary rules: the former define social rights and obligations and the latter "stipulate how, and by whom, such primary rules may be formed" (Dworkin 1972). Like Calabresi and Melamed's (1972) first-order conditions, primary rules are the boundaries of social behavior. Notice that by introducing secondary rules, Hart established a way of legitimating the judiciary's enforcement of primary rules. That is, if primary rules are conceived in a manner consistent with accepted democratic practice, then the "power" of the judiciary to enforce rules has an external validity based on the society at large. But there is a degree of circularity in this argument because the courts also adjudicate the application of secondary rules. We could image situations where adjudication deliberately aims to legitimate certain primary rules.

It would be misleading, however, to conclude that sytems of rules are completely deterministic. Though the popular press would argue that law is just a matter of applying rules, positivists like Hart would argue that there is more to the rule of law than simple application. Indeed, Hart recognized that many rules are open-textured (borrowing a phrase from J. L. Austin).[18] That is, laws are only generally specified, using language that is vague and open. Because of this open texture, ambiguity abounds in how rules should be interpreted, applied, and even considered relevant. Consequently, judges have tremendous discretionary powers.

Reason for open texture vary from the most obvious to the most subtle. It should be obvious that the more specified the rule, the more particular the circumstances and events have to be for it to have relevance. For instance, if a state law prescribes local sewerage capacity according to population density and size, then all cases relating to sewerage capacity must take account of population. The specificity of this kind of rule obviously means that other rules may be needed if the state wishes to legislate other aspects of the provision of local sewerage services. The problem with specific rules is that they can only cover specific, anticipated issues. Moreover, with many specific rules covering all kinds of possibilities, there is a great deal of potential for conflict between rules. Specific rules may minimize judicial discretion with respect to specific cases, but at the same time make discretion inevitable when judges have to decide on the relative significance of one rule in relation to another. Judicial discretion is necessary in these cases because the alternative would be institutional paralysis.

One alternative to tightly defined, highly specific rules is a rule that can cover a multitude of potential cases. This would introduce a measure of discretion, but at the same time place boundaries on legitimate judicial review. For example, a state legislature could prescribe local sewerage capacity through general rules such as need, as appropriate, without actually designating specific criteria. It would then be up to the courts to define need in particular instances and even to change their definitions as events and situations change. Of course, rules become very fuzzy in these situations, although the extent of judicial review is still circumscribed by the subject matter at hand. This option is not only consistent with Hart's conception of law as rules, it also describes the everyday practice of courts in many jurisdictions. The open texture of rules is a practical necessity and reflects the limits of rules—their specificity, contextual contingencies, and dependence on past experience. Judicial discretion is similarly a practical necessity and also reflects the limits of rules—their applicability, relative importance, and consistency with principles.

While I would agree with Hart that the practice of law can be usefully described in terms of legal formalism—indeed this mode of organization is more than a theoretical ideal, it very much reflects the dominant practice of American law—it would be a mistake to suppose that the structure of rules is a separate issue from questions of moral virtue. This is most obviously the case where rules are standards. For instance, "need" is only interpretable from a normative position: how local conditions should be valued in terms of "need" is an issue that has no obvious and immediate technical answer. Standards imply relative values and a hierarchy of values, and thus judicial discretion inevitably involves adjudicating between competing claims of right and wrong. As was noted above, even the most tightly defined set of rules cannot be completely arranged so as to deal with all events (known and unknown). A multiplicity of rules inevitably means that judges have to adjudicate their relative importance as events change and as rules overlap in terms of their relevance for specific instances. Hart has argued, in this context, that acts of adjudication are acts of ascription, that is, acts which assign moral judgment as opposed to acts of neutral determination.[19]

To put the issue most plainly, procedural rules of adjudication cannot be separated from outcomes. Indeed, to define a rule requires that there be an intended outcome; otherwise the rule would have no obvious merit or even form. This does not mean that outcomes need to be exclusively conceived. It is entirely plausible that a multitude of rules can achieve specific outcomes. For instance, we can imagine many different rules that would ensure peoples' voting rights. As a general principle, it remains to be interpreted and applied to specific contexts. Here, of course, is a major opportunity for judicial power: the discretion to interpret policies and statutes in accordance with their relevance to principles. The rule of law in this context must be understood as being open-textured, flexible, and discretionary. Paradoxically, it is the rule of law that consequently provides judges with wide discretionary powers.

There are at least three ways of defining the dimensions of discretion. In terms of the preceding discussion, it is plain that judges have a good deal of discretion to interpret rules and standards given both their prior existence and origins in the democratic caucus. If we assume that the only role of judges is to act within the letter of the law, there still may be significant judicial discretionary power. The extent of power in this context depends on the detailed specification of rules. The more specified a set of rules, the less the discretionary power up to the point where the rules themselves become so detailed, unwieldy, and complex that determinant meanings dissolve into confusion and paralysis. We could term this kind of discretion as *rule-constrained* decision-making power since it supposes externally conceived definitions of the rules themselves. Notice that at their limit, highly specified rules are given determinant readings by the political process, not the judiciary.

Even so, as we saw above, there are limits to rule specification. There can be no rules for unanticipated events except at the most absurd level (for example, there may be a rule that unanticipated events deserve their own rules). Moreover, and more plausibly, a plethora of rules may give rise to situations where there is a choice between a priori specified rules. In these situations, judges have more discretionary power than in the simple rule-constrained situation. Not only may judges have the power to choose between rules, they may also have the discretion to identify choice situations. By doing so, judges can then create further avenues for the legitimate exercise of their rights of interpretation and determination. To suppose that judges would deliberately seek such situations is, of course, to assume that they act as Weberian goal-oriented agents to secure their own legitimacy and influence—surely an entirely reasonable assumption.[20] In these situations, judges have what may be loosely termed *rule adjudicative* or judgment powers, those discretionary powers based on their right to set the ground rules of adjudicatory discourse.

A third type of discretionary power has to do with the structural arrangement of institutional powers, that is, there is a type of discretionary power which flows from institutional position vis-à-vis other associated institutions. In our context, such power derives from the extrademocratic position of the judiciary vis-à-vis the elected democratic caucus. Although judges are bound by convention and, to a lesser extent statutes, their mandates are general and non-specific. While good behavior is expected of judges, there is little in the way of institutional structure to ensure good behavior. Moreover, because judges are so isolated from direct democratic control, it is entirely plausible that judges themselves can define "good behavior" and in doing so create their own arenas of power. The very ambiguity of the judiciary's position in modern democratic society provides judges with extraordinary discretionary power. In these situations, judges have nonrule powers, or more strictly defined, *institutional* or structural powers.

For all the reasons enumerated above, the judiciary is very vulnerable (and legitimately so) to the charge of being unrepresentative. Furthermore, there is a presumption of paternal authority, which does not square well with popular democratic sentiment. Its validity in terms of liberal theory is hardly complete. There are other persuasive theories of the proper role of the judiciary that do not depend on claims of the untrustworthy nature of individuals. In this respect, *institutional* powers must be continually justified, as must the rationales for particular interpretations of rules and their contexts. While appeal to paternal authority is a plausible claim for such discretion, it is not enough. The processes of judicial decision making can be also used to sustain the judiciary's power.

Interpretive Practice

It is tempting to believe that even if legal rules are indeterminant, there are recognized and authoritative procedures that can circumvent these "problems." Periodically, legal scholars proclaim the arrival of new, more successful procedures for interpretation, which reduces the uncertainty (and power of judges) in creating determinant meanings (see, for example, the special issue of the *Ohio State University Law Journal* 1981, on Ely 1980).[21] Typically, these procedural devices are argued to be better because they are somehow more objective and/or they depend upon a consensual majoritarian value (like Ely's claim for the virtue of maximum political participation). Even so, there can be no one "best" interpretative procedure. Whatever the justifications surrounding procedural devices such as originalism, precedent, authoritative cases, logic and rationality, and even contextual adjudication, we must immediately recognize that these devices are simply social practices.

These social and interpretive practices are designed to establish determinacy according to quite specific lines of reasoning. As social practices, they have relative virtues and relative vices and, whatever their relative advantages, they do not remove the need for judgment. As Hart (1961) noted, we cannot retreat to procedural neutrality and efficacy any more than we can conceive of one dominant (and determinant) social value. Having acknowleged this, we should nevertheless recognize that these interpretative procedures have their own peculiarities, which should be explicated so that we understand the various modes of interpretation that will be reviewed in subsequent chapters.

First, *originalism* is a mode of adjudication that depends on the original intent of legislation to adjudicate competing social interpretations. Conservatives often favor this method and invoke, for example, the original intent of the Founding Fathers of the U.S. Constitution or some other original figure to provide a means of resolving interpretive disputes (see Berger 1977). For proponents of this method, originalism holds the promise of a certain consistency of meaning as well as judicial neutrality vis-à-vis disputes at hand. Judges can claim to apply only received interpretations, based on the historical record. But critics charge that originalism is not possible because historical interpretation itself, is dependent upon the values of the judge or the interpretor.[22] Accordingly, there cannot be any neutral facts nor, for that matter, need there be any consistency in interpretation over time because social values vary as does the historical context in which "facts" are constructed. Brest (1980) has been especially critical of those who assume that facts are like truth, to be found, not constructed. And, in these terms, his criticism is entirely consistent with Hart's (1961) notion of judicial ascription.

Even more difficulty to justify is the essentially antidemocratic flavor of this mode of interpretation. Radical political reinterpretations of social values would be denied by originalism in favor of the dead hand of the past. For instance, Huntington (1981) has complained that student radicals' interpretations of equality do not fit with the original meaning of equality as found in the debates among the Founding Fathers.[23] It is little wonder that conservatives cling to the notion of originalism, and it is not surprising that its practice may represent a danger for the judiciary. After all, if the judiciary is already in an ambiguous position vis-à-vis democratic society, claims of originalism may simply serve to emphasize the extrademocratic nature of the judiciary.

The claim of the neutrality of originalism in terms of current disputes is also somewhat problematic. No original text is unambiguous and can be read in many ways (see, for instance, Said 1983*a*). Use of originalism simply magnifies the problems of arriving at determinant solutions to current disputes. Despite these problems, it would be misleading to say that original intent has no place in interpreting law. Since rules cannot stand by themselves, some understanding of what they could have been designed for is almost a necessity. Indeed, rules and statutes would have no meaning unless some objective could be established. The danger with originalism is to believe that it is a technique which can tell truth like no other technique.

Precedent has virtues similar to originalism in that judgments have a measure of consistency based on past events. Precedent also provides a datum point from which to begin the process of interpretation and rule application. This technique depends on associations, that is, finding the commonalities of current and previous cases and then applying the relevant rules. In this manner, precedent is also assumed to provide a shelter for judicial neutrality. By indicating association, judges can then declare a case resolved without going into the specific details of current disputes. Moreover, judges do not have to declare their own preferences openly because by invoking precedent the courts can argue that they are "only applying the law." Of course, there are obvious problems with this kind of exercise. Just finding association requires judgment and selective interpretation. Highlighting the important commonalities can be incredibly controversial and may involve the courts in essentially readjudicating (through reinterpretation) old cases as well as the latest cases.

The logic of precedent depends on treating like cases alike. To do so, however, requires a certain consistency in interpretative practice and principle, for there must be consistent ways of establishing which cases are alike. Otherwise precedent could hardly provide the ordered interpretive structure it is claimed to represent. Thus, precedent itself is not an independent procedure—it depends on how judges interpret cases. In this manner, precedent is constructed just like original intent—neither are discovered like some natural laws. Appeals to principles as the underlying logic of precedent is also problematic. For this datum point to be relevant, principles must have clear, unambiguous, and noncontextual (ahistorical) meanings. But, of course, this is just the problem; judges are called upon to adjudicate alternative interpretations of principles. To use precedent without principles to guide correlative analysis seems arbitrary, but to use principles to ascertain precedent is to use circular logic.

Although precedent cannot provide an unambiguous means of arriving at determinant interpretations, it can be useful as a reference point. The danger with precedent, like originalism, is that the past can be used to invalidate the present. Moreover, there is a danger that in treating like cases alike, grave injustices will be done to those present in the current situation.[24] Universal rules may well deny the unique aspects of current disputes; aspects which actually make the disputes.

Another option related to precedent, but not completely bound by historical circumstance, is to use *authoritative* or leading cases. Instead of depending on the historical record of similar cases, some instances may be isolated as being crucial in the development of certain doctrines or rationalizations. For whatever reasons, perhaps their complexity, their conjunction of events, principles, and background, or their position vis-à-vis other cases, these cases may be invoked as benchmarks in related adjudication. Dworkin (1978) termed these cases as hard cases and Unger (1983) termed them exemplary cases.[25] However they are defined, their importance in legal reasoning is undeniable. Notice that these cases need not be so different from previous cases, nor unique in terms of their qualities. To some extent, their identification is arbitrary and dependent on the situation at hand. There is little in the way of universal rules of identification in the literature even though they assume a great deal of importance in actual interpretation. For example, the U.S. Supreme Court has willingly accepted the notion of test-cases as a means of collecting related cases around a theme and so disposing of related litigation through the use of a standard judgment.

Two other options are available to those who do not wish to be bound by original meaning, precedent, or authoritative cases. The first option is to deny the relevance of past experience and assert the fundamental importance of rules such as economic efficiency, maximum national growth, and the like. This ideal that disputes should be settled so that some larger *all-embracing principle* is satisfied depends on two assumptions. First, it is assumed that principles like economic efficiency have unambiguous and ahistorical meanings. Second, it is also assumed that there is no debate over the empirical measurement of categories such as efficiency. Both assumptions seem implausible. For a start, Dworkin (1980*a*,*b*) has noted that the concept of economic efficiency collapses into a myriad of interpretations. Moreover, even if everyone could agree on the relevant definition of efficiency in a particular dispute, measurement seems very problematic. Debate over the meaning of such a category could not be resolved empirically because such a resolution would depend on the existence of a mediating third-party principle. If prices are used, it has to be acknowledged that prices are relative, dependent upon scarcity and the institutional structure of markets. No absolute measurement of efficiency seems possible (Coleman 1980). In any event, it is unlikely that we would have a dispute if all parties agreed to a universal definition of efficiency.

An alternative interpretive technique is *contextual adjudication*; allowing events and circumstances to play the major role in determining outcomes. Although some writers have suggested that this method is too arbitrary and open to abuse by the courts and other political agents, in reality it is no more and no less problematic than the other techniques noted above. Its advantages are twofold. First, instead of applying without question universal rules of precedent or original meaning or efficiency and the like, the particular nuances of each case would have a large role to play in the adjudicatory process. The subtleties of agreement and disagreement can be played without fear of being denied because they do not fit the existing template of legal opinion. Second, the historical contingencies that give rise to disputes over meaning, even the applicability of alternative principles, can also be taken seriously. Principles can be allowed to vary in interpretation, as can the relevance of circumstances and events. As Morris (1982) suggested, contextual adjudication allows us to be fair to real people and events, not just their universal shadows.

In this context, standards of behavior, of the goodness of actions, may be more resilient than universal but empty rules of interpretation. For many theorists, however, *just behavior* as an alternative metric to procedural rules such as maximum participation represents fundamental problems for the judiciary. For a start, justice or fairness can only be evaluated with respect to outcomes. Otherwise how can anyone know whether or not the intent of the standard was achieved? Outcomes imply substantive decisions of who is to benefit and who is to lose. Once outcomes are involved so too are the initial allocations of wealth and power. Consequently, the entire social structure is implicated. In this manner, contextual adjudication would involve the courts in justifying their decisions with respect to the underlying social structure. Universal rules, however, eschew these issues by shifting concern from power to procedure, from specific outcomes to how decisions are to be reached. In this context, the previously reviewed techniques of interpretation are almost inevitably conservative.

Counterclaims are sometimes made to the effect that contextual adjudication is somehow irrational or illogical (Fiss 1982). But these claims do not seem warranted any more than the claims of exclusive truth made by proponents of procedures such as precedent. In contextual adjudication, principles and their interpretation are still the central questions to be resolved. Fish (1982a p. 501) argued in this context that "the assumption [of liberals is] that in the search for truth, historical and institutional perspectives are obstacles which must be seen through or set aside or gotten beyond. I have been arguing, on the contrary, that beyond historical and institutional perspectives there is nothing to know." Presumably space should also be added to this notion of social relativism. The problem is as much the method of liberalism as it is its substantive concern. Universality is an empty, formal image (compare Clark 1982).

It is obvious then that judges cannot hide behind a screen of procedural neutrality in these circumstances. In contextual adjudication, judges are immediately targeted as the purveyors of determinant meaning. This inevitably places a great deal of strain on the principles underlying adjudication as well as on the credibility of interpretive decisions. But perhaps this is how it should be! All other, non-contextual procedures seem shallow devices more useful for legitimizing the courts than for providing good judgments. Thus, we should understand these procedures to be means of rationalization—social practices which have no natural virtue given social heterogeneity. Consequently, use of these interpretative techniques cannot be independent of the position of the judiciary vis-à-vis democratic society. They are not neutral in application and they are not neutral in terms of their political power.

Manufacturing Determinacy

So far these interpretive techniques have been treated as separate devices used in specific instances to enhance the veracity of the judiciary. In reality, it would be fair to expect these procedures to overlap and to be used as situations demand. For instance, precedent can be quite readily coupled with originalism, just as noncontextual rules such as economic efficiency can reasonably be associated with authoritative cases and leading judgments. The limits to such procedural heterogeneity are permeable and weak. As judges confront new cases and new circumstances, they need a wide array of techniques to fashion determinant interpretations. Indeed, we could imagine circumstances where a narrow vision of adjudicative practice would threaten the legitimacy of the courts. For instance, a narrow formalistic application of precedent carries with it the threat that real events are ignored. At the extreme, those parties affected could argue that courts are unresponsive, even undemocratic in proclaiming their own version of which events matter and which do not matter.

From my perspective, I do not believe that such procedural heterogeneity is wrong or inadequate or an indication of poor legal practice. Interpretations are the source of formal social structures and are themselves produced in a social environment. Fish (1980) argued in this context that interpretative communities are socially conceived associations which define what constitutes scholarship, critical enquiry, and even adjudication (as in this instance). The rules of creating interpretations need not be explicitly stated, for their logic comes from the acceptance of certain social conventions and, ultimately, a world view of which both are clearly a product of social position. The crudest conception of this image would be of judges who come from specific class backgrounds, schools, and training. But, as we have seen, interpretative communities are more than simple instrumental products of social structure; there are many interpretative communities, all vying for dominance.

To deny interpretative hetergeneity would be, in effect, to proclaim the existence or virtue of one determinant technique. Not only does this presume the existence of a truth (which is inappropriate to the logic of my argument), it also denies the fundamental character of judicial practice: interpretation is an institutionalized social act, conceived and constructed in a world of social heterogeneity. Fish (1982a, p. 497) also made this point: "facts can only be known by persons, and persons are always situated in some institutional context; therefore facts are always context relative and do not have a form independent of the structure of interest within which they emerge into noticeability." To suppose otherwise would be to return to a theory of the world which is monolithic and totalitarian. The various advantages and disadvantages of each technique of interpretation indicates that no one procedure can claim an omnipresent virtue. Thus, the heterogeneity that characterizes moral belief is embedded in judicial procedures.

Conservatives often accuse the courts of making law, in contrast to their proper role, which should be only to implement law. For conservatives, law is a particularly troublesome issue. On the one hand they believe that law is made politically, according to the will of society. Thus, any attempt by the courts to interpret law in terms that do not exactly correspond with original meaning is argued to be an improper use of judges' discretionary powers. But conservatives are also bound to distrust the political system, believing that group interests may dominate more general notions of individual virtue or, worse, suppress the freedom of some of its citizens. Thus, the courts should sustain the veracity of principles even if this means denying public policies arrived at in the democratic arena. Courts in this kind of world occupy a special place—an extrademocratic place that allows significant powers of discretion and coercion.

The difficulties conservatives have in sustaining the idea that principles are received, not made, in the social system are well known and need not be repeated in detail here.[26] It is sufficient to observe that principles, like local government autonomy, have an incredible variety of meanings and values which buttress their social significance. It is then inevitable that the courts make law because they have to sustain determinant interpretations of social ideals. In an American world of social heterogeneity, the courts have the major functional role in maintaining social determinacy. This does not mean that none but the courts can do this job. It is entirely plausible that this role could be carried out by the democratic parliament. What is most interesting about the American system is its reliance on the courts as an extrademocratic institution of social determination. Unlike many other countries, the United States, with the institutional arrangement of American society, takes seriously the supposed dangers of majoritarian politics.

Yet, for all its virtue derived from conservative ideology, the judiciary is in a vulnerable position. Its existence does not square well with liberal notions of democracy. Moreover, its wide discretionary powers make it a formidable political institution, a reality which is also at odds with the supposedly dependent nature of liberal institutions. This ambiguity in the role of the judiciary is as much a product of social heterogeneity as its functional character. Inevitably this ambiguity is both a source of judicial power and a continual threat to its legitimacy.

4

Models of Local Autonomy

For all its rhetorical appeal in the United States, the concept and meaning of local autonomy remain incredibly opaque. In principle, local autonomy is desired by the left and right even though, in practice, it is often interpreted quite differently by these different groups. So as to understand the substantive bases of these agreements and disagreements more systematically, an analytical framework is needed which can accommodate these different interpretations. In this chapter, the principle of local autonomy is developed by reference to two related strands of theory. First, we consider contemporary social theories of autonomy, beginning with individual-centered notions, then moving to aspects of institutional autonomy. Here, I contrast the work of Nozick (1981) and Rawls (1971), who follow the Kantian deontological mode of social enquiry, with the work of Berlin (1982) and Dahl (1982), who are more teleological in their analysis of autonomy. The former, Kantian logic is essentially procedural in nature, given basic principles. The latter, teleological model, is more consequentialist in nature; procedures must be matched with desired outcomes.[1]

I then turn to local power and autonomy as it relates to the relations of local governments with higher spatial tiers of the state. The theory proposed is about institutions and their relative powers. Generally, this theory of local autonomy is based on Bentham's (1970 edition) theory of local powers. However, use of this theory should not be construed to mean that we follow the utilitarian path in analyzing social structure. In point of fact, as Hart (1982, chap. 5) has noted, there are good reasons for interpreting Bentham's theory in structural terms, despite the fact that we may not agree with Bentham's derived interpretations of individual autonomy.[2] By extension and reinterpretation, two key principles of local autonomy are proposed: *immunity* and *initiative*. Inevitably, these two principles are quite general. But while they exist at the highest level of social abstraction, they are also obviously related to current American legal doctrines. Their virtues are twofold. First, they allow us to develop

60

an ideal taxonomy of social institution relationships, and, second, their generality allows for wide disagreement on their interpretation.

This sketch of basic principles, implied assumptions, and social values is followed by a description of four ideal types or models of local autonomy. The particular underlying assumptions and philosophical lineages of each type are emphasized and current models of American local government placed in context according to this typology. From that point, American local-state arrangements are similarly considered and an example, drawn from Illinois, is used to illustrate the theory.[3] It should be stressed that the concern here is with principles and ideal types. The issue of how ideology is used to legitimate specific hierarchical and spatial arrangements of local government powers is left to Part II of this book. By way of conclusion, I look beyond these theoretical categories, using the principles and discourse established in this chapter.

Autonomy and Society

Every president of the United States since the Second World War has had a plan for a new, revitalized federalism. Wood (1970) has documented these plans for the immediate postwar era, and Hanson (1982) has similarly reviewed the more recent policies of Nixon, Ford, and Carter. It is apparent that the new federalism movement finds favor with Republicans and Democrats alike. The rhetoric that accompanies these plans is familiar to many, evoking images of de Tocqueville and Jefferson and a proper spatial division of governmental powers (Maass 1959).[4] Thus, for example, President Reagan's agenda for "returning significant responsibilities to the states and local governments" (U.S. Department of Housing and Urban Development 1982) finds a ready and surprisingly large audience, even if his methods do not.

But determining the issues appropriate for local control seems to vary widely, depending upon the specific issues at hand. For example, President Reagan has attempted to gut the Clean Air Act and the Voting Rights Act by suggesting that environmental concerns and political participation are best left to the local level, in accordance with local interests. Yet with questions of local economic development policy, the president has proposed restricting states and localities from implementing their own development policies. The president has argued that local autonomy in these circumstances would compromise national concerns. Many liberals also argue for local autonomy and yet have their own ideas about what is appropriate for local control. Some suggest that voting rights should not be local, and others suggest that economic development policy should be local (Clark 1983a).

There are similar theoretical confusions, although the local autonomy question as such is rarely considered directly. Most academic theorists place their work in the context of an existing, albeit unacknowledged, institutional framework that assumes the existence of some kind of local autonomy. For example, those who analyze the geographical allocation and distribution of public goods and services take as given a model of interjurisdictional responsibilities based on notions of efficiency and sometimes equity (Bennett 1980). Few analysts have acknowledged that the existing institutionl arrangements of powers between tiers of the state in most western countries have little to do with efficiency (for an exception see Ladd 1977). Nevertheless, theorists who have studied local political participation and electoral politics rarely place local government powers in the context of higher tiers of the state, preferring, perhaps, to believe the processes of local democracy to be more important than the question of local institutional powers.[5] In short, local autonomy is either trivialized through a choice-oriented, efficiency theory of local public goods or is ignored by those who emphasize the processes of local politics as opposed to the substantive powers of local government.

These theoretical and practical examples point to a definition of local autonomy that would include some measure of independence. But it should be readily apparent that there is no one definition of autonomy, as there is no one best theory of society. Like the theories of society reviewed in chapter 2, social theories of autonomy can be usefully dichotomized in two broad groups, liberal and structural. The former set of theories are centered upon the individual, and the latter set of theories are more society-centered. Here, I wish to consider briefly the range of interpretations of autonomy before moving on to legal principles. It will become apparent that liberal and structural theorists agree that autonomy is best characterized by notions of independence, agency, and the like, although how they get to these characteristics varies widely.

Liberal theories of autonomy are generally deontological; that is, they refer to the capacity of individuals or instituions to pursue their varied interests, given three initial assumptions: individual freedom, rationality, and consciousness (Richards 1981). At one level, these assumptions are principles for human conduct reflecting a more general belief in the overriding value of human life. As was mentioned previously, at the heart of liberalism is almost a fundamentalist conception of the uniqueness of individuals (see Couclelis and Golledge 1983 for instance)—a uniqueness which can only be completely expressed through its own agency. As a theory of institutional action, liberalism is more a procedural theory of allowed action than a substantive guide to correct action; that is, the proper role of institutions in this theory is to facilitate individuals' freedom, rationality, and consciousness rather than focus on the outcomes of this trinity of apparent absolute virtues. The liberal model described here is, of course, utilitarian in that outcomes between people are not directly comparable given their own unique sets of preferences. For liberals, these are absolute virtues; for institutions, their legitimacy is conditional upon the protection and facilitation of these basic values.

Given this conditional notion of institutional legitimacy, how might institutional autonomy be understood from the liberal perspective? Nozick (1981) suggested that there are two basic characteristics of autonomy. First, autonomy is agency, or the ability of an individual and/or institution to actively pursue their goals free from the coercive force of others. If we assume that social agents act in accordance with underlying principles, those agents must have a significant sphere of discretion in which to act on their own initiative. For Nozick, this dimension is crucial in that he assumed autonomy to be central to any person's self-definition and self-worth. Without an adequate sphere of initiation, individuals and institutions would be others' prisoners. Notice that "an adequate sphere of initiation" is vague and difficult to define. Nozick (1981, p. 501) suggested that it covers "a range of important and significant choices . . . as well as a vast range of trivial choices."[6] What is important and what is trivial is obviously open to debate and, in the liberal model, subject to institutional interpretation.

In the liberal theory of society, individual initiative is not boundless; it is conditional upon observing the rights of others. Similarly, institutional autonomy must be subject to review at least in terms of the consistency of actions vis-à-vis the trinity of liberalism. Thus, relative immunity of social agents is also an important characteristic of autonomy, and this indicates that both initiative and immunity are conditional. Rawls's (1971) theory of autonomy is very similar, being explicitly Kantian and procedurally oriented. He suggested that social agents act autonomously when they act "from principles that they would acknowledge under conditions that best express their nature as free and equal rational beings" (p. 515). Of course, for Rawls there is a further criterion: justice. Yet even this is procedurally conceived by individuals rather than imposed by a state organization.[7]

The structuralist social theory uses very similar concepts, although derived from different assumptions. For example, Robert Dahl (1982), following the lead of Isaiah Berlin (1982), suggested that autonomy exists when an individual or institution is "not to be under the control of another" (p. 16). He also suggested that autonomy presupposes some measure of independent action, a measure of initiative power. The first kind of definition could be equated with the immunity notion introduced above, while the second concept obviously refers to initiative powers. According to Dahl, both powers are necessary for autonomy as both allow for *significant* actions to be planned and undertaken. In this re-spect, Dahl's contextual theory of autonomy is little different from Nozick's despite his attempts to distance himself from liberalism. It would be wrong, however, to say Dahl and Nozick depend on the same theoretical roots. Dahl suggested that "significant actions" can only be given substantive definition through the study of particular outcomes. Thus he would begin with *social* standards of behavior and desirable outcomes and evaluate autonomy in terms of whether these standards were met or not.

Dahl suggested two types of power for institutions: a type like initiative and immunity which enables action, and a type of discretion in standard-setting which could then be used by these same institutions to adjudicate the virtues of their own actions and the actions of others. Because outcomes matter in this contextual theory of autonomy, institutions have to be on both sides of the fence—as actors and adjudicators—while acting at some other level to define the standards used to adjudicate actions and outcomes. Indeed, I believe that these institutional roles are inevitable once we move from procedural structures to substantive outcomes, from noncontextual principles to questions of the justness of outcomes, and from individuals' noncommensurate desires to social goals. Dahl quite clearly expressed the structuralist imperative: whatever the individual aspirations of social agents, they act within certain a priori defined spheres, their actions are liable in terms of the outcomes they cause, and social determinacy is the overriding objective of social institutions.[8]

Richards (1981) defined this type of autonomy theory as teleological, a theory which presupposes that good outcomes can be defined a priori. In this respect, the structuralist autonomy argument is entirely consistent with our previous discussion in chapter 3, to the effect that procedures cannot be separated from substantive ends (Tushnet 1983). We need some idea of what we wish to achieve when a social policy is designed. A further implication is that we can only evaluate the virtue of procedures with respect to the outcomes they cause. In this sense, contextual ad-judication is at the heart of all social adjudication. Even so, there need be no agreement on the desirability of certain outcomes. Social heterogene-ity carries right through to the whole question of social action to institu-tional autonomy.

The previous chapter suggested that the liberal vision is internally incoherent; procedures and outcomes are necessarily linked. This is the case, even though it means that adjudicatory institutions have a great deal of power as a consequence. Thus, I would remind the reader that the question of defining autonomy is little different from the question of interpretation. While we start with ready agreement on principles—in this instance initiative and immunity as the basic dimensions of local autonomy—how they are interpreted is subject to wide debate. Any resolution of competing interpretations must assert the dominance of one interpretation, one underlying value, and one dominant interest. By necessity, any such resolution will reflect particular social interests.

Principles of Local Autonomy

In analyzing local autonomy as a theoretical category, we will depend upon a distinction between social institutions as utopian blueprints and institutions as arenas of dispute resolution and hegemonic control. Institutions can be both at the same time. For example, the legal system defines the structure of our institutions and legitimizes certain modes of social behavior. This distinction is actually between two levels of appearance. The first level is the realm of social aspirations and social transformation, the realm of moral values and conceptions of the proper form of society. At this level, moral conceptions of social life are given formal expression through constitutional mandates. Such moral visions are essentially utopian, conceiving a better social life in reaction to existing structures (Clark 1981b). It would be a mistake, however, to believe that the first level of appearance is somehow imaginary. In point of fact, the first level of appearance is born out of existing class tensions, group conflict, and debate over the proper form of society. Thus, the first level of appearance exists in concrete forms (like constitutions, rules, and standards) and is accompanied by explicit justifying, normative language.[9] Local autonomy is, at this level, a utopian conception of how the powers of social institutions ought to be geographically arranged.

The second level of appearance is essentially the realm of practice and political interpretation of the role of social institutions; that is, given a prior arrangement of rules and procedures, the issue becomes their application and adjudication. At this level, conflict abounds. The exigencies of specific circumstances have to be transformed, or adapted, to the framework of rules, which define social life. Which rules are appropriate and in what circumstances, which rules are inappropriate, and how the rules should be implemented are all points of contention. Moreover, as we noted in the preceding chapter, the meaning or interpretation of social rules and institutions is also open to debate, despite their location at the first level of appearance. The search both for the rules of application and for their meaning implies that the first level of appearance is not, and cannot be, static.

Much of the analysis of local autonomy in this book is conducted in terms of institutional power and legal structures. Definition of local autonomy will then depend on understanding two basic principles. First it is important to acknowledge that legal power can be thought of as being composed of two elements. Following Bentham (1970), we can identify the right' or liberty of a person or institution to act, given certain a priori specifications of rights and privileges. Bentham termed this power the "power of contrectation," the power to act, whatever the circumstances, provided there are prior rights to do so. In terms of individuals, the implications are clear. You and I may decide to migrate and be perfectly able to do so, *given* that we are free to choose our location, place of employment and so on. Our right to do so, however, depends on more general principles conceived at the first level of appearance. We must also respect others' rights to do so. Thus, the power of contrectation is essentially permissive, it allows action (unspecified), given what Calabresi and Melamed (1972) termed first-order conditions.

The second dimension to legal power is the "power of imperation." According to Hart (1982), Bentham conceived this power as that which is active as distinct from passive. In other words, the power of imperation is the power to review, amend, negate, and/or enforce. For an individual, this legal power enables a person to use the state and its apparatus to change the behavior of others (Clark and Dear 1984). This kind of legal power is legitimately coercive, enforcing the rights and privileges of individuals and thereby sustaining determinant outcomes. It should be acknowledged, however, that there is much debate over how to define coercion. Nozick (1974) claimed that only illegitimate force is coercive, not legitimate, state-sanctioned force. But in this context I prefer to define coercion as that which obtains if a person is *forced* to do something that he or she would not otherwise do.[10]

The reader may have noticed that these two dimensions of power are not independent of one another. Indeed, Bentham (1970, pp. 137–39) argued as much when he suggested that the power of imperation is secondary to, or "rests ultimately upon," the power of contrectation. Without an initial definition of a "just order" or right to do so, the exercise of state power would be illegitimate. Yet this argument can be turned around so that contrectative power depends on imperative power. For instance, if a person's right to do something was not backed up by state power, what real meaning would it have? A more useful way of understanding their relationship to one another is to acknowledge that both contrectative and imperative powers derive from the first level of appearance. As such, I assume no specific hierarchy of powers; both are required to give society its normative image, and both exist at the same time. This also means that social analysis begins by assuming some kind of social structure that gives individuals their social identity (Clark 1982).

To translate these two types of power from individuals to social institutions, a further set of assumptions is needed. First, it is assumed that institutions like local government can be treated as purposeful, goal-oriented actors. Like corporations, governmental institutions can be conceived as entities, not simply conglomerations of individuals. In this respect, my theory of institutions has much in common with Weberian notions of rationality and formalized goal-oriented structures (see, more generally, Saunders 1983). This does not mean that institutions act neutrally; rather, given their objectives and the situations at hand, institutions act to maximize their power (Eldridge 1971). In terms of American legal history this assumption is quite strong, and perhaps overstated if we were to analyze existing arrangement of local powers. Even so, as Frug (1980) has pointed out, there is little stopping such an interpretation. Indeed, many policymakers act as if this were true, even if the underlying structural arrangement of power is ambiguous.

For instance, the judgment of the U.S. Supreme Court in *White v. Mass. Council of Constr. Employers* (No. 81-1003 delivered on 28 February 1983) held that local governments have an active and legitimate corporate interest in the welfare of their cities. In this judgment, the Court conceived local governments as social agents with their own agendas and interests. In making the argument for the majority of the Court, Justice Rehnquist argued that when a state or local government acts as a "market participant," as opposed to a "market regulator," then it is not subject to review under the terms of the Commerce Clause.[11] Here, it is the language of the Court that is crucial, because it conceives of local government as a social agent, not simply an external regulator of private behavior. In this case, the crucial issue for the Court was the City of Boston's proprietary interest in a large construction project. There is, of course, a set of larger issues (considered in detail in chapter 5) especially related to the question of geographical discrimination in local hiring practices. For our immediate purposes, the crucial issue is the corporate identity given to local and state governments by the Supreme Court, as well as the more general social conception of institutional action.

Second, it is assumed that democracy and democratic procedures do not necessitate a unique form of local government. Again this is a strong assertion, but I would defend it on two grounds. One is that I wish to analyze social institutions as entities as well as in their relationships to one another. Thus, I am not concerned to derive their necessary form. All we need do is assume they exist. I am not concerned to derive natural or original conceptions of local autonomy. The other defense is that the match between specific institutional forms and their justifying ideologies is not as strong as one might initially suppose. As has been seen, local autonomy can be justified by theorists of many different, even antagonistic, political persuasions (see Castells 1983 and compare Clark 1984).

Definition of local autonomy is then based on a translation between individual powers and institutional powers. Specifically, in the language of contemporary legal theory (Frug 1980), two primary principles of local autonomy can be identified: the power of *initiation* and the power of *immunity*. The first principle, *initiation*, should be thought as being equivalent to contrectation and refers to the actions of local governments in carrying out their rightful duties. Of course, it is entirely possible that local government powers of initiation can be extraordinarily broadly or narrowly circumscribed. It all depends upon the initial specification of the rights and privileges of local government vis-à-vis other tiers of the state. For example, if local governments have the power to regulate and legis-late with respect to land use and zoning, then they are also able to initiate plans and designs for the formal spatial configuration of local economic activities. Similarly, if local governments have the power to legislate in the field of economic activity and employment, then they could *initiate* residential hiring quotas, minority employment requirements, even plant-closing regulations. Inevitably the power of initiation is the power to regulate private individuals. Without such powers, local government could hardly affect any private activity.

Before moving on to the power of immunity, we should also recognize that the source of local powers of initiation remains, at this point, an open question. There are a number of options. It is entirely plausible that initiation powers are assigned by local residents.[12] It is also plausible that initiation powers are assigned by states or provinces or even the nation-state. Once we begin to analyze specific examples, knowledge of the source of initiation powers becomes crucial for understanding local autonomy. After all, if states assign initiation powers to local govern-ments then local autonomy depends on state legislation. In these cir-cumstances effective local autonomy may be quite limited. I shall return to this issue throughout the book, for it has major implications regarding the arrangement of democracy, among other issues.

The power of immunity is essentially the power of localities to act without fear of the supervisory authority of higher tiers of the state. In this sense immunity allows local governments to act however they wish within the limits imposed by their initiative powers. An example of immunity would be local governments' regulating land use (in accordance with their right to do so), without any outside review agency. To make the example even more concrete, imagine that state governments allow local governments to legislate in the field of land use and that they cannot review or amend local decisions within that field of local government power. This would be equivalent to having no state or federal court of appeal as in the United States, or an Ontario Municipal Board, as in Ontario, Canada. Without immunity, however, higher tiers of the state would be able to enforce their own standards of administration and implementation. In the absence of immunity, local governments would have their every decision reviewed and perhaps even amended. In this sense immunity is a principal sphere of local autonomy.

Local government autonomy is thus defined by two specific powers: initiation and immunity. Autonomy also defines the extent of local discretion in terms of local government functions, actions, and legitimate behavior. For example, if local initiative were tightly circumscribed and the conditions in which local powers are exercised similarly prescribed, then local discretion would be quite limited. Moreover, if immunity were limited, then local discretion would be doubly constrained. Autonomy in such a world would surely hardly exist, if at all. In this context, discretion and autonomy are closely related. Local governments have the discretion to act, depending upon the prior definition of local government initiation powers. Similarly, discretion is limited by the review functions of higher tiers of the state.

More formally, discretion is defined by Dworkin (1978, p. 31) as that "area left open by a surrounding belt of restriction." He likened discretion to the hole in a donut in that discretion is always relative and specific to the structure or logic of surrounding rules. Notice that he also distinguished between three types of discretion: two weak kinds and an alternative stronger sense. The first weak kind of discretion arises in situations where previously agreed rules and standards cannot be applied in a mechanical sense. Thus local governments may have the discretion to interpret their initiative powers because these powers are so general that they cannot be automatically applied to every situation. Either judgment is required in interpreting these powers and/or there are questions of applicability in specific situations. In either event, discretion is within the existing set of rules or parameters, and discretion must be consistent with the underlying principles. The second weak kind of discretion arises in circumstances where institutions have final authority as ultimate decision makers or final interpreters of statutes.

But there is a third, stronger sense of discretion (see chap. 3). Instead of defining discretion in terms of exogenous rules and standards, an institution may have the powers of initiation and immunity to set standards themselves. Thus, instead of working with essentially fixed parameters, strong discretion would allow changes in parameters. This is like Warwick's (1981) notion of an institution being able to legislate about its own actions and responsibilities. Indeed, it is like local governments being able unilaterally to amend, change, or restructure their constitutional responsibilities. This kind of discretion is obviously more powerful than the two kinds of weak discretion noted above, although the power of final authority could in effect accomplish the same result as strong discretion. Notice that discretion in all these situations depends on both initiative and immunity; without initiative powers, localities could hardly have any discretion to act or respond, and, without immunity, any discretion that resulted from initiative powers could be sharply curtailed.

For those familiar with American local government law and legal practice, these principles can be used to describe a situation in which local autonomy has been systematically negated over the past two centuries (Frug 1980). Local autonomy has become more and more limited as state governments have narrowed local initiation powers. Even land use regulation, once thought the sole preserve of local government, has become a minor power of localities as state and federal governments have narrowed the exercise of that power through equal opportunity laws, and the like.[13] And, as local governments are the creatures of state legislatures, local initiation powers are very vulnerable to the intrusion of state governments into fields of local planning such as local education, sewerage, transportation, housing, police protection, and economic development. Attempts to define exclusive areas of local affairs have often failed, because local governments have had no ability to structure or define their own initiation powers.[14]

At the same time, immunity has all but disappeared (if it ever existed). Federal and state courts now review all kinds of local decisions for their compliance with the terms of higher-tier legislation. Even when local initiative powers are clearly spelled out, state courts in particular have been unsympathetic to local government interests when disputes involve local governments, their citizens, and the states. But, this brief sketch of American practice should not be taken as being the necessary rule, nor should the denial of local initiation and local immunity be taken as indicating the narrowness of the range of options available for structuring local autonomy. In fact a number of types of local autonomy can be envisaged.

A Typology of Local Autonomy

Combining the two principles of local power introduced above allows us to identify four ideal types of autonomy. The power of localities may be characterized in these terms:

> Type 1: initiative and immunity
> Type 2: initiative and no immunity
> Type 3: no initiative and immunity
> Type 4: no initiative and no immunity

Notice that these ideal types are extreme positions, being essentially paired opposites;[15] that is, type 1 is essentially the opposite of type 4, wherein the former situation could be characterized as complete or total local autonomy, and the latter could be characterized as absolutely no local autonomy. Types 2 and 3 have limited autonomy but for different reasons. For instance, type 2 allows local governments complete authority to regulate and legislate in their own interests but makes their every decision subject to review, modification, or outright negation by higher tiers. In contrast, type 3 provides no powers of local initiation, implying that whatever local governments do, their agendas, regulations, or even actions are set by higher tiers of the state. Even so, in this type of autonomy, local immunity allows local governments to operate without fear of review or supervision once their tasks have been set.

In terms of discretion, the most powerful type of local autonomy is obviously type 1, wherein local governments are able to initiate their own structural parameters free from outside (higher-tiers) interference. This type is consistent with Dworkin's notion of strong discretion. But, there are more subtle distinctions to be made. Even in type 3 there remains potential for discretion. With complete immunity these types of local governments are the final interpreters of their actions; immunity protects them from higher-tier interpretations even though their discretion in terms of initiative may be nonexistent. On the other hand, in type 2 situations, there may be wide local discretion in terms of initiation, but ultimately limited discretion in terms of the decisions of higher review agencies. In this sense, type 2 has a kind of weak discretion most consistent with Dworkin's notion of *judgment* while type 3 is most consistent with Dworkin's weak "final interpreter" notion of discretion. Just as obviously, type 4 has no discretion, although it is hard to imagine that higher-tier rules and standards could be so exhaustive of all possible events and circumstances.

We must also recognize at this juncture that there has been some debate over the utility of ideal-type analysis, with some Marxists arguing that such modes of analysis ignore history and are idealistic. As Saunders (1983) noted, Max Weber, and the branch of sociology dependent on his thought, has been vociferously attacked for perceived inadequacies thought to stem from such analytical techniques. While I would be the last person to deny the fundamental utility of Marxian categories for urban analysis (see for instance, Clark 1981*a*, Clark and Dear 1984), I believe that this type of criticism is largely misplaced. We still require an analytical prism which is relevant to the institutional character of the state and its apparatuses. State power is not simply a derivative category; it must be interpreted and given distinct form. Use of these ideal types of local government autonomy will obviously place the theory within a particular context, but I would argue that this is inevitable because of the need to create a framework flexible enough to accommodate various interpretive communities, using the term coined by Fish (1980).

A more telling, and less pragmatic, objection to Marxist criticisms of ideal-type theories has to do with their own vantage point. Like logical positivists, Marxists believe in a readymade world, a world fully constructed around principles which require discovery and explication. Indeed, critics of ideal-type theories suffer the same problems as structuralists in that they have to assume *one* determinant and fully inclusive theory of society. And, like positivists, they have to believe that their analytical prism is conceived outside of their experience, for, if position were crucial, interpretation could not be general or universal. The irony is, of course, that ideal types are historical by necessity: they are images of what is possible *given* underlying principles. And both *images* and *principles* are historically derived; they don't just *appear*. Moreover, their idealistic character is a reaction to the present; we could imagine materialist conceptions as well as theological conceptions. The real point of any disagreement must be further back in the construction of underlying *principles*, not their imagery. Even at this point, it is difficult to envisage disagreement. It was Karl Marx, after all, in *The Jewish Question* who pointed to the emancipatory logic of U.S. state constitutions using language quite consistent with notions of *initiative* and *immunity*.

The simplest way to proceed is to describe each type in some detail, paying particular attention to how each might be justified and what their relationships are to more general normative conceptions. A type 1 locality, characterized by both the power of initiative and immunity from higher tiers of the state, could be summarily described as an autonomous *city-state*. What it chooses to regulate and legislate is its own business. Higher tiers of the state are irrelevant, both as institutions defining the arena of local autonomy and as watchdogs over the legitimacy of local actions. Local officials have complete discretion in how they act. The limits to action are imposed not by other institutions, but, presumably, by the local population. Hence, legitimacy derives from those local citizens who have significant power. We need not imagine a democratic caucus or even a liberal theory of justice. All that need be assumed is that the local political system is fully integrated with the local state and that the institution is totally autonomous from other local and higher tiers of the state (if they exist).

The autonomous city-state is essentially a Platonic vision of society that assumes minority interests are either of no importance or are fully protected by the local institution. As such, it is an optimistic and compassionate image of society, a vision of decentralized human interaction and regard for one another's rights (Cornford 1941). The city-state as an institution is assumed fully responsive to local needs and its citizenry. In American terms, the city-state is a Jeffersonian conception of a decentralized, agrarian republic. Despite its ready conceptual identification, historical examples are harder to find than one might at first imagine.

Manuel and Manuel (1979) described Italian city-states in similar terms, although it must be acknowledged that Venice and Florence were quite powerful relative to other city-states, even imperialistic. Perhaps the walled cities of feudal times come closest to this image.

In direct contrast, the local state with no initiative powers or immunity (type 4) must be described as having no autonomy. Its agenda, actions, and responses are set by higher tiers, and its compliance with instructions is continually monitored. Such local governments are, essentially, administrative arms or apparatuses of higher tiers of the state. In these terms, such local governments would be best described as *bureaucratic apparatuses*. Notice that such a local state would have no discretion; it could not initiate legislation and would act according to the letter of received instructions. Both authority and responsibility for local actions are highly centralized. In this respect, legitimacy devolves from higher tiers to lower tiers and depends on the extent to which lower tiers of the state faithfully carry out their instructions. Notice that the local citizenry have no *direct* say in what the local state does. This does not mean necessarily that such a system is undemocratic; it may simply be that political discourse is conducted at higher tiers. The local state in such a system is simply a vehicle for carrying out instructions.

There are a number of ways of providing such a type of local autonomy with a philosophical basis. At one level, type 4 autonomy conforms to a Weberian image of a rationalized, bureaucratic, rule-oriented instrument. Elsewhere, Michael Dear and I (Clark and Dear 1984) have described in detail the local state's place in capitalist power relations. These institutions are run by a cadre of expert bureaucrats whose function is to implement higher-order tasks efficiently. At the same time, such a local state could be described as an expression of conservative ideology. For instance, a Hobbesian world would be so hierarchically arranged that local, even state, agencies would be completely dominated by the sovereign authority. Local agencies would be totally dependent upon the sovereign for legitimacy and task definition. Similarly, one could also argue that a nonautonomous local state would be entirely consistent with Edmund Burke's distrust of the masses. By centralizing power and stripping away any local autonomy, localities could neither alter existing arrangements of private property rights and the like, nor would they be able to escape the domination of elites located (geographically and administratively) in higher tiers. Such a normative image is clearly authoritarian (compare Sack 1983).

The third ideal type—immunity but no initiative—is related to the bureaucratic apparatus model of local autonomy, perhaps more so than to the city-state model. With no initiative powers, the type 3 local-state must respond to centrally defined functions and orders. Local residents cannot mandate specific tasks to be carried out by the local state. And yet, because of immunity, there need be no fear of higher tiers of the state reviewing the actual implementation of centrally defined tasks. Thus, the local state in this system has a measure of discretion. Although it cannot choose what to do, once given a specific task it can implement it in any way thought consistent with its tasks. Thus, to the extent that local constituents have power to affect the implementation practices of local governments, there may be significant differences between localities in *how* they implement higher-order tasks.

This type of autonomy is very much that described by Mill (compare McPherson 1982 and Bennett 1980). The local state is *representative* of higher-tier interests and is responsive to local concerns regarding appropriate forms of implementation. Conceivably, local residents vote to elect higher-tier representatives who in turn design policies to be implemented at lower scales. Legitimacy in such a system is predominantly top-down; that is, higher tiers have the ultimate responsibility for the actions of local governments. To the extent that local governments respond to these interests, then local governments will be legitimated and protected by state legislatures. This model or type could also be described as Aristotelian in that claims for justice and equality must be balanced against the tendencies of groups to monopolize power and dominate minorities.

More generally, this checks-and-balances system reflects a concern to narrow and constrain the powers of social institutions by other institutions. Thus, we could also describe the American relationship of state governments to the federal government in these terms. Pocock (1975) has demonstrated the congruence of Florentine political theory with American Republican Constitutionalism. He suggested that American republicanism draws a great deal from Machiavellian political theory, especially with regard to the design of the spatial and functional fragmentation of institutional powers. Decentralized political institutions which are balanced by higher-tier institutions could be interpreted as one consequence of this conception of political theory and practice. Notice, of course, absolute immunity of local governments, even state governments, is not approached in reality. *Representative autonomy* remains very much an ideal type.

The final ideal, type 2, can be described as *decentralized liberalism*. Like city-state autonomy, local governments in this model decide their own agendas, functions, and actions. Presumably they are democratic, although this is not required for the model to function. All that is required is that initiative rest with local government. But discretion is not complete, for lack of immunity means that local actions are closely scrutinized and reviewed, perhaps even negated. Either there are external standards of justice and freedom that must be observed, or, for whatever reasons, society has a larger interest in ensuring some measure of conformity between local governments. In any event, autonomy is limited, but in a way different from the *representative autonomy* model. Legitimacy resides with the local government, its action can only be constrained, and in this manner legitimacy flows bottom-up.

Perhaps the reader will have recognized Aristotelian dimensions to this ideal type of local autonomy here too. Indeed, similar notions of checks and balances work here, although I believe type 2 is qualitatively different from type 3. The power of initiative is crucial, and in Nozick's (1974) terms the role of higher-tier review agencies makes type 2 significantly different from type 3 local governments. For instance, to ensure that no city-state is imperialistic or dominates the others, all local governments might combine to set up an enforcement agency to guarantee that each local government respect the integrity of the others. This would in no way deny local initiative that responds to local concerns. However, local initiative that interferes with other localities could be policed. The logic of this model is very much based on assumptions of a heterogeneous preference, choice-oriented society.

Theory and Practice of Autonomy

So far discussion has been concerned with the theoretical logic of local autonomy. To understand the implications of what has been proposed, we need to become far more specific regarding both current models of local government and existing arrangements of local powers. Here I shall attempt to situate the dominant American theory of local public finance, the so-called Tiebout (1956) hypothesis, and Dillon's (1911) rule of local autonomy, into the typology presented in the previous section.

Tiebout's model is so well known that the reader may be excused for wondering why we should reconsider it at all.[16] Even so, I believe that it occupies a very special place in current theoretical debates concerning the provision of local public goods and services. For some theorists it is simply an analytical, objective model, but for others it is a normative blueprint for social organization (Whiteman 1983). Whenever questions of efficiency and the proper spatial allocation of functions dominate, the Tiebout hypothesis is invoked. Yet, Tiebout's theory of local autonomy is quite inchoate; we need to go on a detective mission before its elements can be identified according to our theory of local autonomy.

Most simply stated, Tiebout's model is a consumption-based theory of voter preferences and service provision. Voters are assumed to be rational, utility-maximizing agents; they are assumed to have distinct and identifiable preferences either indicated by voice (as in voting) or in loyalty (as in remaining located in a particular jurisdiction). There are, of course, many complexities including problems of uncertainty, inadequate knowledge, even racial, ethnic, or income exclusion. I do not wish to reconsider these issues; it is enough to point out that the Tiebout model is hardly an adequate description of reality (Archer 1981). But what of its theory of local government? The most obvious answer is that the Tiebout hypothesis has no theory of the local state. In the Tiebout world, local government hardly exists as an institution; it has no organizational structure, no real interests or agendas, and no real power except as a purely derivative symbol of local preferences. Few analysts treat local government as a corporate institution, but even fewer have internal theories of local governments as distinct political organizations (Michelman 1977).

Nonetheless, this answer is hardly sufficient because most analysts are not explicitly concerned with developing such a theory. They are primarily concerned with the definition and geographical allocation of public goods and services. Implicitly, however, there are in Tiebout's model elements of a theory that can be brought to light using the principles of immunity and initiative. In terms of the latter, a principal assumption of the Tiebout model is that local governments respond to local preferences. If local residents want swimming pools, this preference becomes a task for the local government. If some local residents (a minority) do not want swimming pools, then they have the option of moving to another locality that takes their preferences into account. In responding to local residents, local governments presumably have the power of initiation. Otherwise, the model would not make sense. If residents' preferences were denied because of higher-tier limits on what local governments could do, then the model would hardly be appropriate.

There are, of course, some limits to this analysis. Most obvious is the possibility that some functions may not be reasonably provided at the local level; that is, for reasons of efficiency (scale) or equity (access), higher tiers of the state may be better placed to carry out those functions. It is also possible that society as a whole may decide that some functions such as public opium dens should not be provided at any scale. Notice, however, that this model presumes that legitimacy resides with the voters, and local voters at that. Higher tiers of the state draw their legitimacy in terms of initiative from local decisions about the best scale at which to provide goods and services—legitimacy in this model is a bottom-up concept, derived from the process of decentralized democracy (Nozick 1974). So far then, local initiative is presumed to be a very important power of local government constrained only by specific cases. What of immunity?

For voters to be able to express their preferences clearly, including if necessary to vote with their feet, local governments must be restricted from coercing their residents and other local governments. The most obvious way of ensuring non-coercive and non-imperialistic behavior would be to review local governments' actions; that is, ensure that they comply with the rules of the game (Simmons 1979). Local governments under such a regime would not have complete immunity. In fact, quite the contrary, immunity may be very limited, the actual dimensions being dependent upon the trustworthy nature of the behavior of local governments. This conception is very much associated with the logic of Nozick (1974) and could be identified as a type 2 model of local autonomy. The Tiebout model assumes, albeit implicitly, a *decentralized liberal* model of local autonomy.

This should not be too surprising given that Nozick and Tiebout depend on (and defend) very specific assumptions regarding the primacy of individual choice, freedom, and decentralized democracy. These are values central to many American visions of the proper arrangement of society and its institutions. Although it is difficult to be precise, I would locate the Tiebout hypothesis closer to type 2 than type 4, but, of course, I should stress that this is a conceptual judgment.

Dillon's (1911) rule is the major judicial model of local government powers and dominates American debates of the proper role of localities with respect to state governments. The essentials of this rule in terms of local powers are these: Local governments have only those powers expressly granted by state legislatures, those powers implied by those powers expressly granted, and those powers essential to the accomplishment of local government objectives (Michelman and Sandalow 1970, pp. 252–53). Local initiative powers are tightly circumscribed and limted by this rule in two ways. First, as local governments are creatures of the state, they cannot choose what to do or what functions they should carry out; rather they are assigned their initiative powers by the state. Second, even after powers of initiation are assigned, Dillon's rule supposes that local governments must remain true to the letter of the law and its meaning. Deviations from this rule have been dealt with harshly by the courts, so much so that Dillon's rule has come to be interpreted as a purely *instrumental* definition of local powers. In this respect, American local government begins to look like the *bureaucratic apparatus* of a state government.

To complete this picture we must also ask whether or not local governments under Dillon's rule have any immunity. The answer is an emphatic no. State courts have the power to review, amend, and negate local decisions in areas as diverse as sewerage, education, and zoning. Under Dillon's rule, the courts ensure that the intent and provisions of state grants of power to localities are followed to the letter. One extreme example of this arrangement of local powers is to be found in Ontario,

Canada, where any zoning decision by a locality can be appealed by a resident or the province to the Ontario Municipal Board (OMB).[17] And if there is any room for local discretion within these grants of powers, state courts or review boards like the OMB decide on the appropriateness of local actions. In this context, with very limited initiative powers and very limited immunity, local autonomy is incredibly constrained. Thus, Dillon's rule appears to be best represented by type 4 local autonomy.

In reality, local immunity may not be so restricted, and there may be some local initiative powers. Once we assume, however, that state governments allocate procedural powers, whatever immunity exists would place the local government concerned between types 4 and 3 in terms of autonomy, rather than between types 4 and 2. This distinction is crucial because the state grant of power to local authorities means that state governments have complete control over local initiative. Whatever local governments do, they must receive the blessing of their state or province. The distinction is between localities being *granted* powers and localities *giving up* powers.[18]

In the Tiebout model, local autonomy means that localities have the power to define their own functions subject to the review of higher-tier agencies; in Dillon's rule, localities have no autonomy. In Tiebout's model, localities are primarily responsive to the preferences of their residents; in Dillon's rule, localities are the creatures of the state. On the one hand, decentralized democracy is the source of legitimacy, and on the other, decentralization is imposed and centralized authority retained. And in Tiebout's model functional diversity is a product of local residents' choices; in Dillon's rule, whatever functional diversty exists is the choice of state legislatures.[19]

Local Autonomy in Illinois

Not all American states depend upon Dillon's rule. There have been attempts to increase local autonomy through home-rule provisions (even though, of course, state legislatures retain ultimate granting powers). There are two basic classes of home-rule provisions: *imperium in imperio* (imperio) and the National League of Cities model (NLC). The imperio model is the older of the two, having its origin in Missouri's home-rule provision (passed in 1875). Imperio creates a sphere of action labeled "municipal affairs." Illinois state courts have interpreted this sphere quite strictly. In doing so, in limiting local powers to local affairs—an empirical category which has itself shifted and changed over time—their arguments have been based on what has been interpreted as the intent of the Illinois Legislature. This narrowness of interpretation has been felt in areas such as property law, zoning, banking, sewerage provision, utility rates, and the like (see O'Malley 1980 for a comprehensive review and the following sections and chapters for more details).[20] Nonetheless, within the sphere, municipalities have initiative powers and are free to pass laws. Outside of that sphere, they must obey and conform to the general laws of the state. Within the defined sphere of municipal affairs, imperio home rule gives local governments some initiative power and immunity from state regulation.

In 1953, the American Municipal Association, subsequently renamed the National League of Cities, published a report advocating a new model of home rule. The league proposed that all delegable powers be passed on to local governments, with the legislature able to take any power back by passing laws. Advocates of the NLC model argued that imperio provisions had been unworkable and unsuccessful. Essentially, imperio was thought to restrict local actions so narrowly that democracy at the local level was a sham. Moreover, it was also apparent that there could be no stable definition of municipal affairs. The NLC model in contrast was to encourage the use of muncipal initiative power. In subsequent litigation, however, courts have often read imperio-type language into the NLC provision, restricting the muncipal initiative to the sphere of local affairs (see Vanlandingham 1975).

Illinois adopted a home-rule provision as part of its 1970 constitution. The grant of power is contained in Section 6(1):

> Except as limited by this Section, a home rule unit may exercise any power and perform any function pertaining to its government and affairs including, but not limited to, the power to regulate for the protection of the public health, safety, morals and welfare; to license; to tax; and to incur debt.

At first sight, this appears to be an NLC home-rule provision. Other sections of the constitution, however, modify this general grant. Section 6(i) gives home-rule units the power to exercise the powers given in 6(a) concurrently with the state as long as the state does not "specifically limit the concurrent exercise or specifically declare the State's exercise to be exclusive." Section 6(l) sets up two areas of city immunity from state regulation involving local improvement by special assessment and powers to tax areas within their boundaries to pay for the provision of special services. These grants of power are limited by specific provisions within the home-rule provision. The most important is the imperio-type limitation contained in Section 6(a). This limitation is perhaps better understood as the outer bounds of Section 6(a) grant—home-rule units have no power to regulate national, state, or regional affairs.

Moreover, the provision contains other, quite specific limits. Section 6(d) prohibits home-rule units from incurring debt payable by property taxes maturing more than 40 years from the date of incurrence and from defining and providing for the punishment of felonies. Dillon's rule is reimposed for punishment by imprisonment for more than six months, licensing for revenue, or taxing income, earnings, or occupation (see Section 6[e]). And Section 6(f) places particular limits on the form that local governments can take.

Finally, the home-rule provision sets up the procedure by which the state legislature can limit the power of home-rule units. Section 6(g) allows the legislature to deny any power to a home-rule unit other than those listed in Section 6(l) by a three-fifths vote of each house. Section 6(h) allows the state to preempt any home-rule power except taxation and those protected in Section 6(l) by actually regulating the area concerned. Only a majority in each house is required. Sections 6(j) and (k) allow the legislature to exercise some control over indebtedness of home-rule units (see Clark and Dear 1984 for more details regarding similar constraints on local autonomy in other states).

The Illinois home-rule provision is not entirely based on the imperio or NLC models; it also has elements of grant theory and limitation theory. The grant is bounded by the "pertaining to its government and affairs" language of Section 6(a). Presumably, initiative powers are limited to that sphere—much narrower than the NLC models. The sphere of immunity from state regulation is also much smaller, containing only the areas enumerated in Sections 6(k) and (l):

1. Localities make local improvements by special assessment;
2. they exercise this power jointly with other counties and municipalities;
3. they exercise this power jointly with other units of local government that have been given the power by law;
4. they levy taxes on areas within their boundaries in the manner prescribed by law for the provision of special services; and
5. for home-rule municipalities, they incur debts payable from ad valorem property taxes up to percentages of assessed value specified in Section 6(k), subject to referendum if the legislature votes to require one.

All other powers can be taken away or limited by the state legislature. If the power involves taxation or an area not regulated by state government, a three-fifths vote of each house is needed. But only a majority is needed to preempt home-rule powers through specific regulations that express the legislature's intent to preempt. Structurally, home-rule units lose the major advantages of both types of home-rule provisions: initiative power is limited to an imperio-like sphere of local affairs and the scope of immunity is much smaller than the sphere of local affairs. This example is one of many that could be culled from American and Canadian local government law. It serves to emphasize the structural limits to local autonomy, as well as the crucial importance of the two principles of autonomy itself: initiative and immunity. As in so many other states, local autonomy in Illinois is very close to type 4.

Looking Forward

Local autonomy is at the center of many theoretical models of local public finance and urban politics. Yet there has been little explicit theorizing on what autonomy is. Too often it is assumed that local governments exist as independent units, at the extreme implying a kind of autonomy most would associate with Florentine city-states. This chapter reexamined the notion of local autonomy by proposing a theory of autonomy that placed city power in relation to higher tiers of the state. As such, the proposed theory treats local governments as active social entities, not simply the derivative symbols of decentralized democratic politics.

Following Bentham's conception of legal power and other liberal and structuralist theories, a theory of autonomy was proposed based on two principles: the power of initiative and the power of immunity. The former refers to the power of local governments to regulate and legislate in their own interests. The second principle refers to the immunity of local governments from the authority of higher tiers of the state. From these two principles, a typology of four ideal types was established, running the gamut from complete or absolute autonomy (the city-state model) to absolutely no autonomy.

It was noted in the introduction to this book that local autonomy means different things to different people. The framework outlined above will be used in subsequent chapters to identify the range of possible interpretations and the sources of disagreement. In these terms a number of more general research questions remain to be resolved. First, the gap between local autonomy in theory and practice must be explicated in terms of both the language of democractic politics and the structural arrangement of institutional power. How the language of local autonomy is used to justify spatial exclusion, for example, must be seen in a wider context. It is not enough to implicate local elites; the whole edifice of institutional power must be considered. Second, strategies of political change, whether conservative or radical, must confront the centralized nature of determining local powers. For example, President Reagan's claims of a new federalism would leave cities as constrained as before unless there are major state-level changes in local powers. All that may be changed are the functions that local governments are permitted to undertake and the extent of discretion a local government may have within the terms of such grants of power.[21]

II

Manufacturing Determinacy

Our language can be seen as an ancient city: a maze of little streets and squares of old and new houses with additions from various periods; and this surrounded by a multitude of new boroughs with straight regular streets and uniform houses.
—Ludwig Wittgenstein, *Philosophical Investigations*

5

The Politics of Local Jobs

On 11 September 1979 Kevin White, then mayor of the City of Boston, signed an executive order (to be implemented on 15 October 1979) requiring construction firms working on city funded or administered public works to employ at least 50 percent Boston residents, 25 percent minorities, and 10 percent women out of their total work forces.[1] This policy went far beyond the city's existing, but nascent, affirmative action policies by specifying exact quotas and penalties for noncompliance. No other American city had implemented such a resident-preference employment quota, and few cities had gone much beyond requiring good-faith efforts in combating discrimination from local construction contractors and unions. Mayor White signed into being an exciting new way of distributing the benefits of local economic development planning to local residents. This policy promises to become a major tool in many other American cities' efforts to improve the employment opportunities of their poor residents.[2]

At the outset, the executive order received great support from the local media including *The Boston Globe* and Boston-based community action groups such as the Boston Jobs Coalition.[3] Yet for all the media's support of the order, it was immediately surrounded by controversy. Construction unions and contractors were bitterly opposed to the order, contending that it discriminated against union members who were not city residents and placed an inordinate (and uncompetitive) burden upon employers. Within a month of the order being implemented, the construction unions and contractors had begun proceedings in the Massachusetts Supreme Judicial Court in an attempt to have the order ruled unconstitutional. Only after three and half years of litigation did the U.S. Supreme Court uphold the legality of Boston's resident-preference hiring policy, a decision that surprised many urban planners and legal scholars.

This chapter is concerned with two interrelated issues. First, I am interested in the politics of Boston's resident-preference policy: how it came into being, who supported it, and how it was implemented. While Mayor White rightly claimed the Supreme Court's decision on 28 February 1983 upholding the order as his own, any reading of the events leading up to his signing of the order in 1979 would lead one to conclude that the mayor was quite cautious in lending his support to the policy.[4] The politics involved pitted community groups against unions and contractors with the city often playing an ambiguous role of negotiator, rather than an advocate. Once White signed the order, however, it became his own without qualification. At the same time, the unions and contractors, having lost the political campaign, sought to overturn their political loss through an aggressive legal campaign. The second part of this chapter has to do with the legal challenge to the local jobs policy, including an analysis of the basis of the challenge, the doctrine and statutes invoked, and the rationales used by the courts in deciding the complaints.

My argument here is that the politics and legalities of social discourse are very much related. The legal challenge to the executive order grew out of the political fight over signing and implementing the order. This dispute was based on obvious underlying patterns of racial and residential discrimination in the construction industry. Thus, the legal challenge could be interpreted as a stratagem designed by the unions to thwart the objectives of the dominant political and city interests. Not only did the challenge remove the dispute from the local arena, it also transformed it into a different problem, one based on legal precedent and interpretation. But implied here is a further proposition: law is more than politics transposed. The political texture of an original dispute need not enter into the legal picture. Indeed, that is some of the power of the courts.

Community Jobs for Community Workers

A basic concern of a group of Boston community organizers operating in Boston's poor black neighborhoods over the period of the late 1960s through to the early 1980s was community jobs for community workers. In the beginning, it was the rallying cry for black construction workers who wanted access to the predominantly white and racially discriminatory construction unions. In particular, "community jobs for community workers" was the slogan of a group of workers who came together in the later 1960s under the banner of the United Community Construction Workers (UCCW).[5]

Around 1968, access to construction jobs was a hot political issue in black neighborhoods. The issue involved organizations such as the Urban League, NAACP, the U.S. Department of Housing and Urban Development (HUD), and local community (Roxbury) groups. According to Mel King (1982), a recent mayoral candidate and lecturer at MIT in Cambridge, the issue surfaced over a HUD-sponsored housing rehabilitation demonstration project located in Roxbury. At that time, HUD depended upon the goodwill of a number of white landlords for the success of the rehabilitation project. This dependency upon white landlords created a good deal of racial tension, especially since the local black community had good reasons not to trust them. And, as reconstruction progressed, a second problem became evident: almost all the construction contractors employed white union labor. These workers were drawn from the union hiring halls and almost always lived outside the local community. The savage irony of white workers rehabilitating white landlords' properties in the middle of black, working-class Roxbury was not lost on the black activists or HUD, the project's sponsor.

For blacks, their exclusion from working on projects in their own community was another bitter blow. Not only were they excluded from construction unions, they couldn't even work in their own community. In response, the UCCW was formed in this period with the support of the Urban League, based on the slogan "community jobs for community workers." Demonstrations and racial confrontations ensued, involving an undersecretary of HUD, Robert Weaver, who had chosen Roxbury because of its obvious needs and importance in the northeast region. At one time, the tensions were so great that there was speculation that HUD might have to abandon support of the demonstration project. While little of direct benefit came out of these confrontations, at least in the form of black employment in local construction projects, a major organizational success was achieved. The UCCW was recognized by the U.S. Department of Labor (DOL) as a legitimate representative of black community construction workers.

In 1969, the DOL brought together the UCCW with organized labor (including the Boston Building Trades Council [BBTC]) and the construction contractors (including the Associated General Contractors of Massachusetts [AGC]) in what was called the "Boston Plan." This was modeled on an earlier Philadelphia plan that sought to provide blacks with a route into the construction industry through an alliance between unions and community organizations.[6] In Boston, DOL proposed and funded a construction recruitment and training program administered jointly by the UCCW, BBTC, and AGC through a local representative organization. Basically, the UCCW was to funnel black workers into union-sponsored apprenticeship schemes. Some local Roxbury organizations were brought in to train black workers for construction jobs even though actual recruitment to real construction worksites remained very limited. But only one year later, 1970, the UCCW decided to withdraw from the alliance, believing that they had no power in what turned out to be an alliance between the BBTC and AGC against the UCCW. But DOL continued to fund the BBTC-AGC training programs, which survived through the early 1970s, using a variety of community leader organizations. Yet it could hardly have been judged a success. In 1983, a decade after the initiative, the assistant attorney general of Massachusetts considered racial discrimination in Boston's construction industry to be rampant.[7]

Although unsuccessful in their attempts to penetrate white construction unions, the UCCW remained a potent political force during the early 1970s. Demonstrations were staged, construction sites picketed, and the unions harassed. The major turning point, however, came in 1974 through an institutional change. Because of a change in HUD's funding arrangements, the City of Boston became the principal conduit of federal community development funds, including Urban Development Action Grants. Until 1974, HUD administered their own projects directly throughout the country, bypassing state and local governments. But this arrangement was unsatisfactory for a number of reasons. For a start, HUD's priorities were thought by many to be inflexible when it came to specific local needs. By being centrally administered, it was argued, HUD's decisions were unresponsive to local situations (Hanson 1982). Moreover, during the Nixon administration a great deal of effort had been put into developing a new plan for sharing local, state, and federal responsibilities—Nixon's so-called new federalism plan. The upshot was a certain measure of local autonomy and decentralized power: federal funds were applied for and administered by cities and towns throughout the nation according to federal guidelines.

Since HUD was the principal source of construction funds (both public and private) in Boston during this period (indeed, through the late 1960s, 1970s, and early 1980s), this change in funding administration suddenly made the City of Boston a major force in the local construction industry. (See table 5.4 for more details on the volume of construction in Boston from 1966 to 1979.) In early 1974, Mayor Kevin White announced a new policy for city-funded or city-administered public construction projects: there was to be affirmative action in the hiring of minorities and women. The mayor brought the UCCW in as the principal black representative, forcing the BBTC and the AGC to negotiate once again with an organization they considered to be extremely radical. At that time, the city sponsored a series of meetings between these groups to foster negotiations, which, it was hoped, would lead to greater black participation in the local construction industry. Again, however, negotiations did not go well, for the unions practically refused to consider quotas. Nevertheless, a major organizational breakthrough was achieved by the minority groups involved.

Chalres Turner, who was involved in these negotiations at the request of the city on the side of the UCCW, suggests now that these negotiations facilitated the formation of an interracial community referral agency (made up of blacks, Hispanics, Chinese, and native Americans) for construction jobs. During 1974, black representatives met with other minority groups to create a new alliance around the idea of a city-sponsored referral agency that would place minority workers in construction jobs. In early 1975, this idea was proposed to the BBTC and the AGC by the UCCW negotiating team. While initially favored by the BBTC—principally because one of the BBTC negotiators was also involved in the leftover Boston Plan, which was foundering at the time—and the AGC, both groups quickly withdrew their support and protested to the mayor. The unions were concerned that the new referral agency would reduce their power as the principal source of construction labor, a fear that came up time and again throughout the next few years in many different guises. For instance, the unions also contended that there are many skills involved in construction and they are the only reliable source of good quality labor. Similarly, the contractors claimed that they would have to bear the cost of training poorly qualified labor referred to them by the new community organization. Again the skills issue was raised, although in a slightly different way.

Despite these protests, the mayor decided to support the new agency, and so the Third World Jobs Clearing House (TWJCH) was formed. It was given a budget of about $200,000 and began operations in late 1975 under the leadership of Charles Turner. The TWJCH brought together many different community groups with interests in construction employment. It was able to create an alliance between blacks and Hispanics who had been antagonists over a number of issues relating to employment in the immediate past. Even so, like the Boston Plan of five years before, it quickly became obvious that the TWJCH was to be largely ignored by the BBTC-AGC. Employers refused to send job referrals to the agency, and the unions made no attempt to involve TWJCH workers. Since the TWJCH depended on the good faith of the BBTC and the AGC to work, it was not surprising that it failed so quickly. Even so, as a political alliance, the TWJCH became a very useful device.[8] To create political agitation, the TWJCH called a meeting in early 1976 to inform their worker-clients that they had been stymied by the unions and contractors. This set the stage for a series of direct confrontations and racial fights between the BBTC and AGC on the one hand and the Third World Workers Association (TWWA, the political action arm of the TWJCH) on the other.

Demonstrations, picketing of contractors, and work-site confrontations did increase the rate of referrals to the TWJCH, and the city did announce a new formal policy of affirmative action: all city-sponsored construction work must hire 30 percent minorities and 10 percent downtown workers. So, for the first time, some recognition was given to the claims of the earlier UCCW that community workers should share in community jobs, although the city policy was very much a token effort.

Even so, during this period, Boston was a city under siege. Court-ordered busing of school children had created a highly charged racial climate, with rooftop sniping, rock-throwing, and open fighting occurring on many city streets.[9] In this climate, the actions of the TWWA and the city were met with a series of violent counterdemonstrations by the overwhelmingly white construction unions. A major demonstration sponsored by the BBTC at City Hall effectively intimidated the City Council and ultimately the mayor. The council voted unanimously to defund the TWJCH and the mayor, apparently reluctantly, agreed. Only the intervention of the DOL with financial support saved the TWJCH. But, at that point, many TWJCH activists concluded that their fight was over. While the city had implemented an affirmative action policy, it was clear to TWJCH activists that it would remain a token policy; little progress could be made given the tremendous racial turmoil in the city. The TWJCH could no longer be used as a vehicle for effecting change in the hiring practices of local unions and contractors.

During the early 1970s Charles Turner, among other TWJCH leaders, had observed that their effectiveness was stymied on a number of occasions by a union argument to the effect that it was difficult to implement an affirmative action policy for the construction industry because it would mean replacing poor white Boston residents with poor black residents. The implication was that it would be unfair to whites, given their own needs for local employment. And since the construction industry had laid off many workers during the early 1970s, union leaders contended that an affirmative action policy could only exacerbate the plight of all Boston workers. But it was not clear to the TWJCH that most white construction workers were, in fact, Boston residents. With the collapse of the drive for greater black and Hispanic representation in construction unions in early 1976, a new strategy had to be developed.

In a series of discussions with white Boston workers and a number of local community development agencies, a new strategy was formed, and the old UCCW's slogan was resurrected, this time as "Boston jobs for Boston people." What Turner and others discovered in their discussion with Boston community groups was that white residents were also being excluded from local construction jobs by the unions. City-based community development groups were finding it hard to control the employment benefits of their local spending policies. Over forty community groups with remnants of the TWJCH formed a new organization in early 1977 called the Boston Jobs Coalition (BJC). Over the next two years it met with white and black community groups and developed a new policy for targeting local construction jobs to local residents. This involved coming up with a set of target quotas, the 50 percent Boston residents notion, and an appropriate legal framework to legitimate their proposed policy.

Charles Turner suggests that the quota idea was borrowed from the earlier UCCW group, a group of activists associated with the Boston office of the Urban League in the late 1960s. As for the legal framework, a late nineteenth-century Massachusetts statute was discovered which actually requires counties, districts, towns, and the state to give preference to their own residents in any local publicly funded construction project. Actually, the 1896 statute, Massachusetts General Laws, Chapter 149, Section 26, was still law even though it had been forgotten and never enforced in the recent past.[10] Some suggestions have been made by BJC activists that it was used extensively during the 1930s depression, but there is little solid evidence to support that claim. Lawyers for the BJC also sought to integrate the resident-preference quota notion with current city requirements for affirmative action. Using the language of current requirements, the lawyers for BJC framed a series of possible regulations and codes of compliance. By late 1978, the BJC was an important voice in the community. This was helped as well by *The Boston Globe*, which ran a series of articles on the proposed idea of "Boston jobs for Boston people." Essentially, organizers like Turner began to use the rhetorical framework of unions' antiaffirmative action arguments to frame a new idea that would appeal to black and white Boston residents alike.

The year leading up to the mayor's signing of the resident-preference executive order was an election year. In early 1979, the BJC announced plans to hold a large community meeting to promote their resident-preference policy. At that time the mayor's office invited the BJC to City Hall to begin negotiations with city officials and, again, the unions and contractors. During this period, city officials were generally supportive of the idea and encouraged their legal staffs to prepare a model of the proposed policy.[11] However, the mayor did not publicly support the policy, and it was left to his mayoral opponents to carry the banner. Indeed, as late as 5 August 1979, *The Boston Globe*'s editorial writer questioned why Mayor White was silent on the policy, even though it was clear that the mayor had given a tacit go-ahead in bringing the BJC into the mayor's office. Finally, just before the Democratic primary and in response to BJC pressure, the mayor announced his support of the policy. He signed the executive order on 11 September. But, even then, there were some issues unresolved, particularly the applicability of the order to the city's so-called 121A projects—those private projects financed through city tax rebates and incentives. Again under political pressure at a candidates' night in October, the mayor decided to make the order apply to *all* construction projects.

Up to this point, the construction unions and contractors had been reluctant partners in the city-sponsored negotiations over the new resident-preference policy. As in previous negotiations over affirmative action in construction employment, they resented the involvement of community organizers like Charles Turner and were reluctant to heed the city's existing affirmative action policy. But, because of their dependence on city projects, they were forced to be involved in negotiation. Moreover, because of the nature of the policy and the rhetorical strategy of people like Turner, the unions were effectively limited in their objections. However, once the Executive order had been signed and it became evident that it would be enforced, both the BBTC and the AGC voiced a great deal of alarm and threatened to sue if some compromise was not reached. Ultimately, the unions refused to consider *any* resident-preference quotas, and in October 1979 the unions and contractors began the process of appealing the city policy to the Massachusetts Supreme Judicial Court.

Implementing Boston's Jobs Policy

One of the striking dimensions of the political fight over the access of minorities, women, and residents to local jobs has to do with the various institutional roles the city played vis-à-vis other levels of government. I suggested above that an important turning point in the political wrangling was the devolution of HUD's administration powers to the city in 1974. Previously, the city had little effective leverage over the behavior of local unions and contractors or, for that matter, HUD. Although the city still had to apply for funds and administer them in accordance with HUD regulations, Boston gained considerable power from the shift in congressional policy. Simply put, Congress gave the cities a measure of initiative, a sphere of autonomy, and control over local public works. As long as the city acted in accordance with HUD rules of administration, the city could spend its funds in ways which would best advance its own objectives. The fiscal leverage, coupled with the initiative powers, gave the city a large measure of institutional power.

In addition, finding the Massachusetts General Law, Chapter 149, Section 26, also gave the city a much-needed measure of autonomy. This statute reads, in part, "In the employment of mechanics and apprentices, . . . and laborers in the construction of public works by the commonwealth, or by a county, town or district . . . preference shall first be given to citizens of the commonwealth," and "Each county, town, or district in the construction of public works   .   .   . shall give preference to veterans and citizens who are residents of such county, town, or district." Boston could defend its actions in terms of an existing broad grant of powers, recognizing that all American cities are "creatures of the state" (Frug 1980). Again, initiative was limited to the wording and framework of existing legislation. The city had to act within an a priori legal framework. Even so, this framework provided initiative powers which, once chosen to be used, could make a tremendous difference to the city in attempting to implement its goals. In this respect, the legal system was an opportunity for the city to carry out its politically conceived goals. As we shall see in a moment, however, the legal system provided almost no immunity to the City of Boston. Thus, having signed the order and begun to implement its requirements, the city had to contend with a challenge that sought to deny the constitutionality of its policy initiatives.

Before going on to the legal challenge, it is important to consider, albeit briefly, the city's attempts to implement the policy as well as the local economic circumstances of this period. Both issues have bearing upon future analysis of the legal opinions, and both reflect the importance the city attached to the policy.

Generally, the integrity of the policy owes much to the diligence and institutional power of James Younger, director of the city's affirmative action compliance office. Younger moved quickly to implement the resident-preference policy in the first few months after the mayor's order had been signed. He met with the city's major administrative units, formally notified the various economic development authorities (including the Boston Redevelopment Authority [BRA], the Economic Development and Industrial Commission [EDIC], etc.) and conducted training sessions for the various departments' contract compliance officers. Prebid work schedules were developed for construction firms and included lists of appropriate city employment referral agencies, manning tables, and copies of the executive order's requirements. Over October and November, the order's provisions were incorporated into many city-financed and city-administered projects, running the gamut from the Public Facilities Department's new pumping station, the Ambulatory Care Center at the Boston City Hospital, to a tunnel contract let by the city's Real Property Department. Younger, a black, was strongly committed to the resident-preference policy and in an interview on 28 April 1983 said, "I wanted to be very much involved in formulating that policy and also [to] have responsibility for monitoring and implementing it."

As part of the city's compliance-monitoring efforts, contractors were required to fill their apprenticeship training programs with at least 50 percent Boston residents. This policy, coupled with the city's previously announced (30 June 1978) policy on minority business enterprises, gave blacks and Hispanics a new chance to share the benefits of local economic growth. The minority business policy required that in general, "at least 10 percent of the value of all construction goods and services procured by the City . . . be obtained from minority business enterprises" and that at least "30 percent of all construction work to be performed in impacted areas shall be contracted to minority business enterprises" (City of Boston memo, dated 9 January 1980). These "impacted areas" included large sections of Chinatown, the South End, Roxbury, South Boston and Dorchester, Hyde Park and Jamaica Plain, and Mattapan, basically Boston neighborhoods with significant numbers of minorities and the poor. Contractors were required to ascertain the residences of their workers, the minority status of their work force, and the minority status of subcontractors—both their work force's residency and their ownership.[12]

In the first year of the new policy (December 1979 to December 1980), some 128 contracts were monitored involving 131,934 work hours. Of those total work hours, some 40 percent were performed by local residents. This was judged to be a good effort since the policy was new and was being challenged in the courts by the unions and contractors during much of 1980. However, in the subsequent year, compliance dropped to 34 percent when the Massachusetts Supreme Judicial Court voted unanimously on 28 August 1981 to strike down the policy. Thereafter, voluntary compliance could only be asked for, although it should be acknowledged that even in the first year the order lacked effective legal status. Over the year 1982, under voluntary compliance, the percentage of Boston residents' work hours fell to just less than 30 percent, far short of the 50 percent goal. Since the U.S. Supreme Court upheld the policy in February 1983, the compliance percentage has dramatically increased so that at last word (January 1984), the resident-preference policy was finally being *effectively* implemented.

To understand the extent of racial and residential discrimination practiced by construction unions and contractors during the late 1970s and early 1980s, we can only depend on fragments of data and evidence. The unions have been very reluctant to release membership data. One survey in 1977 by the Massachusetts Department of Public Works (DPW) estimated that less than 30 percent of construction workers working on DPW Boston projects were Boston residents. The same survey found that this percentage varied by neighborhood so that only 19 percent of workers at an East Boston site were Boston residents while 45 percent of workers at a South End project were Boston residents (King 1982). It has also been observed by James Younger that these figures vary by skill and size of firm (personal communication, April 1983). Small firms employing unskilled labor tend to hire local residents more than outside residents while larger firms employing more skilled, union-certified workers tend to employ non-Boston residents. It should come as no surprise to learn that these latter types of firms are the most union-organized.

In 1982 I surveyed Boston unions and found that they used goals of 5.5 percent and 21.9 percent for minority and female representation in apprenticeship programs (obviously the unions had no locality goals at that time). These percentages roughly conformed to 1980 estimates of the proportion of blacks and women in the Boston SMSA labor force (for some reason, the union halved the female labor force proportion of 47.8 percent). Actual city data for the same period suggest that blacks were about 22.8 percent and women about 53.1 percent of the Boston work force. Use of Boston SMSA labor force data by the unions was obviously an attempt to legitimate low—only token—affirmative action goals. Indeed, as a commentator on urban labor market policy has noted, the federal courts have ruled that city labor force data provide a far more reasonable basis for evaluating the affirmative action plans of unions because it is the innercity area that is the most likely "area from which they would draw the vast majority of workers for apprenticeship . . . purposes" (Gould 1977, p. 282).

In addition, specific apprenticeship programs revealed that racial and sexual discrimination was widespread (personal survey, 1982). For instance, of 299 electrician apprentices 6.7 percent were minorities and 7.4 percent women; of 276 ironworker apprentices 18.1 percent were blacks and 2.9 percent women; of 120 apprentice painters 11.6 percent were women, with no evidence of minorities; and, of 95 bricklayer apprentices, 18.9 percent were blacks and 6.3 percent women. But, the practice of discrimination goes far beyond entry into apprenticeship programs. Graduating apprentices still have to be hired. The Massachusetts Division of Employment Security estimated that in 1982 less than 10 percent of all active Boston construction workers were minorities.

The reader should remember that an argument often made by the unions through the 1970s was that economic circumstances in the construction industry were so bad that nothing could justify replacing a poor white Boston worker with a poor black worker. Of course, the evidence noted above fundamentally questions the veracity of this argument on two grounds. First, it is obvious from tables 5.1 and 5.2 that few construction workers were in fact Boston residents. Second, it is also apparent that the unions systematically discriminated against black workers so that their representation in the construction industry was far below their numbers in the overall city work force. Of course, it was true that economic circumstances were very poor during much of the 1970s for Boston's construction industry. In 1970, the estimated rate of unemployment for Boston was 4.3 percent, in 1975 the figure was 12.8, and in 1980

Table 5.1   Residency of City-Funded Construction Work Force

Month	Total Workers	Boston Residents		Non-Massachusetts Residents	
December 1978	433	172	38.0%	5	1.1%
March 1979	114	41	36.0	8	7.0
May 1979	534	215	40.0	1	0.2
September 1979	641	209	33.0	7	1.1
August 1980	128	50	36.0	11	8.0
September 1980	120	53	44.0	11	8.0

Source: Appendix E, Massachusetts Supreme Judicial Court, No. 80-115-Civil p. A48.

Table 5.2   Residence of Work Force, December 1978

	Employees	Percentage
I. Breakdown of work force		
Total number of workers	433	
Total Boston workers	172	38.8
Total non-Boston Massachusetts workers	259	58.5
Total non-Massachusetts workers	12	2.7
Total non-Massachusetts workers employed on projects with less than 50% Boston residents	7	1.6
II. Breakdown of employers		
Total number of employers	67	
Number of employers who employed non-Massachusetts residents	8	11.9
III. Employers who employed non-Massachusetts workers and had at least 50% Boston residents		
Napoli Wrecking Co., Dorchester, Mass. (4 Boston, 3 N.H., 1 other Mass.)	8	
H. Piker & Co., address unknown (5 Boston, 1 N.H., 1 R.I., 2 other Mass.)	10	
H. Carr & Sons, Providence R.I. (1 Boston, 1 R.I.)	2	
IV. Employers who employed non-Massachusetts workers and *did not* have at least 50% Boston residents		
Wexler Construction Co., Needham, Mass. (15 Boston, 1 R.I., 25 other Mass.)	41	
Old Colony Crushed Stone Construction Co., Quincy, Mass. (3 Boston, 2 R.I., 9 other Mass.)	14	
Erection Specialists, address unknown (2 Boston, 1 R.I., 4 other Mass.)	7	
National Plate & Window Glass Co., address unknown (1 N.H., 1 other Mass.)	2	
E.T. Ryan Iron Works, Inc., address unknown	13	

Source: Appendix F, Massachusetts Supreme Judicial Court, No. 80-115-Civil pp. A49–A50.

the figure was 7.2 percent (table 5.3). The Massachusetts Divison of Employment Security (private communication) estimates that unemployment rates in the construction industry for these three dates were about 9 percent, 47 percent, and 33 percent, respectively. More precise figures are hard to come by, mostly because the unions have been reluctant to release figures on the employment status of their membership.

Over the same period, the estimated construction cost of city-issued building permits varied from $313 million in 1970 to $153 million in 1975, and $209 million in 1979 (the latest data available), all measured in current dollars (table 5.4). Given steep increases in price inflation over this period, it is clear that the Boston construction industry went through a severe economic depression during the 1970s. To summarize, Boston's construction industry has been characterized by racial and residential discrimination at all levels—entry to apprenticeship schemes, referrals to jobs, and employment. The efforts of the City of Boston notwithstanding, the city had little chance to affect patterns of employment discrimina-

Table 5.3 Local and National Unemployment Rates (Percent)

	1970	1975	1976	1977	1978	1979	June 1980*
Boston	4.3	12.8	11.1	9.5	7.2	6.5	7.2
Boston SMSA	3.7	10.5	9.1	7.8	5.9	5.2	5.9
Massachusetts	4.6	11.2	9.5	8.1	6.1	5.5	6.6
United States	4.9	8.5	7.7	7.0	6.0	5.8	7.8

*Not seasonally adjusted.
Sources: U.S. Bureau of Labor Statistics; Massachusetts Division of Employment Security.

Table 5.4 Estimated Cost of Construction for Building Permits Issued by the City of Boston

Period Ended	New Construction	Alterations	Total
31 December 1966	$ 61,597,600	$ 40,475,600	$102,073,200
31 December 1968	167,630,200	30,037,900	197,668,100
31 December 1970	260,331,700	52,878,200	313,209,900
31 December 1972	118,890,675	61,193,100	180,083,775
30 June 1974 (18 mos.)	113,867,787	88,651,302	202,519,089
30 June 1976	40,811,716	112,903,729	153,715,445
30 June 1978	45,792,575	113,453,800	159,246,375
30 June 1979	67,801,637	141,203,000	209,004,637

Source: Boston Building Department, Massachusetts Supreme Judicial Court, No. 80-115-Civil.

tion until passage of the executive order and, even then, litigation severely hampered its implementation.

The Legal Challenge

Having won a political fight for the adoption and implementation of the
resident-preference policy, the BJC and the mayor of Boston faced a
legal challenge based on quite different grounds. On 20 March 1980, Paul
Kingston, attorney for the unions and contractors, presented their legal
challenge in a civil suit (under Massachusetts General Laws, Chap. 231A)
before the Massachusetts Supreme Judicial Court. The plaintiffs sought a
ruling that would declare as unconstitutional and therefore void the
resident-preference policy (Executive Order, 11 September 1979), the
minority business enterprise policy (Executive Order, 28 June 1978), and
the Massachusetts public works citizens and veterans hiring preference
statute (Chap. 149, Sec. 26). The defendants named in the case were the
city, the mayor, the City of Boston's Redevelopment Authority, which
was responsible for the administration of Chapter 121A tax incentives for
privte construction, the city's Economic Development and Industrial
Corporation, and the Department of Labor and Industries of the Commonwealth of Massachusetts, which was responsible for the enforcement
of Chapter 149, Section 26. The plaintiffs sought to remove, by one
integrated legal challenge, the whole structure of city and state policies
that directly affected their rights to employment and hiring in the public
construction industry. Moreover, the plaintiffs sought to shift the focus of
the challenge away from the immediate political arena to the constitutional realm, thereby attempting to restructure the logic of the whole
debate.

   In their brief to the court, the construction unions and contractors
argued the effects of the executive orders and Chapter 149 (the "rules"
hereafter) to be fivefold. First, it was suggested that because these rules
applied to local and federally funded and locally administered projects,
there were inconsistencies and conflicts between these rules and the
provisions of Title VI of the Civil Rights Act of 1964 (42 USC 2000d).
Second, they argued that the private contractors faced the prospect of
"serious economic disadvantage and irreparable harm" if, as a result of
these rules, they were forced to refrain from bidding on Boston public or
121A-related construction works. They argued that this was especially
relevant for out-of-state contractors and named the W. T. Rich Company
as an instance in which the new rules had dissuaded a company from
bidding on the Boston City Hospital construction project. Third, they
argued that the rules conflicted with existing collective agreements which
do not allow for discriminatory hiring on the basis of residence, race, or

sex. It was also suggested in this context that any variation from the terms of these agreements would make contractors liable for breach of contract under the National Labor Relations Act. Fourth, the plaintiffs suggested that there were not enough qualified and resident construction workers and minority businesses which could reasonably be employed or used in Boston construction projects. Thus, there was an implied cost or burden to be borne by the contractors. Finally, it was argued that the residency requirements discriminated against noncitizens of Massachusetts and nonresidents of Boston, causing them serious economic harm by virtue of being denied work opportunities.

Under the terms of the court's procedures, the plaintiffs and defendants conferred and came to an agreement on a number of effects that could be construed to follow directly from the city's new rules. They agreed that the rules would result in unemployment of certain construction workers who were nonresidents of Boston and nonresidents of Massachusetts. They also agreed that some out-of-state and out-of-city contractors would be discouraged from bidding on construction projects, thereby limiting competition and increasing the costs of public construction work. But it was also agreed that the rules would alleviate unemployment of Boston residents, reduce the social costs associated with high unemployment, generate further tax revenues for the state and the city, and match the ethnic and racial composition of Boston residents with construction workers working on city projects. It was further agreed that the new rules might alleviate racial tensions, increase tensions between city and noncity residents, and interrupt or speed the work of construction projects.

More specifically, the construction industry's challenge to Boston's employment policies was based on three grounds. Kingston argued that the rules violated the Privileges and Immunities Clause (Art. IV, Sec. 2) of the U.S. Constitution, violated the Commerce Clause of the U.S. Constitution, and violated the National Labor Relations Act. As we shall see, other issues were involved, but these were the principal grounds of objection. Kingston suggested in his brief to the court that the Privileges and Immunities Clause was crucial because it prohibits discrimination by one state against the citizens of another state. This clause holds that "The citizens of each State shall be entitled to all Privileges and Immunities of Citizens in the several States." It has a long history as the principal protection against state-initiated exclusive practices, going as far back, in spirit, as the Founding Fathers of the Constitution (Clark 1981b).

Quoting *Paul v. Virginia* (1869), Kingston argued that both Massachusetts General Laws, Chapter 149, Section 26 and the resident-preference executive order did in fact discriminate against out-of-state residents (albeit very few people were actually involved; see table 5.2). In addition, Kingston invoked the recently decided case of *Hicklin v. Orbeck* (1978), in which the U.S. Supreme Court had ruled unconstitutional an Alaskan statute that required all construction contracts relating to oil and gas pipelines to give preference to qualified Alaskan residents in all employment matters. This case was based upon the Privileges and Immunities Clause, and Kingston argued that Boston's employment policy was much the same in intent and effect.

Part of the logic of Kingston's argument depended on assuming that out-of-state residents were not a major source of the unemployment problems of Boston residents. Thus, any discrimination against out-of-state residents was then arbitrary and against the spirit of the clause. The attorney also pointed to a similar decision in New York wherein the New York Court of Appeals ruled that a statue similar to Chapter 149, Section 26 requiring preference to be given to New York State residents in public works projects was unconstitutional (*Salla v. County of Monroe* [1979]). Again, the crucial issue for Kingston was the ruling that out-of-state residents did not represent a special threat to the employment chances of New York residents. Thus, a parallel was again drawn to the Boston situation. As a side issue, Kingston also suggested that the Boston rules had a further defect, for while the Alaskan statute at least recognized the need for qualified personnel, the Boston rules did not.

Another very important part of the plaintiffs' argument was based on the Commerce Clause.[13] As the policy would unfairly discriminate against out-of-state workers, it would also act as a de facto impediment to the right of out-of-state contractors to do business in Massachusetts and the City of Boston. In this respect, Kingston argued that the policy would violate the Commerce Clause of the U.S. Constitution, which is understood to be a means of countering state-based protectionist economic policies (Clark 1981*b*). Most generally, this clause holds that "The Congress shall have power . . . to regulate Commerce with foreign nations, and among the several states , and with the Indian Tribes." This clause has been interpreted by many academics and Supreme Court justices to be the vehicle of national economic integration. Indeed, in the early 1920s and 1930s, the courts used language such as the "current of commerce" to suggest that the United States was best understood as an integrated system of exchange and production (Clark 1981*b*).

It was also suggested that the size and influence of state and local governments in the construction industry is such that, in the absence of the Commerce Clause, the whole industry would be balkanized. And, Kingston suggested that it was precisely this kind of balkanization that the Commerce Clause was designed to protect against.

Even so, an important distinction had to be made to separate the Boston case from other precedents. In two recent cases, *Hughes v.*

Alexandria Scrap Corp. (1976) and *Reeves Inc. v. Stake* (1980), the U.S. Supreme Court had held that when a state acts as a market participant as opposed to a market regulator, then its actions in preferring its own residents may not violate the Commerce Clause. In the first case, the Court upheld a Maryland statute related to vehicle registration, arguing that as long as the first and direct party concerned was a Maryland resident, then by virtue of the implied contractural nature of the relationship, the state would be interpreted as simply acting in its capacity as an equivalent private actor. Similarly, this argument also held for the latter case. Kingston argued that Boston, by requiring all contractors and their subcontractors to fulfill certain quotas regardless of the performance of their private contractual duties, acted as a market regulator, not participant.

A related objection to a possible state sovereignty exemption from the Commerce Clause was also mounted by Kingston. He suggested that the so-called doctrine of state proprietary immunity was not relevant here because statutes like Chapter 149, Section 26 have a great deal of potential in affecting the current of commerce between the states. Again, by virtue of the size and influence of state governments, if all states undertook this policy, then the construction industry would tend to become spatially fragmented and balkanized—again, an implication which, Kingston argued, went against the intent of the Commerce Clause.

The third principal objection to Boston's employment rules was that these rules interfered with the contractual obligations between unions and contractors, thereby conflicting with the National Labor Relations Act. The Supremacy Clause of Article VI of the U.S. Constitution provides that federal statutes are supreme when compared to state actions and this clause holds that "This Constitution, and the Laws of the United States which shall be made in pursuance thereof; and all treaties made, or which shall be made, under the authority of the United States, shall be the supreme law of the land; and the judges in every State shall be bound thereby."

On the basis of this clause, Kingston argued that Boston's residency rules ought to be declared unconstitutional. He cited a number of cases as precedent, most of them relating to state statutes interfering with established private employment relations. In this respect, Kingston quotes Archibald Cox as arguing that the NLRA and LMRA frameworks would be upset if a State could enforce statutes or rules of decision resting upon its view. While there is a great deal of dispute regarding the grounds for applying preemption or supremacy, Kingston argued that the Boston case clearly came under the preemption doctrine. He cited the case of *Local 24, Teamsters v. Oliver* (1959) in support, wherein the State of Ohio attempted to apply Ohio antitrust law to the conditions of an

NLRA-sanctioned employment contract. The U.S. Supreme Court suggested that the issue at hand was part of the internal logic of the contract and therefore outside the control of the state ("absent any Congressional intent to the contrary").

A number of other issues were raised by Kingston, including the possibility that the Boston policy violated the Equal Protection Clause of the Fourteenth Amendment of the U.S. Constitution and Articles I, X, and XII of the Massachusetts Constitution. Here Kingston cited an older Massachusetts case, *Commonwealth v. Hana* (1907), to the effect that discrimination based upon residence interfered with an individual's right to pursue his or her own interests. Similarly, the previous cases of *Hicklin* and *Salla* were invoked to provide evidence for the federal issue. Another issue raised concerned the consistency of Boston's resident policy with the rules and regulations of two federal departments, the U.S. Department of Commerce and the Department of Housing and Urban Development. Problems raised here concerned the availability of qualified labor, the restrictions imposed on contractors in hiring suitable labor, the degree of target efficiency (i.e., relating to low-income residents) of the Boston resident policy, and the limits of Boston's autonomy in designing employment policies in federally funded construction projects. Finally, it should also be recognized that questions were raised about the exercise of city powers under the state Constitution. In his initial brief, Kingston argued that Mayor White had gone beyond his powers as specified in the Massachusetts incorporation of the City of Boston.[14]

While all these issues are interesting in their own right, the Massachusetts Supreme Judicial Court chose to concentrate on the three principal grounds of objection. The Commerce Clause, the Privileges and Immunities Clause, and the National Labor Relations Act all involved federal sovereignty and preemption. The more local city-based issues were left behind. Notice, however, how the initial political dispute was transformed. Instead of dealing directly with the local racial roots of the conflict, the case Kingston argued practically ignored these issues and concentrated on the rights of a few out-of-state residents. Instead of dealing with the claims of metropolitan unions to unimpeded access to city construction jobs, Kingston chose to emphasize the possible, but remote, likelihood that similar state policies would balkanize the U.S. construction industry. Furthermore, he invoked a notion of "private" contract law to suggest that the "public" had no right to affect the relations between private unions and contractors. It is obvious that the specific local political context was transformed by simultaneously making the issue one of state-level discrimination and of discrimination against out-of-state residents, not the existing local patterns of discrimination in the Boston construction industry.

On 28 August 1981, the court found that: (*a*) the Boston resident-preference policy violated the Commerce Clause; (*b*) Chapter 149, Section 26 violated the Privileges and Immunities Clause; and (*c*) neither the executive order nor Chapter 149, Section 26 violated the National Labor Relations Act. In terms of the Commerce Clause, the court agreed with the plaintiffs that *Hicklin v. Orbeck* effectively denied the constitutionality of both the executive order and Chapter 149, Section 26. Moreover, they argued that the intent of the city and agreed facts "clearly" indicated that the executive order was simple protectionism, thereby triggering a "virtually per se rule of invalidity" based on *City of Philadelphia v. New Jersey* (1978). Similarly, they argued that the statute and executive order contravened the Privileges and Immunities Clause as it protects the rights of out-of-state residents to pursue their interests. And the court contended that the city was more than a simple market participant; it contended that as a consequence the statute was unconstitutional. The court did not, however, find that the NLRA was violated and suggested that the city had not intruded into the negotiating process between contracting parties.

To summarize, the unions and contractors won a major legal victory over their political opponents. Not only did the court accept the logic of their arguments, especially the interpretation of the dispute itself, the court actually used the reasoning of the plaintiffs' attorney. Thus very little of the political texture of the dispute made its way into the interpretation and adjudication process. Nowhere in its judgment does the court indicate that it was aware of, or thought relevant, the local political tensions regarding racial and residential discrimination. By going along with the plaintiffs' conception of the legal dispute, the court did not have to deal with any of the substantive political issues involved. Indeed, by linking the issue to matters of U.S. and commonwealth constitutional law, the result was a foregone conclusion. But this time the mayor remained loyal in his commitment to the jobs policy by hiring a new lawyer, a constitutional law expert from Harvard Law School, to carry the dispute to the Supreme Court.

Local Autonomy and the Supreme Court

The City of Boston went before the Supreme Court in early 1982 to have the lower court decision overturned and the executive orders ruled constitutional. In his submission to the court, Lawrence Tribe, the city's new lawyer, sought to reestablish the importance of the executive orders vis-à-vis the nature of Boston's employment and racial problems. And in particular, Tribe posed the issue of "whether the Commerce Clause invites . . . judicial veto over municipal options for coping with inner-city joblessness and urban decay"(p. 10).[15] While he did suggest that "complete reconciliation of Commerce Clause concerns with concerns of State and local autonomy cannot be fairly expected" he also suggested that the Supreme Court might consider the following arguments. First and foremost, he argued that the Court should agree that the Commerce Clause does not invalidate local provisions regarding the arrangement of local public works simply because some out-of-state firms may opt out of the bidding process as a result of local policies such as resident-preference requirements.

Tribe then argued that the Court must make clear that the Commerce Clause can only be used as a relative test of the efficacy of any local policy, not as an absolute denial of local initiative. That is, where the burden of local policies on interstate commerce is minimal and where local job benefits of city-based policies such as resident affirmative actions are considerable, then the courts should uphold such city policies in the belief that many stand to benefit and few, if any, stand to lose. Finally, Tribe also argued that city-based policies should not be invalidated simply because the city carried out its tasks through traditional means (such as direct hiring and public construction) or less conventional means (such as the regulation of private behavior, like private contracts). Tribe implied that the substantive (ends) goals of city policies should have precedence over procedural (means) concerns. In these arguments, Tribe emphasized the importance of maintaining local discretion and a consequent "moderate" reading of the Commerce Clause. For instance, he argued that the Massachusetts Supreme Judicial Court used the Commerce Clause as an obstructive barrier, thereby denying the attempts of the City of Boston to improve local economic conditions.

But Tribe did more than argue principles of law; he also painted a picture of local conditions which suggested that the City of Boston's central concern was the welfare and equity of its residents. Tribe emphasized the relevant facts, as he termed them: high levels of unemployment, past patterns of racial discrimination in the construction industry, racial tensions, the racial and ethnic differences between local residents and construction workers, and the dependence of the City of Boston on the construction industry as a vehicle for improving local conditions. He pointed to the benefits of the executive orders, including job skills and work experience and the tax benefits that would accrue to the city. From Paul Kingston's perspective as the attorney for the unions and contractors, Tribe put a "wash" (a picture or interpretation) on the dispute that made the city's policies look reasonable, indeed necessary. Put most crudely, Tribe implied that the "inner-city residents deserved a shot at local jobs" (Paul Kingston's words). As an argument for local autonomy, the substantive texture of the original conditions which had given rise to the city's jobs policy in the first place became powerful rhetorical tools with the right emphasis.

In detail, Tribe's argument began by noting that the Commerce Clause "protects the interstate market, not particular firms," quoting *Exxon Corp. v. Governor of Maryland* (1978). He also noted a previous case in which the Commerce Clause was interpreted as a relative measure requiring a concrete balancing of "the burden imposed . . . in relation to the . . . local benefits"; see *Pike v. Bruce Church, Inc.* (1970). Given that no evidence had been presented to suggest that Boston's jobs policy would have had a substantial or decisive effect on interstate commerce, Tribe suggested that this case came under the terms of the previously referenced cases. In particular, he used *Exxon* to suggest that the lower court had used the Commerce Clause as a shield for "particular interstate firms." Thus, he suggested, the court had not fully appreciated the subtleties of precedent. He also argued that it had misinterpreted *Hicklin v. Orbeck* (1978) and had misrepresented the intent of the executive orders. Indeed, he was able to turn the court's logic around to demonstrate that resident job preference was a necessary policy for ensuring that the benefits of local public construction are effectively targeted to those in need.

The second crucial argument turned on how local government actions are defined, either as a market participant or as a market regulator. In *Reeves, Inc. v. Stake* (1980), the Supreme Court held that the Commerce Clause did not apply to states' "marketplace behavior." That is, state and local governments have a measure of immunity even under the Commerce Clause when contracting with private parties to buy or supply goods and services. Just because the City of Boston was acting in terms of its "governmental interests" (providing local jobs and employment skills) in specifying local contractual conditions did not, according to Tribe, reduce its sphere of immunity under the Commerce Clause. Even though Boston may regulate private actions through direct and secondary contracts like resident-preference policies that require private firms to hire local residents, Tribe argued that this distinction makes no difference to the applicability of the Commerce Clause. His last point was that, as in *National League of Cities v. Usery* (1976), the Commerce Clause ought to leave intact the capacity of state and local governments to "fashion effective and creative programs for solving local problems and distributing government largesse" (see also *Reeves*, at p. 848, and Tribe, p. 23).

The respondents before the Supreme Court (the unions and contractors represented by Paul Kingston) stood their ground as argued at the Massachusetts Supreme Judicial Court. The lower court's decision was expanded upon and the relevant precedents mentioned again. Again they emphasized the Commerce Clause issues, especially the supposed damage that the executive order would inflict on out-of-state residents and firms. Consistent with the intent of the clause, the attorney for the respondents emphasized the workforce affected, the protectionism implied by such an order, and the overall original intent of the clause itself. For instance, *Toomer v. Witsell* (1948) was quoted to the effect that the Commerce Clause and the Privileges and Immunities Clause were intended "to help fuse into one nation a collection of independent sovereign States," and *H.P. Hood & Sons Ltd. v. DuMond* (1949) was quoted as supporting these clauses as they arrest the "drift toward anarchy and commercial warfare between States," and finally, that the Constitution itself was "framed upon the theory that the peoples of the several States must sink or swim together, and that in the long run prosperity and salvation are in union, not division," quoting *Baldwin v. Seelig* (1935).

Kingston's argument suggests that the order invited retaliation and protectionism of the worst kind and that it would balkanize prosperity against the explicit wishes of the Founding Fathers. In these terms, he quoted *City of Philadelphia v. New Jersey* (1978) to the effect that "where simple economic protectionism is effected by State legislation, a virtually per se rule of invalidity has been erected." A question was also raised regarding the actual interest of the city in the various construction projects. It was noted by the respondents that the city acted more as a conduit for federal funds than as a real partner in public works construction. Moreover, since many projects were characterized by a low government share in terms of funding or equity (the major balance being put up by private financiers), then many projects could be construed as private works, not public works. Thus, according to Kingston, the city's actions could not be protected or immunized from the application of the Commerce Clause. The respondents played out the lower court decision to the final bell.

On 28 February 1983, the U.S. Supreme Court decided in favor of the city, holding that the Commerce Clause did not invalidate the mayor's executive order. Justice Rehnquist, writing for the majority opinion, argued first that since the local government was a "market participant," then the Commerce Clause did not apply. Basically, as a market participant, state and local governments have a sphere of immunity under the Commerce Clause that allows them to require certain conditions, obligations, and the like from their contractual parties. Since no contractor is forced to enter into a contract with local government and his or her behavior is not arbitrarily regulated, then it is up to the contractors to decide if they wish to undertake the terms of the contract. Second, Rehnquist also argued that even if the executive order had a significant impact on commerce, this was irrelevant given a prior determination of the role of the city as "market participant." Finally, it was argued that the source of funds was irrelevant. As long as the city acted within the terms of the congressional mandate, local discretion was valid, indeed legitimate.

The Court argued that there was no indication in the Constitution that the Commerce Clause was applicable to state actions in the private market. Quoting their previous decision in *Reeves, Inc. v. Stake* (1980), the Court argued for a narrow interpretation of the clause which depends upon a clear demarcation between "participant" and "regulator." While it is difficult to make such a distinction in practice, since governments typically do both at the same time (Clark and Dear 1984), the Court suggested that each local government action should be considered independently and on its *narrow* terms. Arguing against applicability of *Hicklin*, the Court suggested that "where State or local government action is specifically authorized by Congress, it is not subject to the Commerce Clause, even if it interferes with interstate commerce," quoting *Southern Pacific Co. v. Arizona* (1945). Thus, as Boston's financing of local construction was made possible by HUD, this arrangement effectively granted the city powers of initiative and immunity under this umbrella. Local autonomy was hence protected and sustained in the first instance by Congress itself. Even Justice Blackmun, writing for Justice White in dissent, agreed that the congressional mandate was crucial in this context, although he did raise a further issue of the narrowness of this grant of power.

Again, the city had won against the unions and contractors. In this instance, the city was able to bolster its political mandate for the resident-preference policy with an affirmative ruling from the highest court of the land. For White, it was a tremendous boost, one which he claimed as his own in the media and in the City Council. Writing in the *Hyde Park–Mattapan Tribune* (March 1983), the mayor reviewed his commitment to the policy over the period 1979–83 and noted that "by a 7–2 vote, the Supreme Court agreed with my original position that the city has the right to favor its own citizens over others." It remains a precedent ruling, one whose implications remain to be explored, as *The Boston Globe's* editorial writer suggested: "White's Executive Order made good political, economic, and social sense . . . The challenge . . . now is to convert a good idea to a good policy by implementing it aggressively" (1 March 1983).

Politics, Law, and Local Autonomy

The lessons of this case study are threefold and relate to the relationship between politics and law, the logic of judicial decision making, and the nature of local autonomy. At one level, it is plain that the legal apparatus is a major actor in political conflict. Even though the unions and contractors had lost the political battle in 1979 with White's signing of the executive order, these two groups were able to fight the implementation of the order through the state and national courts. Indeed, at the state level, the unions and contractors won, reversing their political loss in a way that seemed at first to be a permanent victory. At this level, law is politics in a quite elementary and instrumental way. Depending on who decides the legal challenge and how the various interests are represented in court, the courts act to sustain the interests of one party (or parties) over another. Thus we can imagine that stacking the court is a viable, even desirable policy when attempting to sustain political domination.

Even so, law is more than politics. The texture of legal interpretation, the logic under which political issues are brought to the courts, and how legal precedent is chosen to measure an issue, all contribute to a transformation of the political into the legal. By a forceful argument of law, the issue at hand may be so transformed that the original political texture is to all intents lost in the translation. For instance, at the Massachusetts Supreme Judicial Court, the unions and contractors were able to raise completely different legal issues (like the Commerce Clause) to effectively swamp the political context (racial and residential discrimination). The whole political struggle was lost as an interpretive factor once the court decided to adjudicate the issue according to the terms of the plaintiffs. This is no mere accident or simple play of words; choice of the legal context in which to argue a case is clearly a subtle and highly contentious strategy. So important is the legal *order* of disputes, such as the one considered in this chapter, that ten years of community activism can be effectively dismissed by a strategic legal brief. The translation between politics and law makes law itself a very powerful political device.

Notice, however, that once we enter the realm of legal argument, indeterminacy abounds. For instance, the unions and contractors held that the Commerce Clause was an absolute measure of the executive order's constitutionality. They based their interpretation on what they thought was *precedent*, the *original intent* of the clause, and the controlling significance of an *exemplary case*. But Tribe, the lawyer for the city, argued that the Commerce Clause is a relative measure, not an absolute denial of constraints on interstate commerce. Furthermore, he based his argument on *precedent*, just like the respondents, even interpreting the same cases (like *Hicklin*). And yet, when the Supreme Court made its decision, it neatly sidestepped a number of difficult issues by making the whole problem dependent upon a somewhat arbitrary and empirical judgment about local government as a "market participant" rather than "market regulator." The Court even used *precedent* and *original intent* (in a negative sense—what it did not say) to legitimize its decision. The tools of argument were the same, but the outcomes fundamentally different.

One of the most interesting points in the previous discussion had to do with the importance of the choice of legal terrain—the context from which to argue. Kingston, the lawyer for the unions and contractors, said it well in an interview: Tribe's position on the necessity for local discretion in solving significant unemployment and racial problems made a tremendous impact on the Supreme Court. It was "a very forceful argument," to quote Kingston. But, of course, it was just that—an argument of emphasis and selection. Where Kingston was able to alter the political argument at the lower level by invoking constitutional concerns, Tribe was just as successful at the Supreme Court level in deemphasizing the constitutional issues and reemphasizing the original political context. By taking seriously the political context, the Supreme Court effectively took sides in the matter and decided for the city against established interests. Rhetoric is a skillful technique of persuasion as is the choice of terrain; argument for one position has to be made so that alternatives are denied and a way forward is laid open. The Supreme Court used Tribe's arguments to deny the respondents and were also able to fashion a third option which went beyond a simple reversal of the earlier decision.

Underlying Tribe's argument was a strong claim for local autonomy. Indeed, his whole argument presupposed a belief in the logic of governmental decentralization and local responsibility for local problems.[16] While the Supreme Court's decision was entirely consistent with this image of strong local government, of relative autonomy and discretion, there are certain ironies that should not go unnoticed. For a start, it is plain that local autonomy was made possible by Congress and HUD's own administrative organization. Congress provided the mandate and the funds, and HUD provided the administrative or procedural umbrella. Local immunity was provided by Congress, thereby circumventing the Commerce Clause, and local initiative was made possible, even encouraged, by HUD's loose regulations. Throughout the political fight, HUD provided the impetus and fiscal muscle for local decision making. Thus political power was then translated into legal power, once the Supreme Court became involved.

Local autonomy, like the Commerce clause, must be interpreted in this context as a *relative* concept. It is relative to the interests of higher legislative and administrative tiers and is sustained by *grants* of powers. Not only does HUD provide a sphere of initiative, even Massachusetts provided a sphere of initiative under the terms of Chapter 149, Section 26. And given that Boston's charter resides with the Massachusetts legislature, it must be obvious that local autonomy in this instance depended upon a prior arrangement of institutional powers. But even though Boston was given these spheres of autonomy, enough discretion remained within these spheres for the city to fashion an imaginative and truly innovative employment policy. Here, the bounds of local discretion facilitated action as much as constraining action. In this context, Boston's resident-preference policy is a story of how popular political will was able to triumph in a situation of limited local institutional powers and strongly opposed interests.[17] Judges legitimized this victory in terms that, although not exactly the same, nevertheless retained the underlying political tension of the original dispute.

6

The Structure of Land-Use Adjudication

One of the lessons of the previous chapter was that court adjudication has an intimate relationship to politics *and* has the potential to transform political disputes. In this context, it is tempting to believe that judicial decision making is only limited by the dispute at hand and the capacity of judges to convince others of the virtue of their decisions. However, to imagine this to be the case would be to ignore the structural relationship of law to society and the parameters that define the arena of judicial discretion. My argument here is that judicial decision making is simultaneously legitimated and limited in scope by the dominant ideological language of contemporary North America, that is, liberalism. As the courts appeal to liberal doctrine to justify their decisions, they are simultaneously limited in what they can decide, their logic of decision making, and the range of options before them. Of course, liberalism is not a seamless web of internally consistent doctrines and principles, far from it; however, liberalism nevertheless is the dominant moral order of society, an order which is the reference point for social action.

So important is the logic of liberalism that it pervades how radical intellectuals understand local autonomy and the possibilities of community organization.[1] But as judges are limited by the logic of liberalism, so too are radicals who operate within the language of liberal theories of local autonomy. The language and structure of liberalism allows action and limits action, simultaneously legitimizing decisions and delegitimizing potential options. These arguments are explored here with reference to land-use adjudication in Ontario, Canada.[2] In the subsequent sections, the limits of liberalism are given deeper emphasis than the sketch just presented above. Not only is the logic of liberalism explored with reference to the spatial division of power, local and province-level responsibilities are evaluated in terms of their correlation with liberal doctrine. While the match between theory and practice is not exact, the rhetoric of adjudication depends on the veracity of liberal doctrine to justify decisions. Thus, this chapter seeks to understand local autonomy in the context of doctrinaire liberalism, a language of decision making.

111

Liberalism is evaluated as a pair of counterprinciples. On the one hand, local autonomy is arguably the foundation of democratic individualism—what was termed in chapter 2 the imperative for decentralization. On the other hand, local autonomy is equally a real threat to individual freedom—the imperative for centralization is its counterprinciple. These two principles are embedded in the language and fabric of liberal ideology. To demonstrate how these principles are given concrete expression, two examples of urban land-use dispute drawn from the Province of Ontario are considered in depth. My choice of this subject and political context was predicated on three concerns. First, given a more general interest in urban economic form, I am interested in understanding how responsibilities for land-use planning are institutionally arranged. Second, the Ontario context is one of the most formalized or structured North American expressions of liberal theory.[3] Thus, we have a chance to integrate the structural arrangement of institutional powers with the language or rhetoric of adjudication. Third, and just as important, I am concerned to demonstrate that the formal arrangement of local institutional powers occurs in common law contexts, as much as the U.S. judicial system.[4] Liberal ideology permeates the social apparatus of both Canada and the United States, even if their national legislative arrangements at higher spatial tiers do not exactly match.

The Limits of Liberalism

As we saw in chapter 2, liberals and radicals alike promote the virtues of decentralized democracy, local self-government, and self-rule. Liberals argue that local decision making is more responsive to local interests, as small units of the state are more adaptive to citizens' needs (D. Miller 1983). Moreover, public goods such as safety and fire protection may have particular implementation requirements which depend on attention to local needs if government is to be effective (Bennett 1980). Functional arguments for local autonomy are, however, inherently limited, being simply technical considerations of the efficiency and adaptiveness of local government. By themselves, functional criteria are hardly the most stable bases of local state legitimacy. And, in fact, liberalism promotes local autonomy for moral reasons perhaps more than for purely functional concerns.[5] Local autonomy is argued to be a necessary condition for individual self-determination, an institutional arrangement designed for interpersonal cooperation and community cohesiveness.

Marxist theories of local government are more ambiguous and less coherent than their liberal competitors (see Clark and Dear 1984 for an extended discussion). This is especially true with regard to the question of local autonomy. Nonetheless, many Marxists would agree with liberals that local government can be a veritable crucible of radical democracy. For Mansbridge (1980) the local state is the level of the overall political system most vulnerable to direct political action. Grass-roots activism and highly orchestrated local participation can, according to this theory, make a difference. Evidence of close relationships between local capitalists and politicians has convinced many radicals that the local state can be captured. To that extent, the autonomy issue becomes an instrumental question of who controls the local state. From this position, it is often asserted that by capturing the local state, the whole state system may be attacked from within. In these terms, liberals and Marxists seem to assume a type 2 model of local autonomy, a model consistent with liberal doctrine.

Against these arguments for local autonomy is another which emphasizes the lack of autonomy of the local state. Elsewhere, I have argued with Michael Dear that the powers and discretion of local government are tightly defined (Clark and Dear 1984). Whatever the moral, functional, and even radical virtues of local autonomy, it remains an elusive reality. Everywhere, local autonomy is compromised by centralized authority (Michelman 1977). Federal grants to local governments have transformed local autonomy (if it ever existed) into a hollow (liberal) ideological shell. The categorical nature of so many federal grants imposes upon local governments uniform conditions of implementation, administration, and compliance. Federal grants are typically targeted to specific groups and clients, narrowly prescribing the limits of local discretion. Moreover, so-called block grants require local governments to seek federal approval for the disbursement and administration of funds. Even the projects eligible for block funding are defined prior to local communities actually receiving funds.[6] In these terms, local autonomy is more consistent with model 4, that is, local governments as bureaucratic apparatuses of higher tiers of the state.

More insidious are the limitations of local discretion implied by state constitutions. Whatever the popularity of rhetoric such as home rule, local responsibility for local problems, and the like, local governments are the creatures of state governments (Frug 1980). As we shall see in chapter 8, the class of problems considered *local* has become progressively narrower over time, as state and federal courts have taken oversight responsibility for areas as diverse as rent control, police, and sanitation. Even zoning, once considered the principal source of power of local governments has had to give way to higher-tier concerns with racial integration and equal opportunity. For example, the U.S. Supreme Court implied in the 1970s that towns and cities cannot intentionally zone so as to exclude racial minorities. And recently some state courts have held that communities must provide housing appropriate to the needs,

even income, of their residents. Practically, the rhetoric of local autonomy is difficult to take seriously given overwhelming evidence of the
fiscal, political, and judicial domination of local governments by higher
tiers of the state.

It would be a mistake, however, to argue that empirical reality is the
only problem with the liberal conception of local autonomy. To do so
would be to assume that the logic of the liberal theory of decentralized
democracy is above reproach, even if its actual implementation is not.
That is, whatever the empirical issues, the liberal vision of local autonomy is assumed uncompromised and remains as the principal legitimate
and normative blueprint for society. In fact, it is entirely plausible that
reality is a symptom of a much deeper contradiction that goes to the very
heart of liberalism. This contradiction is a product of the peculiar liberal
conception of society as a pluralistic admixture of individuals coupled
with an internal logical tension between protecting individuals from
themselves (the imperative for *centralized* authority) and protecting individuals from the state (the imperative for *decentralized* authority or local
autonomy).

My argument here is that formal, structural resolutions of these tensions are inherently unstable. Examples, drawn from recent Canadian
experience, are used to illustrate this proposition. In Ontario, local
governments are delegated powers by the provincial government to
legislate in areas of local concern. In matters of land use, urban planning,
and zoning, the Ontario Municipal Board (OMB), a nonelected administrative tribunal, and the minister of housing have the power to amend and
negate local legislative decisions. This formal structure or arrangement of
powers between local governments and the OMB is, however, indeterminant. As local autonomy has become administratively regulated, the
OMB has had to make law rather than simply interpret and adjudicate
alternative interpretations. Furthermore, appeals to the High Court for
clarification of their respective powers have provided local governments
and the OMB with only a very thin veneer of legitimacy. Indeterminacy
has continually forced the courts to redefine liberalism, alternating between decentralized and centralized authority. The whole edifice of
institutional powers is threatened by incoherence at the first level of
ideology, as much as reality.[7]

These tensions between the twin imperatives of centralized OMB
review and decentralized local autonomy could be interpreted as an
opportunity for radical grass-roots action. Liberal formalism and indeterminacy seem to hold out the possibility that concerted radical activism
could effectively dominate at least the lowest tier of the state. However,
the problem with this argument is that it is itself situated within the
dominant liberal ideology of the state. As a consequence, possibilities of

radically transforming society through control of local government is fundamentally limited by the structure of liberalism. Liberalism simultaneously appears incoherent, indicating gaps in the state system for political action, *and* limits the possible autonomy of the local state, thereby limiting the potential for real change. In this regard, the local autonomy question reflects a more general structural issue, the structure of political discourse.

Ontario Local-Provincial Relations

The legislative division of powers in Ontario regarding urban land-use planning between local governments and the OMB can be termed institutional formalism for two reasons.[8] First, as will be seen later, the Ontario Legislature based the division of powers upon a nonspecific, rule-oriented model of institutional responsibility. That is, local governments and the OMB are assigned formal powers in the areas of urban land use and planning without regard to specific outcomes or instances. Their institutional images are a product of liberal principles and their mandates are broadly defined to cover a wide range of circumstances. Second, and very much related, legal formalism classifies specific circumstances according to more general rules of responsibilities. Therefore, actual circumstances are transformed into their formal equivalents, and rules of adjudication come into play, procedurally generating outcomes which are, presumably, coherent with respect to the whole framework of powers and responsibilities. Thus, for a city to decide the best use of a certain parcel of land, it has to decide first whether the issue falls within its jurisdiction, and then it must determine the appropriate procedures for adjudicating competing claims. If citizens disagree, they may appeal to the OMB. Not only is there a quite complex political process implied here, the institutional decision making process depends on classifying specific situations in terms of a larger, noncontextual, and formalized whole. We must begin with the formal apparatus before we can understand what happens in specific instances.[9]

As in most federal states, the Canadian governmental system consists of tiers: national, provincial, and local (including metropolitan or regional). The principal characteristic of the Canadian system is its hierarchical structure of authority, whereby the federal government has influence over provincial entities for certain matters and, in turn, each province regulates the activities of local governments within its borders. It would be wrong, however, to imply that responsibilities are neatly divided into watertight compartments. The precise nature of the distribution of powers, particularly between federal and provincial entities, has been a continuing source of contention and conflict since confederation in

1867. Local governments can be labeled the "creatures of the province" (Simeon 1977) and are "created by, or at least are fully subject to, their provincial governments" (Scott and Lederman 1972). This is certainly the case in formal terms, as set out by Section 92 of the British North America Act, as well as in two other ways specific to Ontario.[10]

First, the fiscal relationship between these two levels of government has shown a pattern reminiscent of the federal-provincial relationship. In Ontario, the importance of the province as a contributor to local government revenue has grown steadily since the 1930s Depression, so that by the mid-1970s, roughly 50 percent of local government revenue came from the province (Auld 1977). This pattern stemmed from the reluctance of local governments to raise property taxes (their major source of local revenue) and provincially set limits on local debt issues. These conditions have led to complaints from local government leaders that in order to meet local service needs, they have been forced to accept conditional grants (almost 90 percent of all provincial assistance is of this form), at the expense of local policymaking power (Young 1977).[11]

Second, and most important to us in this chapter, the Ontario provincial government exerts a powerful influence over land-use and urban development at both the municipal (intraurban) and regional (interurban) levels. The provincial presence in this area has been firmly established through major legislative initiatives which include the Municipal Act, the Planning Act, and the Ontario Planning and Development Act, while the major administrative vehicles are the Ontario Municipal Board and the Ministry of Municipal Affairs and Housing. The OMB assumes a position of key importance by virtue of its role as enforcer of the provisions of the acts noted above, as well as other legislation of lesser significance (for instance, the Assessment Act and the Highway Improvement Act). The OMB functions as an independent administrative tribunal within the executive arm of the provincial government and has general powers to approve local land-use zoning bylaws and official plans, to supervise and monitor municipal capital expenditures and debt financing, and to create, alter, or dissolve municipal corporations (see, for more details, Ontario Municipal Board 1980, and Select Committee on the OMB 1972).[12] The present role of the OMB is the product of a particular Ontario history of local government insolvency.

In the 1880s and 1890s, many municipalities were independently engaged in a variety of public ventures intended to improve local business and living conditions. Foremost among these were the construction of spur rail lines to connect individual towns to major provincial and national trunk lines and the creation of municipal street-car railways. To finance such activity, towns either floated debentures on behalf of private operators or became directly involved through the formation of municipal corporations. Many of these ventures proved to be uneconomical and numerous municipalities faced corporate bankruptcy. In response to local profligacy, the provincial government formed the Office of the Municipal Auditor in 1897, followed by the establishment of the Ontario Railway and Municipal Board in 1906. The latter agency, whose name was shortened in 1932, was created with the express intent of overseeing capital expenditures by municipal corporations, and its existence was clearly predicated on the general belief that such entities were apparently incapable of managing their own affairs (financial or otherwise) in a reliable fashion (Ontario Economic Council 1973). Thereafter, it also acquired responsibility for adjudicating the soundness of all major land-use decisions at the local level. When the 1930s Depression brought another round of local bankruptcies, the province again interceded with stricter controls over issuance of debt by local governments (Auld 1977). By this point, provincial control over local activities was virtually complete.

The OMB has retained most of its considerable powers to the present day. Its paternal heritage is still evident, both in the goal which it set for itself ("responsibility for the sound growth and development of municipalities") and in the range of its activities (for a more detailed account of these, see the Ontario Ministry of Housing 1980a, 1980b). Indeed, its considerable latitude of action has recently been the subject of much study and concern. In his study of the OMB's administration of municipal land policy and planning, Adler (1971) characterized the operating style of the board as conservative and restrictive. He further suggested that the negative or approval-granting nature of the board's power may be detrimental to effective comprehensive planning at the local level (p. 217):

> In the absence of positive guides from the Legislature, the tribunal has generally adopted a conservative attitude and, in determining for itself the validity of municipal objectives, has been concerned more with micro-planning matters that affect the individual than with macro-planning issues embracing the community and its region.

Little has changed since Adler's study was conducted, and even the current efforts of the government of Ontario to review and revise the contents of the Planning Act offer little prospect for increased local autonomy in the planning and regulation of land use and development.

Current legislation affecting local governments, their legal status as governmental entities, their boundaries, responsibilities, and the like resides solely with the provincial government in the form of *statutes*. There is no constitutional division of power between the province and local governments that would define the latter outside of the ongoing political system. This differs somewhat from the United States, where local governments have a presence in the state constitution, for example, Massachusetts (Dear and Clark 1981). Statutes can be altered by the Ontario Legislature through normal democratic channels, and both local governments and the OMB owe their continuity to the Ontario Legislature. In principle this is a significant difference from normal practice in the United States, although in practice the difference may be slight depending on how U.S. state constitutions can be altered with respect to local government powers.

Local governments are delegated powers by the Ontario Legislature and have no residual powers. Although not explicitly noted as such, Ontario statutes follow the logic of Dillon's (1911) rule, wherein local governments have only those powers expressly delegated by the province. Two further powers derive from such delegations, and are (1) those necessary and incident powers needed to carry out the delegated powers and (2) those powers absolutely necessary for carrying out the expressly noted legislation (Dear and Clark 1981, p. 1284). Practically speaking, delegations of power provide local governments with a mandate to enact their own bylaws within specified limits. Delegations of power are also general rules of permissible action. As such, they seek to classify generally as appropriate or inappropriate the possible areas of local government action. In this sense, the delegation of powers to local government sets the formal parameters for justifiable discretion.

Since local governments are created by statute, so are their various powers. Thus, for example, there are specific statutes regarding local health, sanitation, police, and land-use planning, among many other items. One of the major requirements of the Ontario Planning Act is that local governments prepare municipal plans covering land use and zoning. Formal plans adopted by municipalities are enacted through bylaws and must be approved by the minister responsible in the Ontario Legislature. The OMB can also perform this function through its oversight role and may be used by the minister to rule on specific items. Essentially, the OMB acts as an administrative review board and can review any local bylaw as it relates to zoning and land use, bonds, annexation, and the like.[13] It must decide on the propriety of local master plans and must adjudicate objections concerning local ordinances.

The OMB's administrative board is appointed by the lieutenant governor in council. It is like local governments in two respects: it is covered by legislative statute, and it is a creature of the province. The major distinction between local governments and the OMB concerns the formers' initiation powers and the latter's review powers. Conventionally, the former enacts legislation, whereas the latter adjudicates or reviews questions concerning the legality of the formers' actions. And, again conventionally, the former is thought to represent local collective interests, and the latter is thought to protect individual, regional, or provincewide interests. Thus, the liberal vision of local autonomy is formally constituted by allowing local initiative and narrowing immunity. The broad character of delegated powers is counterposed by strictly defined administrative oversight responsibilities.

Adjudicating Land-Use Disputes

In this section I argue that the separation of powers between local governments and the OMB fails to provide determinant solutions to conflicts over their respective powers. This result is somewhat ironic given the fact that the formal division of powers between the OMB and local governments was conceived precisely to accomplish determinant solutions. Through its review of local government actions, the OMB is intimately involved in controversy and dispute. And, as the OMB has responded to specific conflicts and appeals from local residents regarding local land-use bylaws, local governments have sought to reverse OMB decisions by appealing to the Ontario High Court. Essentially, the procedural device of integrating the contradictory pair of liberal principles fails to provide unambiguous, determinant outcomes in specific instances. Not only are there disagreements between local governments and the OMB regarding the appropriateness of different rules for specific circumstances, but the conditions relevant in deciding appeals from local residents and even what the rules include and exclude are points of tension and conflict. Ultimately, specific cases raise questions concerning the coherence of the whole adjudicatory system.

The indeterminacy of liberalism, a common characteristic of procedural, rule-oriented decision criteria (compare Ely 1980 and Tribe 1980), places the Ontario courts in a difficult position. To adjudicate between local governments and the OMB requires a determinant interpretation of the intent and language of Ontario legislation and thus liberalism itself. The court has very little discretion in the matter: it must side with either the OMB or the local government—it cannot agree with both. In doing so, the court must somehow resolve the contradiction implied by the procedural or formal separation of powers. Thus, it should come as no surprise that adjudication is a highly contentious and political affair. Adjudication pits local autonomy against centralized authority, a result of having to deal with specific cases, not simply broad rules of procedure. Thus, adjudication also pits substance against procedure, an issue that goes to the very heart of the legitimacy of liberalism itself. The courts must reach a determinant solution to the liberal contradiction without denying the legitimacy of liberal ideology and its institutional image. Moreover, because each judicial decision is set within a body of precedent and legal opinion, the courts must manufacture coherent judgments—a very real challenge indeed!

To illustrate what is implied by these arguments, we need to consider instances of conflict between the OMB and local governments. Not only is it important to ascertain which side wins, it is also crucial to identify the logic or language of reconciliation, that is, we must consider how the courts sustain the legitimacy of the liberal conception of local autonomy. Two cases are considered in depth: *Cadillac Development Corp. Ltd. et al. and City of Toronto* (1973), and *Borough of Scarborough and Minister of Housing for Ontario et al.* (1976).[14] The *Cadillac* case involved a developer (Gothic Developments, an arm of Cadillac Corp.), the City of Toronto's decision regarding land-use zoning, and a question of jurisdiction: did the OMB have the power to review the city's decision? In detail, the case evolved in the following way.

Sometime before 1963, a certain area of Toronto was zoned for low-density residential use. The density limitation for that zone called for a floor/area ratio (FAR) of 0.6. In 1963, Toronto rezoned the land in that area for high-density residential development (an FAR of 2.0). Between 1966 and 1970, Gothic Developments acquired land in the area that had not been rezoned. In 1969, the policy of up-zoning the land in that area was incorporated in the official plan of the city. The plan designated the land owned by Gothic as high-density residential. But because the plan itself did not actually change the existing zoning, Gothic applied to have a bylaw passed which would rezone its land in accordance with the official plan. In September 1971, the city council passed bylaw 239-71, which rezoned Gothic's land to a density of FAR 2.4. The FAR represented the new density for that zone of 2.0 plus a bonus which was then in effect of 0.4. The city then applied to the OMB for approval and a hearing was set for November 1972.

The passage of the bylaw set off a storm of controversy. There was a great deal of public protest, including objections by local homeowners' associations. The council was forced to reconsider the bylaw, but reaffirmed its passage on 15 March 1972. After the council's reaffirmation of the bylaw, Gothic and the city entered into a series of agreements. The first involved a road closure and indemnification agreement. In the second agreement, Gothic agreed to convey three strips of land adjoining the project to the city for one dollar. The third agreement concerned a 99-year lease by Gothic of surface lands of the Toronto Transit Commission subway right of way.

From there on, events began to accelerate, with a great deal of political argument and appeal by homeowners of the city's decisions. At the November meeting of the OMB, the board adjourned its hearing until 15

January 1973 to allow an objecting homeowners association time for further investigation. In the meantime, on 4 December, municipal elections were held. Nine out of the 23 aldermen on the city council were replaced. And on 5 January 1973 the new city council held a meeting where a motion was made to pass a bylaw repealing bylaw 239-71. The council sought legal advice concerning any liabilities that might be connected with repealing the bylaw. The council also asked the OMB to adjourn its hearing on bylaw 239-71. The board adjourned the matter until 5 February but noted that if the bylaw was still before it at that time, it would proceed with its hearing. On 29 January the city's Committee on Buildings and Development held a public meeting where it was reported that repeal of the bylaw would expose the city to some legal risks. Nevertheless, the committee recommended that the city council repeal the bylaw at a special meeting set for 16 February.

The stage was then set for a showdown between the city, the OMB, and Gothic Developments. Prior to the 16 February meeting a majority of the city aldermen indicated that they were in favor of repealing the bylaw. However, the OMB refused to adjourn its deliberations and opened hearings on the bylaw, which were completed on 12 February. The OMB then reserved its judgment. On the day before (15 February) the council's meeting, Gothic sued to enjoin the meeting from any attempt to repeal the bylaw. However, on 16 February the council voted to pass a repealing bylaw and notified the OMB of its action. Even so, on 1 March the OMB approved bylaw 239-71 with some modifications. On 1 April the Divisional Court granted Gothic leave to appeal to the High Court regarding questions of jurisdiction and law.

Gothic appealed to the Ontario High Court to quash the repealing bylaw on several grounds. First, Gothic claimed that the repealing bylaw was not in conformity with the official plan, which designated the area as high-density residential. The judge held that the city was not required to implement the plan but was merely restricted from passing bylaws that violated the plan. Further, he argued that density designations were simply limits on the allowable density. The city was not obligated to increase density to those limits. Gothic also claimed that the council had no jurisdiction to pass the repealing bylaw while bylaw 239-71 was before the OMB. Under section 35 of the Planning Act, if the OMB had approved the bylaw before the city council had passed the repealing bylaw, the OMB would have had to approve the repealing bylaw before it could come into effect. Gothic claimed that once the OMB had agreed to review the bylaw, the council lost the power to repeal it. However, the High Court held that "to fetter the power of a legislative body acting within the scope of its delegated authority requires clear words" (p. 202).

Because the statute did not restrict the council from repealing a bylaw before the board had rendered a decision, the judge reasoned that the council had the power to do so.

Gothic also claimed that the repealing bylaw was discriminatory because it acted only against Gothic's land. The judge dismissed this contention by pointing out that bylaw 239-71 also only applied to Gothic's land. Finally, Gothic contended that the city council had not held a *fair* hearing before repealing the bylaw, thus prejudicing the council's decision. But again the judge disagreed, contending that the council had good reason to rush the proceedings. If it waited too long, it would need the board's permission to repeal the bylaw. He also pointed out that Gothic's representatives deliberately stayed away from the final council meeting, when the repealing bylaw was discussed. The judge also rejected claims that the decision was in bad faith, given the agreements made between Gothic and the city. The judge pointed out that the board had not approved the bylaw at the time the agreements had been made, so Gothic had to assume the risk that the bylaw would not be approved. The judge dismissed the application to quash the repealing bylaw.

The remarkable aspects of this case and the decision of the High Court rest with the language of adjudication and the decision to sustain the city council's autonomy relative to the OMB. Essentially, the court held that the city was within its powers as an elected democratic body to change its mind regarding zoning and land use. By doing so, the court determined that the autonomy principle (decentralized decision making) held sway over the centralized authority principle (protecting individuals from the parochial interests of the local electorate). The language of the court is pregnant with this implication and meaning. For example, in arguing for the discretion of the council to change its mind, the deciding justice noted,

> I do not consider that the provisions to which I have been referred (by Gothic) preclude the Council, in its judgment as representatives of the electorate, from unilaterally undoing what it has previously done.
>
> . . . .
>
> To hold otherwise would place in the hands of the OMB a control over the legislative process beyond that intended by the Legislature of the Province. (P. 202)

When dealing with Gothic's argument of bad faith and discrimination by the council, the deciding justice noted,

> [The role of the council] was to determine policy and to legislate in the public interest as they saw it as elected representatives. (P. 208)

And finally, when dealing with Gothic's contention that the city council had already made up its mind before the public hearing (which Gothic did not attend), the justice argued,

> A municipal council is an elected body having a legislative function within a limited and delegated jurisdiction. Under the democratic process the elected representatives are expected to form views as to matters of public policy. (P. 210)

In this instance determination of the High Court held in favor of the democratic caucus. In doing so, the court sought to define the relative roles of the city council and OMB by invoking local democracy. Thus, the decision was justified by one side or principle of liberal ideology and presumed a very strong claim for the autonomy of local decision making. In this manner, the underlying logic of the procedural separation of powers between local governments and the OMB was used to classify and hence resolve the dispute.

Even so, the court's view could be quarrelled with, and Gothic could have argued that Section 35 (22) of the Planning Act applied in the *Cadillac* case. This section states,

> Where an application to the council for an amendment to a by-law passed under this section or a predecessor of this section, or any by-law deemed to be consistent with this section by subsection 3 of section 13 of *The Municipal Amendment Act, 1941*, is refused or the council refuses or neglects to make a decision thereon, within one month after the receipt by the clerk of the application, the applicant may appeal to the Municipal Board and the Municipal Board shall hear the appeal and dismiss the same or direct that the bylaw be amended in accordance with its order.[15]

Gothic may have been able to appeal the case straight back to the OMB. To do so, Gothic would have had to argue successfully that the action of the council was the same as refusing the original application for an amendment under Section 35 (22). Gothic would also have had to clarify whether or not bylaw 239-71 was an amendment to a bylaw passed under Section 35 or one of its predecessors. The original zoning was passed as part of a general zoning bylaw. Since Section 35 is the enabling act for the enactment of restricted bylaws, it is likely that the original zoning bylaw would be a bylaw passed under Section 35 or a predecessor of Section 35, as required in 35 (22). If this was indeed correct, the OMB would have had the same powers as the council originally had when presented with the application to amend the bylaw. The OMB would have been free to pass the amendment or alter the amendment any way that it wanted.

It is obvious that the court chose not to consider these types of issues and argued for local autonomy in the strongest possible language. But in reality ambiguity abounds, both in terms of procedure and substantive structure. Realistically, local governments are highly constrained by a top-down delegation of powers. In addition, local governments are highly dependent on the province for fiscal support. None of these issues entered into the logic of adjudication. Essentially, the court used its position to *proclaim* the primacy of local autonomy.

In the *Scarborough* case, the conflict was more directly between local government and the OMB. Instead of the question of autonomy being fought through a third party, as was the situation in *Cadillac* (Gothic Developments), the *Scarborough* case involved an appeal to the High Court by the Borough of Scarborough against an OMB decision. A group of Scarborough property owners held land located about one mile from the boundary between Scarborough and the neighboring town of Pickering. Scarborough had adopted an official plan as required by the Planning Act, and this plan had been approved by the minister of housing in 1957. That plan showed a large shopping center to be built in the vicinity of the owners' lands. In 1972, Scarborough passed amendment 304 to its official plan. This amendment, in part, designated the owners' lands as a regional commercial center. In accordance with the Planning Act, the amendment was submitted to the minister of housing for approval. However, Pickering Township requested that the portion of the amendment that dealt with the regional commercial center be sent to the Ontario Municipal Board, and the minister complied with the request.

Amendment 304, as passed by Scarborough, contained the following paragraph:

> The 55 acre Regional Shopping Centre originally indicated on the approved Scarborough Official Plan, and more specifically located by Amendment No. 23 approved on March 23, 1961, is retained, to be bounded by an 86-foot Ring Road utilizing existing sections of Centennial and Durnford Roads. (P. 390)

The OMB, in approving the amendment, replaced the paragraph noted above with the following:

> A site located within the area bounded by Sheppard Avenue, Durnford Road and Centennial Road is designated for a community commercial centre. Only after it can be demonstrated that a regional centre will have no detrimental effect on the social and economical welfare of the inhabitants of neighbouring municipalities may an amendment be made to this plan to expand the development to a regional facility. (P. 390)

For the borough this was a major intrusion into its autonomy. The designation of a "community commercial centre" was actually a smaller shopping center than planned by Scarborough. The borough appealed the OMB's decision to the High Court.

The borough appealed the OMB's decision on two grounds: lack of jurisdiction and improper procedure. The attack on jurisdiction contained three parts. First, the borough claimed that the OMB had no power to modify a plan or amendment to a plan submitted to it by the minister of housing. However, the presiding judge held that the OMB had the same powers in this situation as did the minister. Section 14 (2) of the Planning Act provides that, when a plan is submitted to the minister for approval, "if modifications appear desirable to the Minister, he shall, after consultation with the council of the municipality affected, make such modifications and cause the plan to be amended accordingly."[16] Since the minister had the power to amend the plan, the judge reasoned, so did the OMB. The second part of the attack on jurisdiction was actually a procedural attack. The borough claimed that the OMB did not hold the consultation required by the Planning Act. However, the judge assumed that the OMB acted in place of the minister; thus, the public hearing held by the OMB on the amendment satisfied the requirement of consultation.

The third part of the jurisdictional attack was that the OMB had no power to include the second sentence of the above paragraph in its order. The presiding judge held that the OMB was entitled to take regional impact into consideration when evaluating a plan or amendment. However, the board did not have the power to force Scarborough to take such factors into account.

The second ground for attacking the board's amendment was that it allowed the minister to appear at the hearing and call witnesses. The borough claimed that this procedure was improper. However, the judge held that the board had the powers of a court of record. He argued that these powers included the right to determine who shall appear before the board. As a result of the court's deliberations, the following sentence was deleted from the paragraph that the board had replaced in the amendment:

> Only after it can be demonstrated that a regional centre will have no detrimental effect on the social and economical welfare of the inhabitants of neighbouring municipalities may an amendment be made to this plan to expand the development to a regional facility.

The OMB's decision to limit the use of the parcel of land in question to a "community commercial centre" remained in force.

The language or doctrine that the court employed to resolve this conflict is one of express delegation. The borough had been delegated general powers to plan, while the OMB had been delegated powers to review and amend plans and amendments to plans. The judge argued that the OMB had no clear statutory authority that would allow it to impose considerations of regional impact upon the city's own plan. This vision is one of local autonomy. The OMB should act as kind of coordinator, adjusting the plan for any regional impact. The court's analysis employs language that creates an image of strong local municipalities with broad legislative powers and an OMB which is limited by specific administrative powers.

Whatever the ideological virtues of this argument, the structure of the relationship between the OMB and the borough indicated that there may have been less substance to their vision than first conceived. Although the OMB, by virtue of this decision, could not require local governments to take regional impact into account, if they want their plans to be approved, they must nevertheless take these factors into account. The court admitted moreover that the OMB

> is entitled to refuse to approve an official plan or amendment because the municipality submitting it for approval has failed to demonstrate that it would not have a detrimental effect on the social and economic welfare of the inhabitants of neighbouring municipalities. (P. 394)

This decision gives boroughs the power to ignore certain factors in planning. But if these factors are ignored, the OMB also has the power to change plans to reflect factors it deems relevant. In substance, the result of the *Scarborough* case was a reduction in size of the shopping center. And in order to get the size of the shopping center increased, the borough would have had to present evidence demonstrating that an increase would have had no adverse regional impact—precisely those considerations which the court's opinion gives the borough the freedom to ignore.

As in *Cadillac*, the court's opinion promotes a view of autonomous local government with powers which the OMB cannot infringe upon without a specific statutory authorization. Yet, the actual structure of the relationship between the OMB and the borough lends support to just the opposite view.

These two cases of jurisdictional and interpretative indeterminacy illustrate in detail the limits of liberal formalism. And I believe that it is difficult to sustain any argument that would claim these two cases to be so exceptional as to be irrelevant. It is true that on a day-to-day basis conventional rules of local legislative autonomy and OMB administrative review function without major controversy. Precedent coupled with the routine nature of many local public policies ensures a degree of consistency in rule application and response. Local discretion is set within a relatively well-known set of parameters. At the same time, however, it is entirely possible that these two cases are two among many potential others. While *Cadillac* was a politically sensitive issue, *Scarborough* was not. While *Cadillac* involved a third (private) party, *Scarborough* did not.

And, while *Cadillac* raised questions of local officials' proper behavior, *Scarborough* did not. They concerned the everyday administration of local discretion and OMB review.

In these instances, the formal rules of local discretion and review powers failed to provide definitive conclusions. Two dimensions to this failure can be identified. First, it was apparent that the existing set of rules was not comprehensive enough to accommodate the specifics of these two cases. As a formal, noncontextual framework of principles and guidelines, the existing structure of powers could not unambiguously accommodate the "facts." This is not to suggest that the respective local governments and the OMB did not have their own interpretations of how the rules should have applied. In point of fact, appeal to the High Court in both instances arose out of firmly held, but divergent, interpretations of the rules. At the margins of all systems of rules there are always problems of deciding the applicability of different rules. This is true in all facets of law and economics; thus, the failure of liberal formalism at this level should be seen as an inevitable consequence of *formalism* itself. There can never be a complete set of rules that can accommodate all eventualities. Not knowing the future means that rules will always reflect the past. Precedent is essentially made for constructing analogies—similarities and dissimilarities (Dworkin 1972).

The margins of interpretation are then, in part, the margins of rules, their application, and adjudication. Thus, the method of using rules to adjudicate specific circumstances is itself the first source of indeterminacy. The facts of *marginal* cases do not have to be sensational, even completely new or in some other way so very different. All that is required is that the facts fall (or be thought to fall) between the cracks of the formal system of rules. To this extent, we do not have to invoke some external argument concerning political interests or some other motivating force to argue that liberal formalism is prone to failure. Unger (1983) suggested that the logic of formalism is not even necessarily the logic of liberalism, even though it is characteristic of liberal social theory. Part of its heritage comes from the enlightenment and the movement that sought to deny the bonds of feudalism. As Kennedy (1976) has noted, formalism has been a liberating device in the past.

At the same time we should also recognize that embodied in the very rules of jurisdiction lies the unresolved contradiction of liberalism itself. That contradiction is, of course, the pairing of two counterprinciples, local autonomy for maximum individual liberty and centralized administrative review for the protection of individual liberty. The comprehensiveness of rules is not the problem at this second scale of interpretative indeterminacy—the whole liberal vision is implicated. Thus, we have two unavoidable sources of indeterminacy.

Indeterminacy of Liberal Formalism

Despite my arguments that the cases reviewed in the previous section are not so exceptional as to be irrelevant, one objection could be that these cases and their internal contradictions are less important than suggested. A *realist* liberal might argue that conflicts between the OMB and local governments concerning their relative powers is, unfortunately, a fact of life. In a pluralist world of conflicting interests, we should not be surprised that there is a plurality of interpretations regarding local powers. By invoking an argument to the effect that conflict permeates the entire local apparatus of the state, the liberal realist might suggest that what I interpret as indeterminacy is actually pluralism in action. The realist might also suggest a further line of argument to the effect that although conflict is natural, a means of resolution is available. If the OMB is not capable of determining unambiguous outcomes, then higher tiers of the judiciary will provide that function. The closing element to the liberal realist's argument would be that in the cases reviewed above, that was what actually happened. Indeterminacy at the High Court level would be dismissed as a misunderstanding on my part or an obvious instance of my misrepresenting their arguments.

The High Court represents an adjudicator located outside the immediate arena of interjurisdictional conflict. Presumably it is above the ongoing cut and thrust of local politics and does not have a stake in legitimating the OMB. From that vantage point, the High Court, according to the realist liberal, presumably functions to take into account the true facts and the overarching interests that the community at large may have in either ensuring local autonomy or reasserting administrative review. In this regard, the High Court begins to sound very much like the initial functional description of the OMB and its role in the formal logic of liberalism. The principal difference is that the court is further removed from the *action* and has, in consequence, an ability to decide the merits of each case objectively and rationally. This is, yet again, a procedural solution to a substantive problem. The only difference is that liberal realists invoke a kind of *super-objective*, rational interpreter and adjudicator of disputes, an agency that presumably can escape the formal indeterminacy of liberalism so endemic to lower tiers of the state.

Of course my description of what a realist liberal *might* argue is somewhat hypothetical, perhaps even a caricature. Even so, there is enough evidence to suggest that many liberals resort to these types of procedural devices when confronted with the collapse of formalism. Fish (1982a), for example, has noted that many liberals believe that the intrusion of events and institutions with associated political interests obscures the clarity of the underlying formal structure. Their response is to invoke reality to both explain away the collapse of formalism, and at the same time attempt to reassert its underlying logic. Thus, we often are confronted with arguments that flip-flop, depending on the circumstances and sources of critical analysis (for more examples, see Unger 1983). One consequence of this strategy of realist (re)interpretation is a renewed claim for the merits of objectivism—a universal order of stable, formal, and invariant rules and procedures that would discipline reality.

Typically, the strategy begins with reasserting the fundamental importance of the *true facts*. Implied is a notion that if political interests can be held in abeyance, then the facts could speak for themselves, indicating the relative virtues of alternative arguments before the court. From that beginning point, the logic of adjudication is very well known. Having established the facts, the court then moves to interpret them, assigning them to various formal categories consistent with the overarching liberal framework. Some facts may be relevant, others not, the point being that they are lined-up in accordance with the various arguments before the court. The next step is to establish a resolution, using the facts to discern the veracity of competing briefs. Since the method is entirely procedural, substantive issues would not enter into the argument. Finally, the court then moves to justify their argument, invoking precedent, the facts, the community interest, and the like.

Simply reasserting the virtues of procedural adjudication is not enough, however, to avoid many of the issues raised in the preceding sections. The indeterminacy of liberal formalism remains. Moreover, it is difficult to imagine what the perfect apolitical court would look like; it would surely have to be dominated by supermen. But there are more telling criticisms that could be noted, criticisms that deny the entire vision. Surely, the step-by-step procedure just outlined above is completely around the wrong way. How can facts be identified without an underlying, socially based interpretive vision? And, if facts require an interpretive framework, does not that mean that judges start from the end point of the process, not the beginning? Essentially, I would agree with Fish (1982a) that interpretation presupposes facts, that there can be no truth separate from the logic which adjudicating agencies bring with them.[17] Of course, this does not mean that all judgments are subjective or arbitrary. Interpretation is an act of classification, of inclusion and exclusion premised on some underlying image. That image may be inchoate and incomplete, even to the point of containing contradictions. Thus, it is entirely possible that interpretative and adjudicating agencies may be hard pressed to provide a convincing *internal* validation (which is the case here).

If adjudicators use interpretative frameworks to identify and sort facts where do these frameworks come from? The only possible answer is that these frameworks are themselves structured and conceived as social entities (or interpretive communities). To believe otherwise would be to believe that knowledge is a natural, ahistorical vision derived ultimately from some deity. Thus, attempts to define an original intent, or even a meaning divorced from the situation or context in which adjudicators function, are doomed to failure (Brest 1980). It is true that originalism is a strategy sometimes employed when judges are faced by indeterminacy; however, it is not true that "original meanings" are somehow separate from the context in which they are situated. Again, I should emphasize that this should not be taken as implying that knowledge need be completely subjective or arbitrary. Quite the contrary, I would argue that interpretations are structurally determined, manufactured by an overarching logic which is socially derived.[18]

To be more specific would require me to recount the principal arguments of this chapter and book. High Court adjudications of interjurisdictional conflicts between local governments and the OMB are set within the language and structure of liberalism. Their object has to be the legitimization of the entire project, using the interpretative tools internal to the liberal paradigm. If we recall for the moment that Nozick (1974) argued that higher spatial tiers of the state derive from local constituents, the fact that it is the province that creates Ontario local governments provides an inbuilt contradiction. Essentially, the practical arrangement of the state hierarchy is inverted when compared to the model implied by classical liberalism. Instead of local communities giving up powers and duties to the provincial government, the process is reversed. Note that this is hardly a problem if the intent of liberal theory is sustained. It simply may be merely convenient to locate the definition of powers at higher tiers.

Even so, a great deal of ambiguity remains. Whatever the intent of the definition of powers at the provincial level, the practice of local government autonomy *appears* highly constrained. Legislative powers rest with the province; it can do virtually anything including denying those powers already delegated to local governments. This contradicts, in spirit at least, Nozick's logic. The everyday practice of provincial legislation enables the province to define its role with respect to local government. The reverse does not, of course, hold true. Moreover, there is hardly any means of redressing this balance. Local governments can hardly appeal to the federal government since, by definition, local government is created by provincial statute. The only option would be for local governments or interest groups to elect local representatives to the provincial legislature on the understanding that they would form coalitions to change local government statutes. This is a vain hope. Political discourse is quite hierarchically structured.

Legitimacy, at least in terms of the dominant liberal ideology, is thus a problematic issue. Not only is there a contradiction and tension within liberalism (of autonomy versus centralization), even in terms of its institutional image, the formal arrangement of powers places local governments in an inferior position vis-à-vis provincial governments. For Nozick and others, local legitimacy is derived out of a moral vision of local governments representing and protecting individual choices regarding their life-style preferences and who they associate with. The extent to which local governments are able to carry out their constituents' desires (limited, of course, by intercommunity choice), then legitimacy will follow. To the extent that local governments are limited in this regard, their own legitimacy will be threatened. It is up to the province then to justify intrusions upon local autonomy.

Sustaining political legitimacy by invoking liberal ideology implies a number of distinct problems for the Ontario political system. The formal organization of powers is very much a top-down system, dominated by the province. Thus, the province must continually justify itself either through outputs or some moral mandate. Set within liberal discourse is, however, a ready solution. Simply by claiming that local governments are untrustworthy, the provincial government can invoke one of the two basic principles of liberalism. And the provincial government could argue that its role in defining local discretion is relatively limited. That is, after all, the function of the OMB. It is, however, a weak argument which depends first on minimizing the initial provincial control of power and second on extolling the virtues of the OMB. This second strategy is more subtle and, ultimately, depends upon the coherence of the distinction between initiation and review powers.

It should come as no surprise, then, to see the court refer to issues such as local democracy and local autonomy. Their obvious inability to reach determinate conclusions that are stable and satisfying regarding their coherence should be seen as part of the very structure and language of liberalism. Since the entire ajudicatory framework is set within an institutional, top-down delegation of powers, legitimization is an ongoing project at the highest levels of the province. Precisely because these highest tiers are implicated in the entire structure, there can be no escape for the liberal realist or theorist.

The Spatial Structure of Political Discourse

In the first section of this chapter, I noted that many radicals believe local government to be vulnerable to direct or grass-roots action. If the electorate or a particularly vocal segment could be mobilized, then local governments could be taken over. One consequence would be a rearrangement of the class priorities of local government. It might also be suggested that local governments can be used to advance more general political interests and perhaps even attack the hegemony of the entire state apparatus. Local governments may well reflect local, even radical democratic interests, and it may also appear to be an institution more vulnerable to changing class coalitions than higher tiers of the state. However, appearances are deceptive; what appear as opportunities for direct political action are actually gaps in the formal arrangement of liberalism. Indeed, it is the incoherence of liberal ideology that opens up the institutional system of local autonomy and administrative review to political action.

Two sources of incoherence were identified; specifically the arrangement of delegated powers and a deeper philosophical confusion that is at the very heart of liberalism. In the first instance it is entirely plausible that as events and circumstances change, so too do the respective powers of local governments and review agencies like the OMB. Politically, this would seem to imply an opportunity for actively changing the structure of local discretion. In fact one of the cases noted in this chapter, *Cadillac*, indicated that direct citizen input through the electoral process can change the orientation of the local state. And, within the context of the liberal principle of maximum local participation (autonomy), such action is quite appropriate, even legitimate. However, notice what this implies: liberal ideology legitimates local participation. It is also the case that liberal ideology can severely limit local autonomy through the equally important counterprinciple of administrative review (protecting individuals from local parochialism).

Local control and radical transformation of local government can be delegitimated as easily as legitimated. It very much depends on the circumstances and the dominant interpretation of the applicability of countervailing principles. Consequently, local radical action within the logic of liberalism will inevitably be limited by the counter side of liberalism itself. In this sense, political discourse is very much structured by liberal ideology and its formal (spatial) image. This should not be taken as suggesting liberal ideology and its institutional image to be a seamless web of internally consistent principles. In point of fact, incoherence is a characteristic of the formal arrangement of local powers and liberalism itself. However, any radical activism that functions within liberal discourse inevitably carries with it the limits of liberalism.

The limits of liberalism are many, and we hardly need reiterate here the entire critique of chapter 2. Liberalism is an individual-centered theory of society which supposes that society is the sum of disparate individuals. Social association is choice-oriented, and localities are conceived in terms of the preferences of their residents. Substantively, this principle is a major barrier to social justice, because it legitimates exclusiveness, and the narrow interests of some communities. If one city has the right to pass radical policies such as rent control, so too must other communities have the right to require certain low-density residential developments. However, once questions of social justice are raised, then liberalism may be of little relevance. As Plant (1978) has noted, the notion of *community* is loaded with very specific philosophical values which permeate the entire state apparatus. Radical activism must deny the legitimacy of liberalism itself if social justice is to be achieved.

7
The Tensions of Urban Public Service Provision

For ten years, from 1966 to 1976, the City of Des Plaines, a suburban community located just west of Chicago's O'Hare Airport, and the Metropolitan Sanitary District of Greater Chicago fought one another in court over a matter of jurisdiction. The district wished to locate a sewerage treatment plant in the city to serve Des Plaines and other regional municipalities. However, the city refused to give permission for the treatment plant unless the district complied with local zoning ordinances. Both organizations, "municipal entities" in Illinois's municipal code, claimed jurisdiction and both claimed statutory authority for their stands. While the political issues involved in this dispute were veiled, formalized, and transformed by legal challenges, politics was nevertheless at the heart of the issue. Put most simply, the city, being dominated by conservative Republican interests, was more concerned with protecting the existing environment of Des Plaines than accommodating the effects of growth of the larger Chicago metropolitan area. The treatment plant was considered a noxious facility, a threat to existing land-use patterns and home owners' property values.

Politically, the city's and district's interests were incompatible. The city had nothing to gain in helping the district, and the district wished to assert its power at the expense of Des Plaines. The district represented pro-growth interests and patronage jobs, with a budget of about $124 million in 1974 and considerable influence within the Chicago Democratic party.[1] As in so many other U.S. metropolitan areas, sewerage provision is a serious public issue in Chicago. The location of treatment plants, the provision of public services, both in terms of their quantity and quality, and the spatial reach of the sewerage network structure the pace and character of suburban development. Indeed, sewerage siting decisions, and service design decisions, often radically alter land values, property taxes, individual wealth, and the whole spatial character of urban growth.[2] In Chicago, again as in so many other cities, sewerage provision is big business, and perhaps only incidentally a public service. As one commentator on the Chicago political scene noted, "sewerage provision stirs passions and interests like no other urban service; these passions are founded on money and power. You don't mess with the district!"[3]

While we have seen the political dimensions of legal disputes in previous chapters, in this chapter I wish to concentrate more upon the jurisdictional dispute than on the political constituencies represented by the two municipal entities. Which entity had jurisdiction and why are the two principal questions addressed in this chapter. I treat the city and district as contending political actors, thus emphasizing their various institutional powers. Here, I follow the logic of state-centered modes of social enquiry, rather than conventional interest-group models of local politics.[4] To understand the jurisdictional powers of the city and district, a series of legal battles are analyzed and the rationales used by the courts to justify their decisions are reviewed in depth. Given the sequence of legal challenges initiated by the city against the district, it is fair to suppose that the city was neither happy with the courts' conclusions nor satisfied with the courts' arguments. And, indeed, a close analysis of the sequence of decisions will likely convince the reader that the courts performed relatively poorly on this issue. Thus, the sewerage battles in Chicago are not only interesting for the passions engendered, the whole adjudicatory framework used by the courts to decide these cases promises to be an interesting case study in judicial decision making.

Even so, this chapter aims to go further than simply demonstrating the limits of judicial decision making in a suburban context. As a point of comparison and analysis, I also wish to consider the relevance of an alternative mode of decision making, one which is thought by some to be superior to judicial decision making—empirical and theoretically based public finance rules. As applied to urban public facilities, theorists such as Bennett (1980) and Inman (1979) have argued that public-finance theories provide a better way of making decisions regarding the optimal assignment of public services between jurisdictions. By invoking neoclassical positivist conceptions of economic analysis, this school of thought supposes that we can avoid what they identify as the "subjective nature of politics," and the "arbitrariness" of judicial decision rules. Expert opinions based on sound theoretical principles are thought by Bennett (1980) and others who follow the neoclassical economics and law tradition (see Posner 1981b) to be more efficient rules for adjudicating between competing jurisdictional claims.[5]

Public Choice Models of Urban Services

Choice models of urban public goods begin with two groups: consumers who are local voters (residents) and producers, typically local governments.[6] From this position neoclassical rules of market structure, supply and demand and the like are applied to the public realm. Basically, a simple but powerful analogy is made between private behavior and public preferences. Thus, the public realm cannot create preferences through manipulation of private individuals. Accordingly, these types of models do not and cannot tell us how preferences are created.[7] Individuals are assumed to maximize their utility by voting for certain bundles of public consumption goods and/or amenities. Individuals are like accountants in this regard, weighing the benefits of various goods against their costs (in the form of taxes, levies, etc.). But, unlike accountants, there are no public standards of benefit. We are in a utilitarian world.

On the demand side, individual preferences, when summed together, are the signals for local governments to supply those public goods demanded by local residents. The formal signal or expression of local preferences is obviously the votes caste by local residents for alternative packages of local public goods. There are further subtleties which deserve mention in this particular context. For instance, there are at least two ways in which public-choice theorists imagine that local choices will or can be evidenced. The median voter model based on Hotelling's theory of spatial competition, assumes that "central" or majority preferences determine the mix of public goods offered voters.[8] This model depends upon candidates for local office offering choices of public goods combined with their fiscal and tax costs. Here, we must assume perfect information, full participation in the democratic process, and rational decision making; that is, people must not only know their preferences but also act by them according to proposed alternatives.

According to Inman (1979), there is some evidence that this model works, empirically speaking. Even so, there are many doubts about the model, particularly concerning the restrictiveness of its assumptions (Clark 1981a). But there are two less restrictive options. One option is to specify what Inman termed the "dominant party model." Here it is assumed that informed voting is costly; size and functional complexity are typically invoked at this point. Well-disciplined organizations run local government and effectively limit choice, both in terms of those who would offer themselves as candidates and the bundles of public goods offered voters by party organizations. Here local majority preferences are less important than how well the local party system can satisfy different minority interest groups who are highly active in the local community. Note, however, that preferences are still important, and the nature and cost of local public goods are similarly important. The difference is that the local government may be able to buy enough loyalty by offering specific types of local public goods to specific local interest groups while spreading the costs of provision across the whole community.

The limit to this kind of redistribution is the mobility of local residents. Assuming choice between local governments, free access and easy mobility, dissatisfied residents may vote not by voice so much as exit (using terms made popular by Hirschman 1970). Since it is also assumed that local governments maximize revenue and minimize costs, the exit option may effectively discipline a one-party democratic community. For example, if some public facilities require certain levels of population to be provided efficiently, the local government concerned will likely amend its behavior so that the required population levels are maintained.[9] By doing so, costs (taxes) are minimized, and local government behavior disciplined. Producers, that is, local governments, are thus only thin bureaucracies (open to constituents' interests). In this model, they cannot avoid local preferences, although how these preferences are expressed range from direct voting (democracy) to representative voting (minority interests) to implied voting (mobility).

Models of local government functions based on Hotelling's solution to spatial competition are really designed to determine a single local government's level of local public services. In this model, intergovernmental grants look like lump-sum transfers which simultaneously allow local governments to provide more services without violating majority voters' budget constraints. Thus, consumers' utilities increase and the demands for service increase (Oates 1979). Residential mobility models, on the other hand, are more complex in that they can create a heterogeneous landscape of public services—communities differentiated from one another according to their mix of local public goods, their sizes, and economies. Indeed, Tiebout (1956) imagined a set of communities which specialize in very different types of public facilities and consequently draw very different kinds of residents. For Tiebout this is a result of rational utility maximizing behavior; for Nozick (1974), who derives a similar landscape, it is the result of morally likeminded people wishing to locate near one another for life-style preference reasons.

On the supply side, we noted above that local governments are assumed to maximize revenue and minimize costs.[10] In the literature, there are a number of ways that this objective function can be sustained. One way which we have already acknowledged has to do with scale. That is, the costs of providing a particular public good may reduce as the population served increases to a point where costs begin to rise again. Implied here is, of course, a kind of U-shaped average cost function, typical of neoclassical microeconomic models of private firms. Whether or not these cost functions are U-shaped or some other shape is of little importance. As long as they can be empirically defined, the theory of optimal population size can then be applied to the problem of designing jurisdictions for the provision of such services. In this kind of model, jurisdictions are designed in accordance with theoretical principles and their empirical images; it is assumed that jurisdictional boundaries are plastic and malleable, what Thrall (1979) has termed elsewhere as "putty" (borrowing a term from the capital controversy; Harcourt 1972). Of course, it is quite possible that different functions will have different optimal population sizes. Thus, the logic of this model suggests, at the extreme, a whole series of jurisdictions of varying spatial scales and population sizes, all derived from the imperatives of maximizing revenue and minimizing costs. For some theorists such as Bennett (1980), there is evidence that this kind of model can explain the existence of special-function districts, such as sewerage districts in metropolitan areas throughout Europe and the United States. Of course, it is an extreme conclusion. Less extreme is an implied notion that cooperative interjuris-dictional service organizations should perform similar functions to single purpose functional districts. After all, with the twin imperatives of max-imizing revenue and minimizing costs, all adjacent and contiguous locales' would have a vested interest in forming such alliances, assuming for the moment that such services are desired by all communities' residents.

For public-finance theorists, these choice models of local public finance provide theoretical, even empirical guidelines for the design and implementation of local government functions. At one level (which we will call empirical-cum-realist), theorists such as Inman (1979) suppose that local governments can be analyzed as if these models were relevant. By that I mean, it is either claimed that the empirical evidence supports these models and/or that reality would be like these models if allowed to be so. The *as if* argument combines a measure of empiricism with theoretical abstraction, culminating in a set of rules for the theory and practice of local public finance. For instance, Bennett (1980) goes to great lengths to demonstrate the existence of optimal city sizes and functional efficien-cies. The object of this kind of analysis is to indicate that these models provide relevant rules for jurisdictional design (the scale of local govern-ments), jurisdictional responsibilities (which level of government ought to be responsible for different kinds of public goods), and jurisdictional relations (the necessity of cooperation, for instance).[11]

The empirical-cum-realist vision of local public finance can be reason-ably dispatched by counterempirical evidence and an internal critique of its assumptions and logic. Indeed, while Inman (1979, p. 284) suggested that "the evidence for or against the dominant party framework is largely anecdotal," he went on in the next two sentences to suggest, "there are numerous studies that attest to voter ignorance, the disincentives to become informed, and the high cost in time and money of running for local office. In many cities the prerequisites for monopoly power in local politics are present." And he noted on page 283 that one-party local governments, controling access to jobs, resources, and the budget are typical of larger cities. He says, "party resources . . . largely control elections . . . favors granted are favors rewarded . . . the result is long runs of one-party rule. Only major scandals, legal limitations on reelection, or long-term demographic shifts can undo control." Inman's reservations have been echoed by Oates (1981) and Yinger (1981) among others.

In terms of Tiebout's assumptions, many more doubts can be raised. For instance, even Tiebout was forced to admit that there may be far fewer opportunities for moving than he implied. And even if there were many opportunities, there is something a little odd about his argument. If it is individual preference that drives choice, Tiebout's model implies in the extreme that we would have a myriad of local governments, perhaps as many as there were individuals.[12] Furthermore, it is obvious that the map of locations is as important as the existence of different locations. That is, people make location decisions on the basis of the spatial position of locations vis-à-vis other locations. This is the lesson of racial discrimination in urban areas, both in how people move and how communities erect barriers to entry by zoning and the like against residents from other nearby communities (Yinger 1979). It is just as obvious that mobility is very difficult; income, social status, and race seriously restrict the set of possible destinations.

We could go on indicating the problems of Tiebout-type assumptions from the perspective of the consumer. And I doubt whether many would disagree with my list of problems with the real world as compared to Tiebout's idealized landscape. However, I wish also to emphasize the supply-side problems of the Tiebout model, and choice models generally, because these issues are hardly ever recognized in the literature although they bear directly upon the logic of choice models.

As was noted in chapter 4, the Tiebout model implies broad powers of initiative and some immunity. In this context we may legitimately question whether local governments have enough initiative power and immunity from higher tiers of government. Dillon's (1911) rule is in force in many states, limiting local governments to narrow spheres of jurisdiction and narrowly defined areas of interest. Dillon's rule seems to counter Tiebout on two counts: it limits initiative to specific tasks, thereby denying local preferences not covered by these specific grants of power, and it enforces jurisdictional homogeneity, not heterogeneity. Dillon's rule treats local governments alike, thereby denying the possibility of different preference communities and of choice between locations simultaneously. Dillon's rule does not allow any immunity. Thus, any local action can be appealed to a higher level dominated, presumably, by a different mix of people and preferences. Thus, institutionally, the supply side of choice models of local public finance seems unrelated to the dominant American mode of local government organization.

Of course, this type of criticism of the empirical-cum-realist model of local public finance is quite appropriate to the concerns in this chapter, and this book more generally. To evaluate adequately the relevance of this type of model for settling jurisdictional disputes in Illinois and the sewerage wars in particular, we have to look at the institutional capacity of local governments. This means evaluating the arrangement of local initiative and immunity powers, as well as the arrangement of specific jurisdictional responsibilities (if any!). Like any analysis of the supply side of choice models, the issues are empirical and internal to the logic of the model. That is, we can say whether or not the model's assumptions are met, whether exceptions exist, and how the practical realities of specific communities may modify the implementation of these choice models. This is, however, an empirical test of the relevance of these kinds of models. While we will consider this issue in more depth in a later section, a more fundamental question needs to be addressed: whether or not these models *should* be applied to jurisdictional disputes at all.

Efficiency and Local Public Goods

There is another version of public choice that is less empirical and more theoretical in content. For simplicity's sake, I will refer to it as the Chicago law and economics school, although it is obvious that others not located in Chicago also proclaim its virtues (compare Kennedy 1981). Posner (1981*b*) suggested that this school has two branches—positive and normative. Both branches suppose, however, that economic efficiency is the fundamental yardstick for judging the efficacy of public institutions like law and local government. On the positive side, Posner argued that judges act as if they follow this maxim. More specifically, Posner suggested that judicial decision making can be interpreted as the application of economic principles leading to, or aimed at, maximizing overall wealth. This, he suggested, is a characteristic of American common law, a practice of judicial decision making reaching back over two centuries. In these terms, the positive approach to law and economics aims at demonstrating the economic effects of the application of legal norms. Thus, like any theory of society, the theory of law and economics seeks to explain the structure and application of social rules. Posner claims that this research agenda is neutral and "purely descriptive."

The second branch is more contentious and has drawn a great deal of argument. Essentially, the normative argument is that "wealth maximization should guide public policy in all spheres" (Posner 1981*a*,

p. 780). That is, judges ought to decide cases according to economic principles of efficiency and optimality, and public institutions ought to be designed so that social wealth is maximized, and thus social costs minimized. While written in terms of wealth maximization, the whole intent of the Chicago law and economics school is to apply principles of neoclassical economics to the design and adjudication of public rules. Wealth maximization is the goal; efficiency rules and optimal concepts are the tools or means by which this goal is attained. Posner distinguished strong and weak versions of this theory. The former presumes that economic principles ought to be applied in all situations while the latter presumes that barring an adequate theory of wealth redistribution judges ought to use economic principles as long as they do not entail radical redistributive implications. Going on what he noted earlier concerning the virtues of maximum national wealth, Posner obviously believes in the strong version of the normative branch of law and economics.

In terms of the preceding discussion of local public finance, the strong normative model of law and economics would surely suppose the following. First, local jurisdictions should be designed so as to maximize wealth. That is, jurisdictions should provide local public goods and services at the lowest cost possible, thereby maximizing the local and national social surplus. Second, the normative model of law and economics also implies that conflicts over jurisdictional authority ought to be resolved so that social wealth is maximized. Thus, this school of thought implies that judges ought to decide in favor of those parties or jurisdictions which would provide local public goods as cheaply as possible. Third, the normative model also supposes that the more social institutions are arranged according to the theoretical principles of neoclassical market economics, then axiomatically, wealth will be maximized. Here, theory provides a datum point by which to evaluate the efficacy of existing local governmental arrangements. This model implies that judges ought to decide cases, and local governents ought to design their programs, so as to mimic the neoclassical market.

For those who despair of ever finding one social rule stable enough be applied to different times and places, Posner's normative rule must seem very attractive. It promises stability and nonarbitrariness—judges would know what to do in any circumstance, and their behavior could be reasonably predicted. Thus, economic rules would be applied to all circumstances; the context would not come back to haunt decision makers.[13]

It is this promise that is at the heart of recent academic attempts at formalizing the theory of local public finance. For instance, Thrall (1979) has attempted to develop a spatially invariant criterion for judging the fairness of property tax schedules. He used an idealized landscape, the tools of neoclassical economics and a spatial equilibrium setting to establish theoretical principles which would guide public policy. And Lea (1979), writing on the structure and performance of the local public sector, suggested that the normative goal of public policy analysis ought to be pareto optimality. He argued that this criterion is "relatively uncontentious" (whatever that means), and can be achieved by applying efficiency principles to public policies. However, unlike Posner (1981a, b), Lea (1979) is content to pursue the weak form of this normative vision.

For Bennett (1980) and so many others, the normative application of economic principles to the practice of local public finance has many virtues. Even so, I would contend that this model is so flawed as to be irrelevant for resolving problems such as local jurisdictional disputes. I would argue that its irrelevance is not so much a matter of empirical irrelevance as it is a matter of theoretical indeterminacy. Clearly, economic rules can be useful in designing public policies. So I do not mean to suggest that there is no place for economic issues in specific circumstances. There are many empirical issues to be resolved at that level. More to the point, I would argue that as *the* normative rule for social adjudication, wealth maximization is incomplete, indeed indeterminant. By that I mean, wealth maximization is ambiguous; it requires outside judicial interpretation to be applied in specific circumstances. Consequently, it cannot replace judicial discretion, because it needs judicial discretion. For those readers who have learned the lessons of chapters 2 and 3 by heart, the problems of wealth maximization must seem obvious. I will concentrate on the central problem: interpreting what maximum wealth means.

There are a variety of reasons for ambiguity and indeterminacy in interpreting maximum wealth as a judicial rule. One issue is its origin, that is, where the goal of wealth maximization is derived from within the logic of neoclassical economics. Posner (1981b) and others claim a theoretical status for the rule, while being quite vague on where its origins lie. If it is imposed from outside of the model, then it is itself arbitrary! There are, however, a number of internal possibilities. For instance, it might be claimed that wealth maximization is a collective preference of all citizens, presumably derived (summed) from individual preferences. If so, many theoretical problems stand in its way and threaten the efficacy of the whole concept. Specifically, Arrow's (1953) "impossibility theorem" (the impossibility of deriving an aggregate social welfare function from individuals' utility functions) is a clear threat at this level of abstraction (see MacKay 1980 for an in-depth treatment).

Since the social welfare function model has been one defense of maximum wealth, efficiency, and optimality, we could reasonably suggest that there is an internal inconsistency with this model which makes it immediately questionable as a judicial rule. While it is reasonable to suggest, as does Lea (1979), that Arrow's critique is extreme and that welfare rules such as the pareto criteria are still useful means of ordering alternative policies, a further rule, or set of rules, is needed to judge when one welfare rule is applicable and inapplicable. Put another way, we could imagine another reasonable criterion, say a social justice rule that requires the rich to give to the poor, which is just as reasonable as a means of ordering alternative policies as any other criterion. The very notion of "reasonable" is vague and unhelpful. Like all appeals to an average informed citizen (e.g., the man on the Clapham Omnibus, made famous by Lord Denning), it can legitimate rhetorically all kinds of policies.[14] Even Posner (1981a) has attempted to put some distance between his notion of social wealth and utilitarian versions based on aggregate social welfare functions.

Actually, Posner's (1981b) version is a variant of Rawls's original position device for deriving social justice. Posner used a method very similar to Rawls's to suggest that maximum social wealth would be a desired end by all individuals located in a presocial, original position. It should be recognized, however, that Posner departs from Rawls's veil of ignorance and does not consult so-called unproductive members of society in creating his social good. For these departures, he has been severely criticized, especially for his implied antidemocratic sentiments (real or imagined; see Coleman 1980). While there is a good deal of force in these criticisms, I would like to emphasize one other issue which has received less attention but which, nonetheless, makes severe inroads on the internal logic of Posner's Rawls-type justification of the normative virtues of wealth maximization. This issue is simply the limits of liberalism itself (cf. Sandel 1982).

Put bluntly, Posner, like Rawls, has no theory of moral sentiments. Indeed, he cannot have such a theory because he begins individual calculation prior to the creation of society. Like Rawls, he imagined individuals to be created prior to society and hence conceived them as rational calculating agents. Yet this is precisely the problem for Rawls, and now for Posner, which we noted in more depth in chapter 2. It is impossible for Rawls to explain how these individuals were so conceived as to be complex individuals with passions and desires prior to society. We can only assume some state-of-nature argument or some innate qualities of individuals which exist prior to and independent of society. At the extreme, we have to assume what Putnam (1981) has termed "brains-in-a-vat," a neutral nondimensional world (perhaps a Marcusian one-dimensional man) which is simply a stage for individual action, not a situation in which action takes place. Granted, Posner did introduce the notion of productive as opposed to unproductive individuals and partially dropped the veil of ignorance so that some context is introduced to give reason for choosing maximum wealth, and yet these modifications are hardly helpful.

On the one hand, Posner used Rawlsian logic to separate context from motivation and then, on the other hand, introduced context to get individuals to choose what he wanted them to choose. This is a very odd way of analyzing the virtues of wealth maximization. It simultaneously depends on-liberal conceptions of individualism and allows for the force of circumstances to define the worth of individuals. Thus, wealth maximization is created as the social goal through a device which classifies individuals into two different social groups. The virtue of Rawls's approach was that he could claim a measure of desirability and legitimacy for any world created through his model. Not only were peoples' positions irrelevant, they all participated in creating the golden rule. Posner's world, however, denies the participation of some members of society and allows material circumstances to enter into peoples' calculations. Thus, Posner's notion suffers both from being based on Rawls's and from not being consistent with Rawls's. Like Rawls, Posner is unable to justify his original position in terms of the character of his individuals but unlike Rawls, Posner cannot claim legitimacy in a liberal democratic sense for any endpoint of his analysis. In Posner's terms, wealth maximization would be a highly controversial rule, requiring "outside" adjudication in application.

Posner's problems do not stop there. Wealth maximization is also liable to need judicial interpretation because it is itself ambiguous. In a thorough review of Posner's argument, Dworkin (1980b) suggested that there are at least four different ways of interpreting wealth maximization. Elsewhere, I have applied this argument to a critique of Reagan's national urban policy.[15] Here I wish to note briefly Dworkin's classification as a point of disagreement with Posner's claim that wealth maximization is the single, simple rule of adjudication that he supposed.

Wealth maximization may be desired as a goal in and of itself. This implies that society would be somehow better off if it had greater wealth, although it remains unclear how we would measure this wealth, even what this wealth would imply in terms of distribution. Posner would surely not worry about its redistributive consequences, although Lea might. A second interpretation of wealth maximization might be that it makes everyone better off or at least no person worse off. We could imagine a Kaldor-Hicks criterion or even a pareto criterion to take account of circumstances where unrestrained wealth maximization created inequality.[16] Notice, however, that this interpretation leaves unstated how to measure "better off" and how to compensate losers. A further set of rules and principles would have to be introduced to give substance to the general claim. A third interpretation would be that wealth maximization enables society to achieve other goals. That is, it is a means to an end (again left unstated). This interpretation goes beyond Posner because it denies the idea that wealth maximization is an end in itself (remember Posner thought efficiency to be the means of wealth maximization). Finally, we might interpret wealth maximization as a surrogate for other goals. For whatever reasons, it may be the case that wealth maximization is an umbrella concept which captures in one unique recipe a set of other desirable goals. The difficulty with all these interpretations is not their individual virtues. We can imagine, I am sure, situations where society might wish to pursue one or two interpretations over others. Rather, the difficulty is that either these interpretations are given meaning or value by circumstances and/or they raise other hidden questions of the meaning of substantive justice itself.

By itself, wealth maximization is neither unambiguous nor determinant. To apply it as an adjudicative rule, we would first need to interpret its meaning by some other rule or sets of rules. Again, this may well be appropriate, even desirable, given the circumstances of particular disputes. But it is just as clear that wealth maximization needs judicial discretion to be given substantive meaning. Thus, while we can imagine using wealth maximization to adjudicate competing jurisdictional claims for resources, we also have to acknowledge that the rule itself would have to be interpreted. Posner's interpretation is one of many and appears flawed—both in terms of liberal conceptions of individualism and in terms of Rawlsian assumptions. To proclaim just one interpretation of wealth maximization would also be undemocratic. And, indeed, Posner's model seems just that—built upon an unequal distribution of resources and an unequal voice in social affairs.

To summarize my argument against the law and economics school of adjudication, I would contend that concepts like efficiency and wealth maximization are two among many others which have a claim to our attention. Generally, they are useful tools for evaluating alternative policies. But they cannot deliver on implied and explicit promises made by public finance and law and economics theorists that they are somehow superior rules of adjudication. At one level, it is not obvious that economic rules adequately describe how jurisdictional systems of local government functions are actually designed. Thus, as a positive model of analysis, it remains to be seen whether or not these economic models can better describe reality. At another level, it is not at all the case that these principles can be unambiguously interpreted or applied. By that I mean that it is not obvious what should be the correct interpretation of wealth maximization, nor is it a priori apparent that any one policy would best achieve this goal, whatever it means. In the next sections, I explore the legal structure of Illinois local government, emphasizing the underlying principles of its design and the ambiguities of interpreting the best allocation of jurisdictional responsibilities.

Local Autonomy in Illinois Again

The state of Illinois entered the Union in 1818 with a constitution modeled on other recently formed states, including Kentucky, Ohio, New York, and Indiana. In its first constitution the county was the major unit of Illinois local government. However, most power was retained by the state legislature, which was given the power to appoint all major public officers except governor, lieutenant governor, sheriff, coroner, and county commissioners. In those early years, the legislature ruled supreme even though citizen movements sought to decentralize certain of its powers to local government. Deriving momentum from a national movement for popular self-government in the 1820s and 1830s, a similar movement in Illinois convinced the legislature in 1826 and 1837 to allow the election of judges and constables. Eventually, this same movement contributed to statewide constitutional reform.[17]

It was widely felt that the state government possessed too much power with too few constraints on its actions. This feeling was galvanized by a number of state actions during this period which undermined its credibility and popular image. First, two state-chartered and-administered banks failed soon after statehood, one in 1821 and another in 1834. Second, the state's ambitious campaign of internal improvements (public works and infrastructure) was largely a failure (including a $10 million debacle involving a state railway system in 1837). The only successful scheme from this campaign was the Illinois-Michigan Canal.

With the state heavily in debt and its credit rating deteriorating, its political legitimacy collapsed, culminating in the constitutional convention of 1848. Of this new constitution, Cornelius (1972, p. 32) wrote:

> [it] was considerably longer and more detailed than that of 1818 . . . because the convention writers were attempting to exercise greater control over State government in the future than had been exercised in the past.

The new constitution provided for the election of more officers, restricted the indebtedness of the state to $50,000, and prohibited the state assembly from extending its credit to aid individuals and private corporations. Municipalities were also given major responsibility for internal improvements and public works. In accordance with this new function, the possibility of a township mode of local government organization was introduced (obtainable by a majority vote of county electors). Local government units were also given the power to assess and collect taxes to finance their activities.

When the constitutional convention of 1870 concluded, the document it produced contained a specific provision to limit local indebtedness and municipal subscriptions to railroads. During this time there was a strong mood against the "extravagance of municipalities" (Lewis 1971). Many legislators representing Cook County and the City of Chicago were frustrated in their efforts to have the new constitution deal specifically with the problems that rapidly urbanizing areas were facing. While they vied for a framework that would grant them greater local autonomy and allow for increasing specialization and expansion of city functions in the future, they were overpowered by rural and southern blocs who were fearful of the potential dominance of Chicago in state politics. The only concession granted to city interests was the creation of special criminal and superior courts to serve the burgeoning needs of Cook County.

Although the constitution of 1870 remained in force for the next one hundred years, in the years immediately following the adoption of the new constitution, recentralization of power to the state level was expressed through legislative initiatives such as the Railroad Act of 1871 and the Railroad Law of 1873, which regulated rates and other practices of railroads and warehouses. The 1873 law became a national landmark of states' subsequent ability to regulate business affecting the public interest when the U.S. Supreme Court ruled in its favor in *Munn v. Illinois* (1877). A successful challenge to state dominance would not materialize for many years, but the push for greater local autonomy began early. The home-rule movement in Illinois was centered in Chicago, where the 1880s and 1890s saw the formation of such home-rule promoters as the Chicago Civic Federation and the Chicago Citizens' Association, as well as the involvement of the National Municipal League. While this movement produced a constitutional amendment for "limited home rule" through the Chicago charter of 1904, it remained largely irrelevant.

A further constitutional convention met in 1920–22 and included among its provisions a more expanded home rule for Chicago as well as greater representation for Cook County in the state legislature. But with state opposition to Chicago still strong, the proposed constitution was never adopted. It was not until 1970 that home rule was fully instituted in Illinois. Prior to that year, the prevailing Dillon doctrine had limited local government powers only to those expressly conferred on them by the state legislature. The new constitution of 1970 brought home rule to all cities over 25,000 in population and to those counties which elected a chief executive officer. Other cities could adopt home rule by referendum.

While the 1970 constitution reflected a new era for local government in
Illinois, it is important to acknowledge the legitimacy of state preemption
of local legislation, even in home-rule situations, which stems from the
U.S. Supreme Court's decision in *Hunter v. City of Pittsburgh* (1907). In
summing up the Illinois situation over a decade ago in the wake of the last
constitutional convention, Cornelius (1972) remarked that:

> All powers would go to local units unless specifically prohibited by the constitu-
> tion, or preempted by the State Legislature. Preemption would determine in
> part how much power the localities would actually have. (P. 158).

Indeed, any reasonable conclusions concerning the extent of local
government autonomy in Illinois cannot be based solely on the latter. It
must be pointed out at this juncture that, even as it was granting home-
rule powers to local units, the legislature was also imposing a uniform set
of regulations for financial accounting and budgetary control on all local
governments. Even though the Constitution decrees that "powers and
functions of home rule units shall be construed liberally" (Art. VIII, Sec.
[m]), the same portion of the document (Sec. 6—Powers of Home Rule
Units) set forth a long list of restrictions on the activities of home-rule
entities (see chap. 4). It is clear, then, that the Illinois home-rule provision is of the *grant* form rather than the *limitation* form. As defined by
Mandelker and Netsch (1977), these two forms of local government
powers can best be understood in the following terms:

> In grant States, constitutional home rule cities possess only those powers that
> are granted by the constitutional home rule provision. Courts in grant States
> may take a narrow view of the delegated authority similar to the approach
> mandated by Dillon's rule for statutory grants of power. . . . In limitation
> States, home rule municipalities enjoy all powers found to be within the
> municipal initiative unless the exercise of these powers is in some way limited
> by the constitution, by statute, or by the municipal charter. (P.187)

All municipalities in Illinois have had their autonomy limited and
constrained by state and even national statutes. In cases such as *Ronda
Realty Corp. v. Lawton* (1953), local planning and zoning initiatives have
been declared in violation of the equal protection clauses of both the
Illinois and United States constitutions. Similarly, in *209 Lake Shore
Drive Bldg. Corp. v. City of Chicago* (1971), the Illinois Supreme Court
declared that the city lacked the authority to regulate against discrimination by private owners in the housing market. Thus, both prior to and
since enactment of full home rule for Chicago, the city, like other Illinois
cities, has remained vulnerable to state intercession.

Finally, we should also acknowlege that there are other limits on local
autonomy which affect cities like Chicago and which are related to the

judicial sphere as well as the economic or fiscal sphere of autonomy. Many state and federal grants are categorical in nature, thus imposing limits on local discretion. Although the U.S. Supreme Court originally ruled that Congress may not control state and local activities by setting conditions tied to particular sources of financing (see *United States v. Butler* [1936]), the use of categorical grants has since been defended successfully (see *North Carolina v. Califano* [1978]). Furthermore, in a famous case involving Chicago, noncategorical general revenue-sharing funds designated under the State and Local Fiscal Assistance Act (31 USC Section 1221 *et seq.* Supp. 1976, and Pub. L. No. 94–488, Oct. 13, 1976) were successfully withheld until the city agreed to comply with the provisions in the act against discriminatory hiring and promotion practices (see *United States v. City of Chicago* [1976]).

Similarly, the judgment in *Hills v. Gautreaux* (1976) affirmed that financial assistance from a federal department (Housing and Urban Development) to a municipal corporation whose official policies were known to be discriminatory (like the Chicago Housing Authority) was in violation of the Fifth Amendment and the Civil Rights Act. Thus, the power of higher tiers of government within these intergovernmental arrangements is strongly economic as well as legal. Cities like Chicago have had to deal with an environment of constitutional, legislative, and fiscal-administrative control. And while Illinois cities have gradually been able to add to their own particular functions and responsibilities, they have remained subject to a whole range of review powers sustained by the state.

For local public-finance theorists who assume a wide range of local powers (so-called supply-side assumptions noted earlier in this chapter), Dillon's rule denies jurisdictional initiative. Specifically, the tasks and responsibilities of local governments are defined through general statutes at the state level. Local preferences can only influence how local governments carry out these tasks (the level of service provision, for instance) although even this possibility is limited by local governments' lack of immunity. With general statutes, local homogeneity rather than heterogeneity is implied. Thus, jurisdictional choice is severely limited; indeed, local government attempts at community differentiation may well be ruled illegal in all circumstances. The empirical expectations of local public-finance theorists must be severely shaken by this evidence.[18]

At the same time, the state government seems to have built into the structure of local government a set of ambiguities and problems of interpretation. I would suggest that it is reasonable to suppose that the Illinois state government could create all kinds of different jurisdictions—ranging in spatial scale, functional responsibilities, and boundaries. If the state government took seriously the notions of economic efficiency and optimality, such as the most efficient design of sewerage treatment facilities in urban areas, then it would be well within its powers to create such special districts as needed. Of course, these districts would owe their existence to legislative fiat, since they would be "creatures of the state" (Frug 1980), not local preferences. Indeed, as circumstances demanded, the state legislature could create, change, even destroy these local governmental units so as to maintain the best arrangement of urban public facilities. As a pure economic issue, local municipalities would be structured according to state-level notions of efficiency, not local, or even regional, interests. Any arrangements along these lines would necessarily change as economic circumstances change. The existence of the Metro-politan Sanitary District of Greater Chicago could be interpreted in these terms.

Yet there are some other issues that may intrude. Specifically, economic efficiency must be justified since, as we saw above, it is not a neutral or necessarily consensual goal. To do that may involve local residents, even notions like local needs. Thus, we could reasonably expect state-initiated local functions to be justified in terms of local interests. These interests would obviously be related to the functions provided, their spatial reach, and the allocation of costs and benefits. In these ways, local constituents would be used to justify state-level local public goods. By invoking local preferences, state-level institutions may find local residents demanding more than they wish to provide. Limited local participation may explode into jurisdictional controversy over whose interests are served by state-level bureaucracies. Similarly, as local needs are invoked to legitimate state-level agencies, it may become quite ambiguous whose authority is relevant in specific circumstances. These issues are explored in the next section.

Chicago's Sewerage War

In late July 1966, the Metropolitan Sanitary District of Greater Chicago began negotiations to acquire a 103 acre site in the City of Des Plaines for a water reclamation plant. This parcel of land was zoned by Des Plaines as an M-1 Restricted Manufacturing District. The proposed reclamation plant was obviously not consistent with the city's zoning ordinance. Apparently, the City of Des Plaines made an attempt to apprise the district of its zoning ordinance and its lack of support for the plant. However, the district "declared its intention to proceed [with the plant] without application to the City for a [zoning] variation" (*City of Des Plaines v. Metropolitan San. Dist.*, 1970). The district then purchased the property, plans were drawn up, and preliminary site clearances were initiated.

In November 1966, the city filed a complaint with the circuit court asking that the district be forced to acknowledge the city's jurisdiction in matters of local land-use planning. The court decided in favor of the city, ruling that the city's zoning ordinance was applicable to the district. An injunction was also issued to halt all construction. On appeal, the district contended that a municipality's zoning ordinance is not applicable to other municipal units in carrying out their rightful, legislatively defined, governmental functions. The district cited two previous cases, *Decatur Park Dist. v. Becker* (1938) and *Village of Schiller Park v. City of Chicago* (1962), in arguing that the courts should respect the integrity of the two parties' separate spheres of responsibility, as defined by the legislature.

The court had argued in *Decatur* that in cases where two statutes conflict, their application is most appropriate in their respective fields of operation. Thus, even if a parcel of land was zoned for a particular use, an agency acting within its powers and spatial arena could use such zoned land for other purposes. In the *Schiller Park* case, the City of Chicago was allowed to use their condemnation powers to acquire property close to O'Hare Airport since the city was thought to have acted within its rights as manager of the airport.

The district contended that their waste water responsibilities were such that they had jurisdiction in this field of government over the entire Greater Chicago area (their operations area as defined by the state legislature). However, the appellate court held that, as in *Heft v. Zoning Board of Appeals of Peoria County* (1964), the district was required to comply with the provisions of local government zoning ordinances. Only if the area in question had been unincorporated would the district have been able to act as if the area was under its sole jurisdiction. Also, the district's claim that a municipal unit cannot interfere with another was held by the court to be an extreme interpretation. The court suggested that the district's failure even to apply for a zoning variation was evidence that an accommodation between the two municipal entities was still possible. Thus, the First District Appellate Court found that the circuit court had acted in a manner consistent with precedent and the facts of the case. The city won the first two skirmishes of this battle.

But, at the Illinois Supreme Court level, the city suffered a major setback. The supreme court ruled against the city and reversed the lower courts' decisions. The issue was interpreted to be "whether plaintiff's zoning ordinance is applicable to defendant's power of eminent domain" (*City of Des Plaines v. Metropolitan Sanitary Dist.*, 1971). The state supreme court argued that Illinois statutes authorized the district to acquire the land in question. They cited the enabling legislation of the district (Ill. Rev. Stat. 1967, Ch. 42, para 327) and specifically its powers of eminent domain to justify the district's decision to acquire the parcel of

land for "its corporate purposes" (p. 430). This statute contained the
following provision:

> Except as otherwise in this Act provided, the sanitary district may acquire by
> lease, purchase or otherwise within or without its corporate limits, or by
> condemnation within its corporate limits, any and all real and personal prop-
> erty, right of way and privilege that may be required for its corporate purposes.
> (Ch. 42, Sec. 327)

The court also suggested that to require the district to act in accordance
with local zoning policy would be to "frustrate the purpose of the statute." While they also conceded that this statute was not an absolute grant
of power, relief from arbitrary or excessive use of eminent domain was
theoretically still possible, and in this instance the court asserted that the
district had acted well within its authority. Finally, the court denied that
Heft was relevant because of issues pertaining to the previous case;
essentially, Peoria County had already submitted itself to the jurisdiction
of the local zoning board of appeals.

   In this first battle, the district ultimately won because the Illinois
Supreme court chose to interpret the case from one perspective on the
basis of one statute. No obvious attempt was made to resolve the underlying problem; the city and district were of equal municipal status in terms
of the state legislature. Indeed, in contrast, the appellate court had
clearly taken a more fundamental view of the problem when it argued
that a mutual accommodation of interests should be reached between the
two parties. The appellate court implied equal status for the two municipal units. The state supreme court, however, chose to evaluate the
district's "purpose" above that of the local government. In doing so, the
court implicitly suggested that the district had a "special purpose," which
went beyond local interests. The court treated the city as a restraint on
the rightful exercise of the district's duties. And it turned around the
appellate court's notion of shared responsibility—instead of jurisdictional responsibility being a question of accommodation, the supreme
court supposed that the district was dominant over local governments
unless a case could be made that their use of this power was excessive or
outside their field of interest. The supreme court used a functional model
of municipal powers to allocate jurisdictional responsibility while ignoring the underlying legislative predicament.

   The first battle was fought under the terms of the old 1870 Illinois
Constitution (as amended), which treated local government units as
administrative arms of the state legislature. Dillon's rule held sway in this
context. Cities and towns had no discretion or initiative powers other
than those expressly authorized by state statutes. Legislative supremacy
meant that localities had only those powers granted in express terms,

those powers implied in those expressly granted powers, and those powers necessary for the accomplishment of their expressly granted tasks (Dillon 1911). As we have noted before, the practice of most U.S. courts has been to interpret these powers narrowly and by the letter of the law (chap. 4).

With the passage of the new Illinois Constitution in 1970, however, a chance was given to localities to assume home-rule status. In late 1972, the City of Des Plaines went back to the courts in an attempt to reestablish their jurisdiction over the district. In this battle, the city argued that its home-rule status now gave it power to regulate special districts like the Metropolitan Sanitary District. The issue was interpreted by the courts to be whether or not the previous Illinois Supreme Court ruling was still valid in these circumstances. The circuit court decided that *res judicata* applied in this instance; that is, since the parties, issues, and subject matter were virtually the same as before, the supreme court's ruling should stand. The city then appealed to the appellate court, claiming that the 1970 constitution had so altered the legal relationship between the parties involved that new questions of law "must be decided" (*City of Des Plaines v. Metropolitan San. Dist.*, 1973). Here, the appellate court held in favor of the city by reversing the lower court decision. Again, the city had won over the district.

The appellate court argued that *res judicata* only applied in circumstances where the facts and conditions of a case were exactly the same from one time to the next. They suggested that the 1970 constitution had radically altered the powers of local governments. Specifically, they suggested that Dillon's rule was no longer the basis for deciding questions of local powers; rather home-rule status now gave the city a grant of inherent powers as noted in Section 6(a) of Article VII. The court cited the following passage of that section in support:

> [A] home rule unit may exercise any power and perform any function pertaining to its government and affairs including, but not limited to, the power to regulate for the protection of the public health, safety. (P. 26)

In the court's view, Section 6(a) "dramatically altered the concept of legislative supremacy," especially since the district possessed no equivalent powers, being solely a creature of the legislature. Here, the court suggested that the city had a broad grant of initiative power which could be exercised in accordance with local concerns. In contrast, the court held that the district had limited initiative powers being still bound by Dillon's rule. Furthermore, it was noted that the constitution was the source of home-rule powers while the district had only legislative support.

At the same time, the court also noted that Article VII did not deal explicitly with interjurisdictional responsibilities. Thus, their interpretation was really an attempt to flesh out the implications of the home-rule provision in terms of interjurisdictional dominance. By doing so, of course, they reversed the order of dominance found in the previous supreme court judgment; the city now held sway over the district unless proven otherwise. Thus, the court implied some democratic virtues to home-rule municipal units which special districts like the Metropolitan Sanitary District did not share in. Here, McBain's (1916) notion of an inherent right of self-government seems to come closest to the court's view, even close to the court's choice of language in their argument (for example, "the grant of inherent power," p. 26).

But again, the Illinois Supreme Court reversed the appellate court's decision, thereby siding with the district against the city. Essentially, the supreme court asserted that *res judicata* was, in fact, relevant, just as the circuit court had argued, and that the adoption of the 1970 constitution had not altered the facts or circumstances of the dispute. In doing so, however, the court implied that home-rule provisions of local powers were no different from legislative grants of power.

The supreme court asserted that "it is apparent that the cause of action, the issues, the parties and the relief sought in this action are identical to those in the earlier case" (*City of Des Plaines v. Metropolitan S.D. of G. Chicago*, 1974). Of course, the city did not pretend otherwise. However, the city did argue that their substantive powers were now very different. But in this regard, the supreme court claimed that the source of local powers was irrelevant, the facts were supposedly just the same. Very little was offered by the court by way of justification for this stand. This was despite an implied argument that the 1970 constitution had only changed the origin of local powers, not the actual dimensions of local powers. According to the court, Dillon's rule was apparently dressed up in a different guise, not radically altered or denied. Again, the functional argument for the district's domination held sway over local interests and, again, the court relied upon a one-sided reading of the state statutes which were interpreted to give the district its exclusive powers. Justice Ryan, in dissent, argued that "instead of resolving the vital issue of this case [local power under the home-rule provision of the 1970 constitution], which was created by . . . this court [in the previous adjudication], the court simply states that it is irrelevant" (p. 11).

At this point, the city had lost two out of two supreme court challenges to the district, although it had had minor successes in lower courts. While it had been successful in asserting the local powers issue in the appellate court, the supreme court had remained locked in to the logic of a functional model of interjurisdictional responsibilities, based on state statutes. Yet, the supreme court's logic in these two decisions was hardly convincing to the city then, and is hardly convincing to an outside reader such as myself now. Its logic seemed arbitrary and selective. The court would not countenance the idea that local governments had any rights over special districts which had wider spatial jurisdictions and specific functions. In the first battle, the court simply asserted the superiority of the sanitary district using an Illinois statute. And, in the second battle, the court simply ignored substantive claims for local government powers. It should not be surprising that the city felt it should continue the struggle.

In June 1974, the city enacted an ordinance requiring any sewerage works in the city to obtain a permit from the city. The city set up a code of standards for the emission of airborne odors, bacteria, and the like. The district, however, refused to apply for a city permit, contending that its State of Illinois Environmental Protection Agency permit was sufficient under the terms of then current Illinois statutes (Ill. Rev. Stat. 1973, Ch. 111 1/2, pars. 1013(a), 1039). On 28 February 1975, the district appealed to the circuit court to rule that the city's ordinance was not applicable. But not surprisingly, the circuit court ruled against the district, arguing that it "was obliged to comply with reasonable provisions of the health ordinance which were not inconsistent with conditions imposed by the EPA" (*Metro. San. Dist. of Chicago v. City of Des Plaines*, 1976). This ruling was then appealed by the district directly to the Illinois Supreme Court.

Again, the issue centered upon the proper dimensions of local home-rule powers, and again the city lost. It lost the third battle and, for the time being, the whole sewerage war. In arguing before the supreme court, the district added a new wrinkle to its position. It asserted that regulation of sewerage was a statewide concern, not a matter of local government interest. And the court took the lead of the district in framing the legal question as "whether the environmental regulation of a regional sewerage treatment plant . . . pertains to the government and affairs of the City of Des Plaines" (p. 718). While the court did agree that the powers and functions of home-rule units ought to be interpreted broadly, it nevertheless argued that statewide interests preempted local interests. It pointed to the fact that the sewerage plant would serve six other localities, as well as Des Plaines. Moreover, it was concerned that if it decided in favor of Des Plaines, this would set a precedent for other cities to question regional authorities. Finally, it suggested that it would be more efficient if one municipal unit (the district) had responsibility for the regulation of environmental matters. For all these reasons, the supreme court reversed the circuit court decision, and the city of Des Plaines lost again.

Obviously, the supreme court again ignored the issue of the substantive powers of local government units. It used empirical-cum-functional considerations of statewide interests, precedent, and efficiency to legitimate its decision. No attempt was made to consider the home-rule issue, leading Justice Ryan in dissent to protest that:

> it is imperative that we not continue to deprive units of local government, especially home rule units, of their right to legislate in this area most essential to the health and welfare of the inhabitants. (P. 719)

It is obvious, in retrospect, that the supreme court felt unable to deal with the local-powers issue. Its interpretation of these cases did not even allow for negotiation between city and sanitary district. And it would not even allow for coextensive regulation as long as the city did not violate state environmental laws, surely a minor local power if allowed. In these ways, the court's decision was quite consistent and absolute, if incoherent. It held fast to its initial position on local powers, articulated in the first battle, that the district had absolute jurisdiction over city interests. By doing so the court ignored fundamental changes in the legal relationships of cities to districts and retained Dillon's rule, albeit implicitly, almost to the end. It is little wonder that home rule in Illinois was so ridiculed by local governments during this period; basically the supreme court refused to acknowledge its existence.

To my mind at least, the appellate court was most sensitive to the ambiguities of local powers and jurisdictional responsibilities. At this level, the court recognized the relative nature of jurisdictional powers and the lack of adequate constitutional guidance in resolving interjurisdictional disputes. Moreover, it took the home-rule provision seriously by attempting to support the broad scope of home-rule powers. The supreme court, however, went out of its way to ignore these issues and assert the district's interests.

Whatever the motives of the supreme court in backing the district, its dependence upon empirical and functional logic to support the district provides us with a good example of the local public-finance model in practice. The court maintained that the district was the municipal unit responsible for metropolitan waste water disposal. The court proclaimed an exclusive and absolute interpretation of the district's powers, a necessary argument if the functional model of local responsibilities was to have any credibility. The other arguments, like efficiency and precedent, were invoked to maintain the legitimacy of that position, even though it is not clear that either argument had absolute virtues. That is, like the appellate court, we can imagine circumstances where efficiency would not be compromised by including the City of Des Plaines in the planning and regulation of public facilities. Similarly, precedent seems a weak argument since it admitted that the district was not immune from outside review and the court itself had (and still has) the power to ignore past decisions and constitutional authority. Indeed, it demonstrated that power by ignoring the 1970 home-rule provision.

Thus, I would suggest that the empirical-cum-functional arguments of the supreme court in these cases were really strategies designed to avoid the larger substantive issues of local powers. It is reasonable to suppose that it may cost less to provide sewerage facilities at a regional, as opposed to local, level. And it is reasonable to assume that interjurisdictional interests may be difficult to coordinate, especially when there are local interests that do not share the philosophy of the larger regional agency. So we would not deny these arguments a place in any analysis of the allocation of local responsibilities. It also seems, however, that these functional issues were given exaggerated importance relative to the minor claims of the city. After all, the city at its worst only wished to maintain the integrity of its zoning scheme, not deny the sewerage facility a site in any circumstances. Further, coextensive regulation of local environmental concerns with the Illinois EPA hardly seems so important once we recognize (as the courts did) that EPA regulations would preempt local regulations in any conflict.

8

The Doctrine of Local Matters

In his dissenting opinion to the U.S. Supreme Court's majority decision in *Schad et al. v. Borough of Mount Ephraim* (1981), Chief Justice Warren Burger argued that courts should not intrude in "local expressions of choice," which are related to "essentially local concerns" (p. 88). A New Jersey borough, Mount Ephraim, had prohibited live entertainment, specifically nude dancing, in its commercial area. In arguments before the Supreme Court, the borough contended that such entertainment violated its zoning ordinance and, as a consequence, the borough was within its rights in closing down the facility. Justice White, writing for the majority of the Court, concluded, however, that the borough's action was arbitrary and in violation of the First and Fourteenth Amendments of the U.S. Constitution. Burger, on the other hand, suggested that the borough had a legitimate interest in protecting the community in accordance with local sentiments. He stated the issue as "the right of a small community to ban activity incompatible with a quiet, residential atmosphere" (p. 85).

In broad terms, Burger's argument was for a sphere of local autonomy and, in particular, powers of local initiative which would sustain the integrity of the "placid bedroom community." He made two claims in this argument. First, he suggested that "a community of people are—within limits—masters of their own environment" (p. 85), implying that there is a geography of government power arranged according to the spatial scale of the issues involved. The second claim made by Burger was that "the towns and villages of this Nation are not, and should not be, forced into the mold cast by this Court" (p. 86), thereby implying that there is some virtue in protecting geographical diversity. Basically, Burger suggested that courts should represent local preferences as they concern local matters, a point he has made in numerous other cases. (See, for instance, Chesler 1983, as well as a previous case, *Wisconsin v. Yoder et al.*, 1972, wherein Burger wrote for the majority that members of a Wisconsin Amish community had the right to educate their own children since "compulsory high school attendance could have [a significant detrimental impact] on the continued survival of Amish communities as they exist in the United States today" [p. 209].)

It is argued in this chapter that the doctrine of local matters is incredibly fragile. While this doctrine is often invoked as a defense for local autonomy, even as a blueprint for local public administration, it has proved to be very unstable in changing circumstances, encouraging pragmatism, not stability, of adjudication.[1] Its American origins can be traced at least as far back as de Tocqueville and his romantic conception of eighteenth-and nineteenth-century New England life. I suggest in the next section that it is de Tocqueville's conception of local autonomy that is embodied in more recent theories of local public finance (Tiebout 1956) and local government legitimacy (Nozick 1974). As such, the doctrine of local matters promotes an idealized image of community life more than any stable principles of how to organize governmental responsibilities effectively. Thus, in general, *local matters* is best understood as a rhetorical device used to justify judicial descretion. In this chapter I use the example of Colorado to indicate how local government powers are organized in terms of local matters. I emphasize the realities of local autonomy in a state that has prided itself in supporting strong local governments through the home-rule provisions of the state constitution.

De Tocqueville Meets Tiebout

Democracy in America, first published in France in 1835, is a record of de Tocqueville's observations as he traveled through America and a treatise on society and the role of the state. It is also a testament to the principles of democracy and its practice in a new land—as he noted (p. 39), a "democracy more perfect than any of which antiquity had dared to dream."[2] As the book is full of praise for American democracy, it is also written in praise of liberalism, especially that American kind of liberalism which draws its inspiration from Locke rather than Bentham (Hart 1982). Interspersed throughout the text are references to natural order, to god, and to a "state of nature," which American democracy had to come closest to matching.[3] Thus, we should immediately recognize that there are subtle and not-so-subtle differences between de Tocqueville, the liberal theorist of some 150 years ago, and Tiebout, whose major contribution to the spatial structure of government was published in 1956. Even so, there are enough commonalities between the two to set Tiebout within the logic and structure of de Tocqueville's treatise.

One way of understanding de Tocqueville is to characterize his mode of enquiry in late twentieth-century terms. To be most general, de Tocqueville presents a society-centered theory of the spatial and functional structure of government power (cf. Clark and Dear 1984, Nordlinger

1981). Sovereignty of the people is de Tocqueville's wellspring of American democracy "adopted in practice in every way that imagination could suggest" (p. 60). In contrast to western European nations, de Tocqueville claimed, sovereignty of the people was not simply a slogan "neither hidden nor sterile," but the guiding principle of American society. And it was the mechanism of social transformation during the revolutionary period which severed the "powers of class and inheritance" (p. 59). De Tocqueville used this principle to argue that since "the people" make the laws, and choose the lawmakers, then executive power and administration directly serve the popular will. De Tocqueville suggested a kind of utopian direct democracy ordained by god; for instance, he said, "the people reign over the American political world as god rules over the universe. It is the cause and end of all things; everything rises out of it and is absorbed back into it" (p. 60).

From that position de Tocqueville went on to outline his model of government structure using functional and naturalistic doctrines to sustain his bottom-up conception of government powers. In most of this discussion he used New England as the basic model, which the rest of the U.S. followed, albeit at times somewhat imperfectly. (De Tocqueville observed that "as one goes farther south, one finds a less active municipal life" (p. 81), perhaps the product of poor education, leadership, etc.) The spatial hierarchy of government is built by de Tocqueville from the bottom up, beginning with the township, then the county, the state, and finally the nation.[4] He suggested a number of times that it came about through history, that it was a peculiar accident of circumstances which conspired to order settlements by locale rather than by some overarching (European) class-dominated plan which would have been imposed on the lower classes (p. 44).

But this "historical accident" is not the most important reason advanced by de Tocqueville for this peculiar spatial configuration of government powers. The basic reason he advanced is that "townships" are natural. He argued "the township is the only association so well rooted in nature that wherever men assemble it forms itself" (p. 62). He also suggested that since European nations do not allow individual liberty, local communities are always threatened, always on the defensive, and always subject to the arbitrary powers of a strong and enterprising government. What he called "communal freedom" (p. 62) is then a necessary condition for the growth of towns. The logic of his argument went as follows. First, he assumed individual liberty and the practical sovereignty of the people. Second, he supposed that townships are the natural spatial arena of human association, and thus it grows by its own accord, albeit encouraged by "laws and circumstances," which consolidate them. Third, he supposed that the "original position" must be the community, and thus, since America was founded at that level (or so de Tocqueville's interpretation went), America itself is favored by nature and god. In these terms, de Tocqueville claimed, "man creates kingdoms and republics, but townships seem to spring directly from the hand of god" (p. 62). Whether he was just reporting American arguments or actually making this argument as his own, de Tocqueville's theoretical logic closely followed Locke's (cf. Clark 1982).

From the township, de Tocqueville then speculated on the nature of men, their interests, and passions. At one early point he claimed, "interests, passions, duties, and rights took shape around each individual locality and were firmly attached thereto" (p. 44). Here he implied two things: first, individuals are conceived, in terms of their interests at least, separately from communities; but that second, once formed, they naturally associate together at the community level. Yet again, this is the logic of liberalism, in this case dependent upon the deity, but nevertheless conceived in terms of individuals' interests.[5] This should not be taken to suggest that he assumed individuals to be virtuous or trustworthy. In point of fact, he thought "men" to be dishonest and guided by their own self-interests rather than higher-order social goals. For instance, he noted that the passions of ambition, the taste for power and self-advertisement, and the pursuit of substantial interests are very "troublesome," threats to the virtue of civil life itself (p. 69). While these passions are concentrated in the townships, the townships work "magic"—they socialize, educate, and limit the natural passions of men so that they actually benefit the collective whole (p. 69). He argued that "local institutions are to liberty what primary schools are to science; they put it within the people's reach; they teach people to appreciate its peaceful enjoyment and accustom them to make use of it. Without local institutions a nation may give itself a free government, but it has not got the spirit of liberty" (p. 63).[6]

Once we leave the "natural" township, however, different issues arise. At once, de Tocqueville was concerned to control the passions of individuals and the powers of higher tiers of government. Judicial powers are introduced so as to control government officials and "prepare men to exercise administrative power" (p. 75). At the state level, being derived out of the constituent townships, the legal system was assumed by de Tocqueville to be of crucial importance. It could make local and state officials accountable, provide avenues for citizen appeal (p. 79), and legitimize the exercise of power itself. Throughout, de Tocqueville emphasized the lack of hierarchy, the pattern of administrative decentralization, and the intimate links between state structure and the people. But even so, he recognized tendencies toward centralization, a condition which he most commonly associated with Europe (e.g., the German Empire, p. 88). He did not assume, however, as he had of townships, that higher tiers of government have a natural claim for citizens' loyalty. Indeed, state legislatures are thought to be so powerful that "nothing can check [their] progress, neither privileges, nor local immunities, nor personal influence" (p. 89). For de Tocqueville, the only way to contain state legislatures was to divide, fragment, and decentralize power.[7]

This was one rationale for local government functions, but, of course, there were others, most obviously, local functions such as education, which were thought consistent with community cohesion. And there were functions that were somehow assumed to be best accomplished at the local level (de Tocqueville mentioned tax collection in this regard, p. 89). Consequently, we can identify at least three justifications for local matters. The first and most important reason, in de Tocqueville's terms, would obviously derive from the natural structure of local communities; whatever would make community association more fulfilling would be a local matter. (Chief Justice Warren Burger's defense of Amish communities' resistance to public education seems relevant here.) This concept was thought by de Tocqueville to be both natural and absolute; that is, it derives its significance from a set of higher-order moral principles—not the exigencies of circumstances. The second rationale for local matters is circumstantial; it is probably better (perhaps more efficient) to collect taxes at the local level than at the state level. And, the third rationale for local matters might be interpreted as procedural; it is probably in the best interests of society to fragment government functions spatially, rather than allow the centralization of administrative and legislative powers. Circumstantial and procedural rationales for government decentralization are, realistically speaking, relative and empirical, that is, based on specific circumstances and events. As efficiency changes with spatial scale, so, too, would the provision of public goods and services at the local level. Similarly, in some circumstances it may be better to fragment one set of functions than another set; it would all depend on the exigencies of the moment.

De Tocqueville's model of local autonomy could be summarized in the following terms. Since the township is man's natural arena of association, it is also the crucible of higher tiers' own legitimacy. Townships give up powers to higher tiers, according to more general (spatial and functional) concerns. A most obvious example is national defense and the protection of every man's rights. De Tocqueville noted, for example, that criminal justice is best administered at the county level (p. 70). Of course, state agencies may still use local communities to administer higher-tier functions (a decentralized administration imperative). By giving up powers, towns give up some of their initiative powers, and by implementing higher-tier functions, they are likely to have limited initiative in those areas, and certainly little immunity from higher-tier review. But, of course, the patterns of local initiative and immunity in these circumstances are fluid and subject to change as circumstances demand. It is unclear, though, how circumstances are to be used in changing the spatial arrangement of government functions and what yardsticks might be used to indicate the relevance of decentralization versus centralization. De Tocqueville preferred decentralization, so perhaps that was and remains the default option!

At the same time, it is also obvious that townships may retain a wide range of powers in de Tocqueville's America. He suggested that townships only give up powers when they have some interest which is wider than their geographical domain. Otherwise, "in all that concerns themselves alone the townships remain independent bodies" (p. 67). Here local matters are defined in accordance with their own interests—a definition which may seem circular at first sight, but which simply reinforced the initial assumption made by de Tocqueville that townships are the natural beginning points for social enquiry. He argued in this context, "I do not think one could find a single inhabitant of New England who would recognize the right of the government of the State to control matters of purely municipal interest" (p. 67). Again, I should emphasize that de Tocqueville assumed that all government powers owe their origin to the local level; if power is given up to higher tiers, it is for specific reasons.[8] Even "social duties" (those interests shared with other townships) are carried out at the state level through the consent of local communities. In de Tocqueville's terms, local matters are the fundamental basis for local autonomy.

Tiebout published his paper on "a pure theory of public expenditures" in 1956. As we have seen in previous chapters, Tiebout's paper has been the datum point for many analytical attempts, in the local public-finance literature, to model the patterns of local public goods. Like de Tocqueville, Tiebout began with an assumption that there are purely local matters which are best dealt with at the local level. But unlike de Tocqueville, Tiebout sought to explicate a logical positivist model of local government functions based upon efficiency, not some normative ideal. At the local level, he suggested that since residents can leave a locality, then there are reasons to expect that local public goods (local matters) can be treated as marketlike commodities. The market referred to here is composed of residents (voters) who express their preferences (demand) for certain public goods through either direct voting or through residence in a locality. On the supply side, localities offer a bundle of public goods hoping to attract a certain clientele (residents) characterized by income and taste. According to Tiebout, one result of a world structured along these lines would be a set of communities differentiated by the types of public goods provided, their quality and price (taxes). Another result predicted by Tiebout was an efficient allocation of resources which would just match the preferences of residents located in different communities. Finally, Tiebout also suggested that the provision of local public goods would be constrained, as it could not be in the national sector, by market forces, so that waste, oversupply, and trivial preferences would all be avoided. In this world, localities would have initiative and immunity powers consistent with the provision of local public goods—the local matters doctrine again.

For Tiebout, the crucial lever in this system was resident mobility. If consumers are dissatisfied with a community for any reason, then they will move, or vote with their feet. And as another locality appeals and as consumers move into that area, local conditions will reflect migrants' tastes and preferences until the costs of providing public goods begin to repel residents. Obviously, it is a system of demand and supply signaled through residential mobility.

Bennett (1980) has taken this model further by introducing a set of complications to the Tiebout world. Specifically, jurisdictional fragmentation is recognized, as well as problems of spillover or geographical externalities (where benefits may spill over into other localities), and what he terms "tapering," the distance-decay effect of the costs and benefits of local public goods. Whatever the complications added to Tiebout's model, the logic remains intact. Essentially, optimal allocations of local public goods can be uniquely determined, quantitative measures of optimal community size can be derived, and public goods can then be exclusively classified according to spatial scale: local, state, even national matters can be given empirical definition.

As was noted in chapter 4, the Tiebout model has only an inchoate, implicit model of institutional responsibilities. He provided little in the way of analysis of local and state responsibilities, assuming, I suppose, that the optimal scale of public goods and services would be an adequate rationale for the spatial structure of government. In these terms local, state, and even national governments would have the same initiative powers since the market would obviously penalize any government that attempted to provide, for example, higher-order functions. Similarly, immunity powers would be somewhat irrelevant since residents would leave a locality if it somehow discriminated against them. The limit to this model is obviously the national level since it is more difficult to exit at this level, and more difficult to voice personal preferences. Tiebout made no attempt to address this issue and actually suggested that his model should be viewed as a rationale for decentralizing all government functions, according to their appropriate spatial scale.[9] Tiebout proposed a model of local autonomy bounded by local matters and an exclusive way of defining the responsibilities of local, state, and national governments.

Compared with de Tocqueville's, Tiebout's model is both similar and dissimilar at the same time. Both utilized a society-centered model to determine local responsibilities: Tiebout called them "consumers," de Tocqueville called them "the people." Both derived the local state out of local preferences. Indeed, both used choice, mobility, and tastes to create spatially and functionally differentiated communities. And both used an empirical rationale to define the functions of higher tiers of the state; what de Tocqueville termed "social interests" and what Tiebout might have called "higher-order consumption goods." Finally, both de Tocqueville and Tiebout defined exclusive domains for local government actions through what are termed "local matters." In these ways, de Tocqueville and Tiebout express a rich and thoroughly American conception of the proper role of local government based on local matters.

Yet there are basic differences between them, the principal difference being found in their initial assumptions about the worth of communities. De Tocqueville, as we saw earlier, thought townships to be natural, whereas Tiebout simply thought them efficient. If they were not efficient in Tiebout's terms, he would not have promoted their virtues. On the other hand, de Tocqueville supposed that communities exist in nature even though they are arranged and bolstered by man. And he even thought that they might be inefficient, but, nevertheless, that they exist before any such calculations are made, even despite such calculations. Basically, Tiebout supposed that communities are a relative concept born out of the exigencies of circumstances. While de Tocqueville recognized many of the same issues of spatial scale and efficiency, his model was based on an absolute belief in the natural virtues of communities. Thus, there are two quite different defenses for local matters: one might be termed empirical, based in part upon de Tocqueville and more generally Tiebout, and the other might be termed idealist sustained by de Tocqueville's romantic image of the virtues of New England community life.

A Theoretical Critique of Local Matters

Theoretically, there are a number of ways to go about criticizing the doctrine of local matters. For example, we could follow Whiteman's (1983) lead and criticize the Tiebout hypothesis for its failure to provide "a reasonable theory of mobility and individual choice" (p. 372). Indeed, the Tiebout model can be shown to be fundamentally compromised because of its own idealization of circumstances and situations faced by most people in contemporary America. Like Nozick (1974) and others, Tiebout is unable to integrate in his hypothesis the realities of economic inequality within the decision framework of residential choice. In these terms alone, the Tiebout model is at best irrelevant, at worst a means of legitimizing inequality (see Scanlon 1976 for a critique of Nozick 1974 in these terms, and Clark 1983a for an analysis of the conditions for local choice in American society).[10] These issues are serious and deserve recognition. However, in this section I wish to raise other objections that relate more directly to the process of adjudication. The first objection concerns the plausibility of de Tocqueville's absolute claims for community integrity, the second objection concerns the indeterminacy of empirical measures of local matters.

At the outset it should be clear that de Tocqueville's claims for the absolute virtues of local government are liable to the same criticisms raised in chapter 2 concerning the reasonableness of exclusive claims to truth promoted by liberals and structuralists alike. In the abstract it is difficult to take seriously the claim of exclusive truth simply because the values implied require belief more than any analytical demonstration of their relevance. By that I mean, like all other normative visions—utopian, romantic, and idealistic—it is difficult, even impossible, to design an empirical test or some other test that would establish the veracity of the beliefs implied. As was noted in chapter 2, tests of beliefs fail in at least two ways. First, it is almost impossible to design tests able to account for systematic differences between beliefs in terms of their moral principles. One way or another, beliefs are more often incommensurate, rarely directly comparable. Thus, second, tests of beliefs often impose so-called "third-party" principles (like simplicity, logic, etc.) which are hardly relevant to the overall design of beliefs.

This means, of course, that de Tocqueville's claims for the absolute virtue of local government can hardly be denied or rejected outright. But it also means that there is no fail-safe way of convincing the skeptic that the principle has any merit. There are, however, a number of issues that should give us pause in pursuing de Tocqueville's logic. A structuralist would immediately be concerned with the logical separation made by de Tocqueville between individuals and communities. His suggestion that individuals form communities in accordance with their interests and passions raises a number of questions. For instance, it is not clear where individuals are located prior to association. Presumably, de Tocqueville would answer along the lines of Locke and the more recent modes of analysis provided by Rawls (1971) and Nozick (1974), that is, individuals are located first in a state of nature or an original position. But this answer only serves to create more problems. For example, how are interests formed in a state of nature? Aren't interests circumstantial anyway? And, don't people calculate and recalculate their interests as their knowledge of other community members broadens and deepens?

De Tocqueville's theoretical model raises exactly the same issues we have raised previously regarding the impossibility of separating individuals from community. A structuralist would argue, of course, that communities create individuals and communities are then formed and reproduced by institutions such as individual self-interest. Indeed, Chief Justice Warren Burger recognized as much when he argued for the right of Amish communities to educate their own children. By education, socialization, and isolation, Amish communities seek to reproduce themselves through their children. They use local institutions to dominate and structure the lives of their dependents. Thus, when Burger noted the "vital role that belief and daily conduct play in the continuing survival of Old Order Amish communities" (*Wisconsin v. Yoder*, 1972), he was expressing an argument entirely consistent with structuralist notions of social causality (what Chesler 1983 has termed "conservative authoritarianism"), and inconsistent with conventional liberal notions of individual integrity (on this last point see the opinion by Justice Potter Stewart in *Yoder*, p. 246).

The problems with de Tocqueville's image do not stop here, since underlying his model of local autonomy is a naturalistic doctrine of the origin of man and local government. His predictable answer that individuals begin in a state of nature is surely yet another instance of his dependence upon the logic of Lockean liberalism. Similarly, his assertion that local communities are the natural arenas of human association implies that local matters are made in heaven rather than by law. Neither the structuralist nor the reconstructed liberal (like Rawls) would agree with this kind of belief, and yet it is at the very heart of de Tocqueville's image of the townships of New England. His belief in nature is absolute; so, too, is his belief in the integrity of communities. Both beliefs are ultimately derived from his belief in god. Liberals often proclaim the virtues of individual integrity, but they are reticent to cloak their arguments in the deity. And structuralists often proclaim the fundamental importance of social association but, again, hardly ever suggest that such associations are somehow natural or necessarily closer to god. Indeed, the whole intellectual movement (which included liberalism) of the post-Enlightenment era could be interpreted as an attempt to strip religion of its influence over the arrangement and interpretation of social life (see MacIntyre 1981 for an extended discussion).

The naturalistic doctrine should not be immediately dismissed by the reader in a belief that such doctrine is somehow out of fashion or only held by fringe minorities. It remains a loud and aggressive stream of thought in American life appearing, for instance, in the judgments of the U.S. Supreme Court. Anyone reading Burger's opinion in *Yoder* is immediately struck by the importance he attaches to religious communities. He not only protects them from the encroachment of the state, but also suggests that the Amish communities represent an earlier, perhaps more valued, way of life close to nature and the soil (p. 210). The virtues of community life are extolled by Burger as he described Amish values such as their attachment to "a life of goodness," of concern for community welfare and manual work (p. 211). Throughout he drew parallels between Amish communities and a lost era of American history, suggesting the Amish are devoted to "a life in harmony with nature and the soil, [exemplifying] . . . the simple life of the early Christian era that continued in America during much of our early national life" (p. 210). It is little wonder that Justice Douglas dissented from the majority opinion. As a liberal in the modern sense, he was concerned that Amish children were being held hostage to their parents' beliefs.[11] For Douglas, the role of the court should be to protect individuals against all-enveloping community values.

Having established that the moral claims for local autonomy and local matters are relative, not absolute, conditional upon argument, not god-given natural orders, I also wish to consider the claims made by empiricists for the virtues of local matters as the rule for deciding the proper sphere of local autonomy. As was mentioned above, the value of this later argument depends upon demonstrating the existence of empirical regularities which would unambiguously allocate government functions to the optimal spatial level. Local matters are presumably those public goods and services best or most efficiently provided at the local level in accordance with local preferences. Local autonomy is thus defined by local matters. This relative conception of local autonomy is also to be found in de Tocqueville and more recently in Tiebout and those who write in this latter tradition. For instance, Thrall (1979) writing on spatial equilibrium analysis has followed this logic, as has Bennett (1980) writing on the distribution of functions between government levels. As we saw in chapter 7, this concept is the raison d'être of economic analyses of the local public sector.

For local matters to have any use as a tool in adjudicating disputes over the proper spatial scale to provide public goods, three conditions need to be met. First, local matters should be reasonably stable, thus predictable rather than arbitrary or solely context specific. This is a weak condition, for all it demands is some consistency in application and measurement. As a standard, it can be made more reliable with more information and greater technical expertise. This condition can be met, I suppose, with the application of enough research and new knowledge. More problematic are the second and third conditions. Specifically, the second condition requires that local matters be exclusively and unambiguously defined. It must be possible to define matters which are exclusively local, as opposed to higher-tier functions; otherwise judges would have to use yet another rule of adjudication unrelated to the internal logic of the Tiebout model to adjudicate competing jurisdictional claims. The third condition is that analytical rules, derived from the internal logic of the Tiebout model, must have an identifiable empirical image. Otherwise, there will be continual litigation over the meaning of different circumstances. All these conditions are required for adjudicative determinacy and can be found in any number of judicial texts.[12]

One way or another, I would argue that none of these conditions can be met and, as a result, any empirical test of local matters is more often arbitrary than principled. The weakest condition is that the test of local matters be reasonably reliable. This depends on knowledge of the optimal spatial allocation of resources and functions gleaned from empirical research. As the simplest condition, it suffers from a simple problem: most judicial decisions have to be made before information is complete. Complete knowledge is a fallacy, circumstances are always changing, and different events call for different knowledge. Since events have their own character, they also transform existing knowledge, making it less relevant, less reliable, and less accessible. Judges, like others who use empirical tests, are limited by circumstances. I would admit that this is an extreme argument. There are techniques which are useful in bolstering existing knowledge. Analogies, metaphors, precedents, and past performance can and are used to cope with this problem. Even so, I must emphasize that judgment and experience are crucial in these circumstances. Judgment and experience make consistency and determinacy and minimize, but don't eliminate, arbitrariness. For all these reasons, I would argue that empirical tests of local matters are not completely reliable but, at the same time, these problems are seriously contended with![13]

More problematic and more difficult to achieve are the second and third conditions. To demonstrate why I believe this to be the case, I wish to briefly review Quine's (1953) most famous paper, "Two Dogmas of Empiricism." Dummett (1978) suggested that this is the most important paper written in the last half-century in the philosophy of language. But it can also be easily interpreted as an attack on the determinacy thesis of logical positivism. Put most simply, Quine argued that empiricism is incapable of delivering unambiguous truths. The structure of his argument went as follows. He began be defining the two dogmas of empiricism: the first he defined as "a belief in some fundamental cleavage between truths which are analytic, or grounded in meanings independently of fact, and truths which are synthetic, or grounded in fact" (p. 20). The second he defined as reductionism, "the belief that each meaningful statement is equivalent to some logical construct upon terms which refer to immediate experience" (p. 20).

In his essay he sought to show that both dogmas are ill-founded. What is particularly interesting in his analysis and critique is that he was able to demonstrate that both dogmas are dependent upon one another; that is, to make an analytical statement depends upon some empirical confirmation of a previously conceived logical argument. Analytical statements are thus derived from synthetic observations and depend upon abstraction to ensure their veracity in the face of "recalcitrant experience." What he implied was as experience provides the seeds for analytical statements, these statements can only be built into a logical edifice if they are so general and so abstract that isolated subsequent observations do not challenge the whole. Quine put this point in these terms: "any statement can be held true come what may, if we make drastic enough adjustments elsewhere in the system" (p. 45). Thus, it is difficult to imagine step-by-step confirmation, information, and revision; experience cannot effectively use small increments of knowledge; paradigm shifts are accomplished through challenges to the whole or "corporate" body of theory. The implication is that empirical facts will only have a very loose association with theoretical expectations.[14]

At the same time, he suggested that "no statement is immune to revision" (p. 43). Thus, experience can alter our synthetic modes of description, although the analytical structure will probably remain intact. One way of understanding the relation of analytical and synthetic statements is to imagine an analytical statement as the nucleus, and synthetic statements as boundary conditions. While a useful analogy, Quine did not believe it to be functional or causal so much as a spatial map of association. Again, it should be emphasized that analytical statements exist by virtue of their abstraction, their denial of boundary experience. From this point, Quine then suggested that science, as represented by analytical statements, is underdetermined by experience. While "the edge of the system must be kept squared with experience; the rest, with all its elaborate myths or fictions, has as its objective the simplicity of laws" (p. 45). Finally, Quine introduced the concept of pragmatism as a way forward. In a world of underdeterminacy, pragmatism is the only rationale for action. And since analytical truths are so distant from experience, there can be no absolute truths.

The implications of Quine's argument for the doctrine of local matters are threefold. First, it is plain that the two strong conditions for its use as a blueprint of adjudication can never be met. Basically the level of abstraction implied in Tiebout's model is such that it is virtually impossible to identify government functions which are exclusively local, or belong to higher orders. While it may be possible to define such spheres in the abstract, actual functions will be far more ambiguous. The implication of the collapse of this second condition is that another pragmatic rule will always be needed by judges to identify local matters. Lack of an adequate set of rules of exclusivity and recognition, based upon the analytical logic of the Tiebout hypothesis, suggests a second implication. Pragmatic decisions will be inevitable, even necessary, if determinacy is to be achieved. But, of course, by its very nature pragmatism is only loosely based on analytical logic—in Hart's (1961) terms, principles will be characterized by their broadness of texture, their looseness of interpretation. In these circumstances, pragmatism requires justification and legitimation, rhetorical claims which are capable of carrying the day.

The final implication to be drawn from Quine's argument is that consistency in adjudication will be a fond hope rather than an achievable reality. Lack of an adequate integration between analytical rules and synthetic experience will continually frustrate the courts as they seek to maintain consistency in the interpretation of principles and consistency in the applications of these rules to circumstances. We can reasonably expect the courts to do the best they can under the circumstances, but we should not expect more than this!

Quine's argument is, of course, consistent with our previous analysis of the limits of judicial reasoning (see chap. 3). The relative nature of circumstances and doctrine, as well as the relative nature of decisions themselves argued previously to be so characteristic of judicial reasoning, has a ready place in Quine's logic. Even so, Quine takes our analysis one step further in indicating the structural limits of knowledge and the necessary realities of decision making from principles. No superhuman judge can overcome these problems, and no one doctrine, even if unanimously conceived and interpreted, will avoid indeterminacy.[15]

Home Rule in Colorado

To illustrate the practical importance of both the local matters doctrine and the indeterminacy thesis, we now turn to an analysis of the dimensions of local autonomy in the State of Colorado. My reasons for choosing Colorado, rather than some other state, are twofold. First, Colorado is conventionally thought to promote the autonomy of its cities and towns. In contrast to many eastern states, Colorado has relied less on Dillon's (1911) doctrine of only allowing localities to exercise those powers expressly mentioned in state legislative enactments of power and more on home-rule provisions which seek to provide a general sphere for the exercise of local initiative. Indeed, there is some irony in these circumstances since de Tocqueville wrote almost exclusively about New England townships. Thus, we can reasonably expect to see evidence of what could be termed strong local autonomy. Second, a major defense of local autonomy in Colorado had been the doctrine of local matters. As we shall see, it is enshrined in the state's Constitution and has been taken very seriously by the courts. Thus, we can explicate the practical realities of the doctrine as well as the inherent problems, in its application to particular cases.

The notion of home rule has a great deal of rhetorical popularity, but much less substantive meaning than commonly appreciated. Sandalow (1964) noted that home rule is commonly associated with local autonomy and referred to the capacity of local governments to act in accordance with local communities' needs free of the interference of higher tiers of the state. While all commentators would now concede that local autonomy is a relative condition, the concept of home rule has been promoted in the past as a counterimage to Dillon's rule. For instance, McBain's (1916) argument sought to suggest the existence of "an inherent right of local self-government" drawing upon language and logic closely related to de Tocqueville's original conception of natural communities. As Dillon's rule tightly restricts local initiative and denies local immunity, home-rule doctrine seeks a broad sphere of initiative by carving out a sphere of exclusive interest. Most often invoked in this regard are local matters, since they offer, rightly or wrongly, the hope that localities can govern themselves according to local preferences and concerns. The ideas implicit in this home-rule doctrine can then be traced back at least to de Tocqueville, and it represents an important historical theme of American democratic life.

Most scholars trace its origins as a legal doctrine to the *imperium in imperio* doctrine, which was first articulated in Missouri in 1875. This doctrine allowed cities to "frame charters for their own government consistent with and subject to the Constitution and laws of the State" (Vanlandingham 1975, p. 1). Over time, home-rule provisions have been expanded beyond the *imperio* model, so that most recently the National League of Cities (NLC) model of home rule seeks to reserve a number of powers to the cities as a matter of principle. I do not wish to go much further with an extended discussion of home-rule doctrine since its practical provisions are less clear than its rhetorical image. Indeed, as we shall see, implementing home rule in Colorado has been a tortuous affair. It is important, however, to recognize the intent behind home-rule doctrines—local self-government—since it is this intent which marks the doctrine as different when compared to Dillon's rule.[16] Moreover, when judges come to interpret the meaning of related doctrines such as local matters, understanding the implied home-rule intent has been of major importance to scholars and judges alike.

Article XX of the Colorado Constitution, first adopted in 1902, is the basic home-rule provision of Colorado. At that time, it was adopted to free the city and county of Denver from state legislative control of its day-to-day affairs. In 1912, a more general provision was adopted which made home rule an option for all cities. Previously, the state legislature had the right to amend and cancel cities' charters and even operate Colorado's cities. Denver, being the largest city and obviously the center of power, was often the target of such legislative actions, so much so that in the late 1890s, Denver was paralyzed by all kinds of special legislation, governing boards, and political turmoil. According to Klemme (1964), the home-rule movement in Colorado was centered upon Denver's problems, leading to the passage of Article XX in 1902.

There are a variety of ways in which localities are protected from state legislation. For instance, Article V, Section 25 prohibits the legislature from passing local or special legislation in areas such as public works, police, justice, deeds, schools, tolls, railroads, etc. Similarly the legislature cannot pass special laws if a general law would suffice. Article XIV, Section 13 also requires that all related legislation deal with classes of cities and towns, not individual towns. And Article V, Section 35 prohibits the legislature from creating special commissions or private corporations to perform or affect the performance of municipal functions. A special commission in these terms is "some body or association of individuals separate and distinct from the city government . . . created for different purposes and not connected with the general administration of municipal affairs" (*Milheim v. Moffatt Tunnel Improvement District*, 1922).

Generally, Article XX, Section 6 (the home-rule provision) has been interpreted as a limit on state involvement in local affairs. Like the two other articles noted above, Article XX prohibits the state legislature from interfering with the performance of local governments except in situations where local government operates in matters of statewide concern. Section 6 grants municipalities a number of specific powers but also declares that local powers are not limited to those enumerated (in contrast to Dillon). Localities have the right to self-government in local matters, and this grant of power is expressed in the following terms (Colorado Revised Statutes, 1953, vol. 1):

> It is the intention of this article to grant and confirm to the people of all municipalities coming within its provisions the full rights of self government in both local and municipal matters. (P. 404)

Furthermore, Section 6 holds that state statutes apply except where they are superseded by local ordinances passed in accordance with local powers; that is, where towns and cities pass local laws regarding local matters, their laws hold above state statutes. In circumstances where localities do not use their local powers, state statutes apply as a matter of course. Local autonomy is then protected by prohibitions against special legislation and is made possible by the sphere of local matters.

In terms of initiative, localities have a wide range of powers as long as they stay within the sphere of local matters. However, as we shall see in a moment, local matters are ambiguous as an empirical category—it is hard to separate *local matters* from *statewide matters*, and especially *mixed matters*—and are subject to two conflicting interpretations. One major theme that is carried throughout the period 1912–80 is that Article XX limits local powers to only local matters (see especially *Mauff v. People*, 1912). But another (counter) theme has been that Article XX was conceived to "bestow upon the people of home rule cities every power possessed by the Legislature in the making of a charter therefore" (*Denver v. Hallett*, 1905). There remains a great deal of ambiguity over the relevance of these two interpretations, the former which we shall call *strict*, the latter *expansive*.

Article XX does not provide cities with any immunity. All actions with regard to local matters can be appealed to higher levels, including the courts. One might, however, interpret the prohibition against special legislation as immunity, since particular cities are shielded by general legislation. But I would argue that immunity in terms of local actions remains virtually nil. Even so, in contrast to Dillon's rule, Colorado's model of local autonomy is more generous, indeed more plausible. In its strictest sense, Colorado's model enables local initiative and does not restrict it to only those functions expressly provided for in state legislation. In its most expansive form, Colorado's local autonomy model provides local governments with at least rhetorical strength, if not immediate legislative powers. Granted, localities remain "creatures of the state," and immunity is nonexistent, yet there are enough qualitative differences to mark Colorado's home-rule provisions as different from Dillon's home rule, certainly different from Chicago's powers![17]

Interpreting Local Matters in Colorado

We begin in 1905 with *Hallett*, the expansive model of local matters which is most consistent with a de Tocquevillian reading of the intent of Colorado's home-rule provisions. And we end with a 1978 case, *Delong v. City and County of Denver* (1978), which is confused and ambiguous in its interpretation of local matters. As will become apparent, the lines of argument throughout this period are never so straightforward nor as consistent as a layman might expect judges to perform. There are many twists and turns in the courts' opinions, with some quite arbitrary shifts in opinion. But, of course, this should be expected since it is the overall thesis of this chapter that pragmatism is inevitable once we come to implement empirical tests in a changing world, far distant from the abstract and idealized theoretical images which provide judges their moral legitimacy. In many respects, the historical record captures ambiguities inherent in the whole notion of empirical standards.

In the beginning, *City and County of Denver v. Hallett* (1905) sets out one of the earliest explanations of the home-rule provision of the Colorado constitution. The case involved a question of municipal initiative. Specifically, could the City of Denver purchase a site for an auditorium and issue bonds for that purpose? The court cited no earlier Colorado cases when stating its theory of how the provision worked. The court held that the intent of the home-rule provision was to bestow upon the people of Denver "every power possessed by the Legislature in the making of a charter of Denver." From this perspective, the test for whether an exercise of power falls within the home-rule grant was: could the legislature have conferred the power upon Denver? I will refer to this test as the *Hallett* test throughout this section. The court went on to say that the legislature had basically plenary power in delegating powers to municipalities, implying that the scope of powers which could have been delegated was extremely broad. The court argued that "the test is whether the power, if exercised, will promote the general objects and purposes of the municipality, and of this the Legislature is the judge in the first instance; and, unless it clearly appears that some constitutional provision has been infringed, the law must be upheld." A narrow reading of this case, then, would give home-rule cities very broad initiative powers, but the case would say nothing about the immunity of cities from state action.

Some twenty years later, in *City and County of Denver v. Tiben* (1925), the courts were involved in adjudicating the extent of immunities of home-rule cities from the action of the state legislature. The state constitution had contained a provision which exempted nonprofit cemeteries from taxation, and the legislature passed a law exempting those cemeteries from local assessment. The court held that the law was valid as applied to home-rule cities. It argued that the legislature had the sole power to declare the public policy of the state, and that "public policy must be applicable to all portions of the State, and where, as with us, there are home rule or charter cities and towns [as well as those created by general statute] . . . this policy . . . still applies to all classes of municipalities." Here, the strict rule was applied, as the court stressed that home-rule cities were given exclusive control in matters only of local concern. In their analysis of whether the subject was of local concern, the court said: "while the matter of the taxation and assessment of cemeteries in this State not organized or maintained for private or corporate profit is, in a sense, local to every city and county in the State, yet in the larger and fuller sense . . . it is a matter of State-wide importance and of governmental import, and not merely of local or municipal concern."

But, in *City and County of Denver v. Henry* (1934), the court then shifted its position. This case involved conflicting state laws and local ordinances. A state law said that right of way at traffic intersections should be yielded to the vehicle approaching from the left. A Denver city ordinance, however, required that right of way should be yielded to the vehicle approaching from the right. According to the court, the question was: "is the control of traffic at street intersections in the City of Denver a local or municipal matter?" Here, the court used the expansive *Hallett* test to define local or municipal, that is "every power possessed by the Legislature in the making of a charter for Denver." It was determined "by ascertaining whether the Legislature, in the absence of Article XX, could have conferred upon the municipality the power in question." The court concluded that under this test "there seems no escape from the conclusion that the regulation of traffic at street intersections in the City of Denver is primarily a matter of local concern because proper regulation is almost wholly dependent upon local conditions." The court also said "if the city had power, prior to the enactment of the statute, to pass such an ordinance as that here in question, it had that power by virtue of the Constitution, and the statute could not take it away."

This expansive test was also then applied in *Fishel v. City and County of Denver* (1940). Here, the City of Denver took some property outside the municipal boundaries by exercising its power of eminent domain. Denver then gave this land to the U.S. government for their use as an air school and bombing field. The court applied the *Hallett* test. It held that because the legislature could have delegated such powers to the city, the city had those powers under the home-rule provision. This was a case involving municipal initiative; no conflicting state statutes were involved.

Yet, only one year later, in *People v. Graham* (1941), the court again shifted its position. The issue in this case was whether a requirement that a motorist involved in an accident should stop his vehicle, give certain information, and help the injured party was a matter of local and municipal concern or a matter of statewide concern. The state had enacted these requirements, but the City of Denver had not. The court phrased the issue this way: "the only question with which we are here concerned is whether the derelictions charged in the information are violations of regulations of motor vehicle traffic of a local and municipal nature, over which a home rule city has exclusive jurisdiction. If not, the general laws of the State apply." The court was immediately faced with the precedent it had set in *Henry*, holding that regulation of traffic at intersections was a local matter. But in this instance, the court argued,

> the words "local and municipal," occurring in Section 6 Article XX, *supra*, is not a fixed expression that may be eternalized. What is local, as distinguished from general and State-wide, depends somewhat upon time and circumstances.

Technological and economic forces play their part in any such transition. As motor vehicle traffic in the State and between home-rule municipalities becomes more and more integrated it gradually ceases to be a local matter and becomes subject to general law.

The court concluded that the state statute did cover a matter of statewide concern. They held that

the investigation and apprehension of a violator of such requirements is not exclusively a local matter. Infractions of these provisions are of general public concern. Moreover, these requirements do not necessarily relate to traffic control, but provide certain necessary actions on the part of the motorist involved to be taken after an accident to protect the life and property of the injured. The offenses charged in the information here under consideration come under the general police power of the State and do not necessarily relate to regulation of motor vehicle traffic of a "local or municipal" nature, although occurring in a municipality.

Here, the court rejected a number of possible interpretations of the local and municipal requirements and concluded that: (1) local matters are not to be defined by reference to a city's boundaries, and (2) the court cannot set up fixed, rigid categories because the nature of a particular subject can change over time. Given the technological and economic factors listed by the court, one final implication was that over time local matters would become statewide concerns and not the other way around.

But again, one year later, the court reconsidered their opinion in *Ray v. City and County of Denver* (1942). This case involved different sets of regulations passed by the City of Denver and the state involving the terms for certain loans. The city conceded that the subject was not one of local and municipal concern, and so it did not have the exclusive right to regulate the subject. But it was also contended that "the mere fact that the State in the exercise of its police power has made certain regulations does not prohibit the municipality from exacting additional requirements." The controversy, then, was over whether or not there was a conflict between the state and city regulations. In the absence of such a conflict, the court seemed willing to allow both levels of government to legislate on the same subject.

The court set out a number of tests for determining whether or not a conflict existed. One of these tests was picked up as "The Test" for determining the presence of conflicts in these cases. The test was: "in determining whether an ordinance is in 'conflict' with general laws, the test is whether the ordinance permits or licenses that which the statute forbids and prohibits, and vice versa." Later cases have interpreted the "vice versa" to mean that the city forbids what the state expressly permits.

This kind of test was reasonably useful for a time. However, in *Canon City v. Merris* (1958), a new wrinkle was involved, a "counterpart ordinance." A counterpart ordinance is a city ordinance covering conduct that the state has made a crime by statute. It holds that if the state statute makes certain conduct a crime, then as a counterpart in the municipal laws of a city, such conduct must be tried and punished as a crime. This principle applies whether the conduct is described as a local and municipal matter or as a statewide concern. This case was most noteworthy for setting out the doctrine of mutual exclusion. Specifically the court used the term "supersede" to "mean that the law of the State is displaced on a local and municipal matter where there is an ordinance put in its place. Where, however, the matter is of State-wide concern, supersession does not take place. Application of State law or municipal ordinance, whichever pertains, is mutually exclusive."

The court seemed to deny the possibility implied earlier in *Ray* that both the cities and the state could regulate the same subject. The regulations in this case involved drunk driving. The court went on to say that the regulation of drunk driving was a matter of statewide concern: "Ordinarily, regulation of traffic is a local and municipal matter [citing *Graham*] . . . But the state has decreed that driving while under the influence of intoxicating liquor or a narcotic is a forbidden act; it leaves nothing for the city to regulate."

In *City and County of Denver v. Sweet* (1958), the issue was whether a constitutional amendment made after the passage of the home-rule amendment (allowing the state legislature to levy income taxes) took away the power of home-rule cities to levy income taxes. The court completely flipped the interpretation of the home-rule provision that had been applied in the earlier cases. Instead of using the expansive *Hallett* test as the definition of "local and municipal," it restricted the *Hallett* test to subjects which were actually "local and municipal." Home-rule cities, under the *Hallett* test, were limited to "powers necessary to carry out (the city's) functions as a charter city which are either not of State-wide concern or not prohibited by other constitutional provisions." And, according to that court, "local and municipal" depended on "the inherent nature of the activity and the impact or effect which it may have or may not have upon areas outside of the municipality." Thus, home-rule powers could be limited in one of two ways, by constitutional amendment and/or by broadening the concept of statewide concern.

In this instance, however, the court held that the amendment giving the legislature the power to levy income taxes preempted the field of income taxation, leaving home-rule cities no power to enact such taxes. They argued that "the mere fact that the wording is permissive to the State does not make it any less an exclusive power to levy this special type of tax."

So, home-rule powers were taken away even though no language existed in the later amendment that exclusively vested the power to levy income taxes with the state.

Using the language of *Merris*, the court then dealt with *Davis v. City and County of Denver* (1959). This case involved municipal initiative, the city having passed an ordinance prohibiting the operation of a motor vehicle by a person whose license was suspended. The court said that under the home-rule provision, if a subject is local and municipal, then the city can supersede a state statute by passing an ordinance. If the subject is not local and municipal the home-rule provision does not come into play. Outside of the provision, the city acts as an agency of the state and is subject to state control. For the court, the test seemed to be whether the subject is predominantly local or predominantly statewide.

The court, however, rejected the notion that any subject that is predominantly a statewide concern can only be regulated by the state. The judges claimed:

> Article XX of the Constitution does not grant to the City authority to regulate matters of general and statewide concern and . . . this power can be exercised by municipalities only if the state consents to its exercise and provided that the matter, although predominantly general, is one in which the municipality has sufficient interest to warrant the delegation of power to it.

The court went on to claim that the state cannot delegate power over matters "exclusively Statewide and general."

This case seemed to provide a means of classifying municipal initiative, ironically negating a previous decision also made in 1959 which explicitly rejected any categorical method or mechanical way of classifying "local and municipal." In *Woolverton v. City and County of Denver* (1961), the court went on to define *strictly local* as when a municipality by enacting an ordinance supersedes an existing statute on the same subject; *exclusively statewide* as when a state can preempt the field by legislating on the subject; and *mixed state and local* as when two sets of regulations do not conflict "it would follow that a city, acting with the express consent of the State, can legislate on a subject within the legitimate sphere of both its interest and that of the State." This logic was later modified in *Vela v. People* (1971) in two important respects. First, a municipality passing an ordinance concerning a local matter did not preempt the state from passing a statute on the same subject. Instead, the municipal ordinance superseded the statute to the degree that the two conflicted. Thus, for a local ordinance to prevail over a state statute, two conditions had to obtain. One, the subject had to be of purely local concern. Two, the sets of regulations had to conflict, as defined by the *Ray* test. If either of these conditions did not obtain, the state statute applied.

Second, almost in passing, the court said that "there is nothing basically invalid about legislation on the same subject, by both a home rule city and the state." This statement completely ignored the requirement, expressed in *Woolverton*, that the city must have the consent of the state to regulate matters of mixed concern. Later cases explicitly held that cities do not need the permission of the state to regulate matters of mixed concern.

For example, in *City of Aurora v. Martin* (1973), the court concluded that an offense of assault and battery could be the subject of "mixed" local and state concern. Both entities could regulate the matter as long as the city ordinance did not conflict with the state statute. Unlike *Woolverton*, the court argued that no express consent from the state was needed for the city to regulate on a matter of mixed concern. The court also rejected the notion that the state had preempted the field by enacting its own statute. It said that more than just a statute on the same subject is needed to show an intent by the legislature to preempt. By dropping the requirement for state consent for cities to regulate matters of mixed concern, the court significantly increased the scope of municipal initiative. And the restrictions on implied preemption of the field had a similar effect on municipal immunity.

In a later case *Pierce v. City and County of Denver* (1977), one concerned with municipal authority to regulate obscenity, the court argued:

> in the area of "local and municipal matters," home rule municipal authority may "supersede within the territorial limits and other jurisdiction of said (home rule) city or town any law of the state in conflict therewith." On the other hand, there exist areas of "mixed" state and local concern in which concurrent state and municipal power to regulate is recognized. Finally, there are areas of exclusively "statewide" concern where local power to regulate is preempted. This preemption is often triggered by a "conflict" between the State and local schemes of regulation."

The court concluded that the city could not license electricians. "Here it requires no great showing to establish a legitimate State interest in establishing a single, uniform system of licensing electricians." Under the terms of this case, the scope of immunities for home-rule cities can be interpreted very narrowly. All the state would have to do is show some legitimate state interest and it would be able to strip the locality of any regulatory powers.

Finally, to end our discussion, but not the obvious problems of determination faced by the courts, local matters were extensively reinterpreted in *Delong v. City and County of Denver* (1978). This case dealt with the subject of the tort liability of municipal officers. Here is how the court described the doctrine under the home-rule provision:

The City and County of Denver is a home rule city and in matters of purely local and municipal concern it can legislatively supersede conflicting state statutes. Likewise, in matters of exclusively State-wide concern, State statutes will always supersede conflicting local enactments. . . . If a subject matter is both local and statewide concern, then a home rule charter provision or ordinance and a State statute may coexist if they do not conflict. A home rule city possesses what has been labeled a "supplemental authority" to legislate on a subject matter of concurrent concern. Of course, if the state and local enactments do conflict, then the state statute would supersede the home rule charter provision.

It is hard to know exactly what the courts meant by these statements. They remain as pragmatic rules for specific situations. Thus, it should be readily apparent that further dispute will generate further twists and turns in interpretation as different circumstances conspire to negate previous interpetations.

The Rhetoric of Local Matters

Is the concept of local matters an adequate umbrella for local autonomy? In this chapter, I argued that it is not. As a moral principle, its primary location is in the kind of natural liberalism most commonly associated with John Locke and Alexis de Tocqueville. Consequently, as a moral principle local matters suffers from being overdetermined; that is, so abstractly conceived by heaven in absolute terms that it is impossible to interpret the concept as being relevant for the ordinary practice of law. While it still retains some relevance as a judicial category, witness the language and logic of Chief Justice Warren Burger and the Colorado courts, it supposes that its strength and relevance are conceived outside the democratic arena. To believe the concept, we have to suspend our belief in the democratic process and the historical advance of *rationalism*. Now, this may well be appropriate for some; however, we should not be surprised when we hear of wide disagreement and even open derision of the concept. After all, it is only one moral interpretation.

As an empirical principle, it suffers from what Quine (1953) termed underdeterminism, that is, only a weak empirical association with abstract principle. As events change, as circumstances alter our interpretations, and as we are forced to revise and re-revise our definitions, it becomes obvious that local matters is a hollow concept. We can theoretically demonstrate à la Quine (1953) that it is inevitably compromised by its very reality, and, we can also empirically demonstrate (as in Colorado) that it is a very loose concept indeed. Yet, it is used, and will continue to be used, as a pragmatic device for sorting jurisdictional powers. And, in these terms, local matters is a rhetorical device, an umbrella for local autonomy which depends more upon the force of an argument in a particular circumstance, than principles. Rhetoric implies an ad hoc use of history; concepts and events woven together by justificatory language. But, its "weave" is loose, even open textured (using J. L. Austin's term), and inevitably so.[18]

One final point also should be made. Throughout this and the previous chapter, I noted that local matters as an empirical category is a strong theme in a great deal of social science literature. It seems that it shall remain so, even though the logic of local matters seems incredibly opaque. By that I mean, it is not clear why local finance theorists believe in local matters apart from very simple (simplistic) notions such as efficiency. As a rationale for local autonomy, it will continue to find favor with the courts to the extent that economists can fashion empirical rationales. But, it is obviously a slippery concept. Empiricism has its own problems, problems which will not go away and which will cause interpretative crises from time-to-time. Rhetoric is bound to be important in these circumstances.

III

Local Autonomy Reconsidered

So you are saying that human agreement decides
what is true and what is false?—It is what human
beings say that is true and false; and they agree in
the language they use. This is not agreement in
opinions but in form of life.

—Ludwig Wittgenstein, *Philosophical Investigations*

9

Local Autonomy in Contemporary Society

In the previous chapters of this book I argued, in one form or another, that law is a relative concept. Like Geertz (1983), I don't suppose that law has any "magical" qualities or a supernatural logic which is somehow superior to contemporary social theory.[1] There does not seem to be any evidence that law has an internal coherence unmatched by any other social institution. In point of fact, it has been argued that legal doctrine is just like all other social theories in that it is necessarily partial, contextually dependent, and riddled with moral pluralism. Thus, I have little sympathy with some legal scholars' claims that law is best described as a set of logically ordered and deduced, neutral principles of social discourse (compare Murphy 1964). The legal dream seems to be an impossible dream, sustained by mistaken philosophical claims for the existence of an exclusive determinacy—one cause, one truth, and a set of exhaustive principles.[2]

While accepting that this dream need not be a description of reality, many social theorists and legal scholars nevertheless seek this kind of truth. In doing so, they reflect, perhaps, their own training as social scientists and the dominant naturalistic mode of scientific discourse (see Goodman 1984, and chap. 1 above). As emphasized in previous chapters, such dogged commitment to logical positivism belies the incredible heterogeneity of social interpretation and the reality of different circumstances and practical reason. More often than not, such claims appear as rhetorical devices designed to legitimate the judiciary.

For example, Charles Tooke (1933) noted many years ago, "while it is true that the decisions of the courts in the construction of municipal powers often seem to the layman contradictory and inconsistent, yet with rare exceptions they are based upon fundamental principles of constitutional law and well-established rules of statutory interpretation" (p. 268). Here Tooke meant to imply, one might suppose, that the latter part of his statement, concerning well-established principles, renders the first part, concerning laymen's observations of the character of adjudication, mistaken or at best naive. Principles are revered by Tooke for their truthlike virtues, and determinacy is presumably obtained through orderly application of principles to circumstances.[3]

My view, however, is that both clauses of Tooke's statement have equal veracity. Scattered throughout this book are many judicial interpretations regarding the meaning of local autonomy, "municipal powers," which appear contradictory and inconsistent. At the same time, it is also apparent that courts attempt to use principles and established rules of interpretation to arrive at decisions. Tooke's two statements seem to me to describe quite well the actual practice of judicial decision making even though legal scholars might argue with my interpretation of specific cases.

To take just one example, while analyzing whether or not the City of Boston had the right to require construction firms to give employment preference to local residents (chap. 5), it was observed that legal principles played a crucial role in litigation and adjudication over this issue at all levels of the legal system. Similarly, it was observed that interpretive practice was based on common modes of doctrinal construction, such as precedent, exemplary cases, and statutory requirements. Yet, for all the application of these devices, indeterminacy and inconsistency seemed ever present; this was the reason that the issue was so contentious. All these devices are, in Austin's terms, open-textured. And, as a consequence, they cannot exclude varying interpretations, differences in emphasis, or differences in application. It was only by invoking the specific circumstances and history of the litigants that it was possible for us to arrive at a reasonable interpretation of the Supreme Court's decision.[4] Again, to draw parallels with Geertz (1983), it is local knowledge which makes legal theory and practice.[5]

This kind of example is repeated through chapters 5 to 8 and it suggests that if a theory of law exists, it can only be at once general and specific. And I would argue that theoretical generality is only possible at a superficial level, where there are broad agreements on social values such as local autonomy which are empty at this level of abstraction. Specificity is not only the application of social principles to circumstances, specificity is actually required to give these general concepts meaning in particular circumstances. Without specificity, the meaning of principles such as local autonomy will always remain empty. But, of course, specificity in these terms turns the whole edifice of legal formalism upside down by moving from circumstances to justificatory principles, instead of from principles to circumstances and back to principles.

This last chapter is devoted to teasing out the implications of my theoretical stance based on the examples that were developed in the preceding chapters. As my goal in this book has been to show why both of Tooke's statements are simultaneously valid, here I wish to reexamine

the principle of local autonomy from a variety of social-theoretical perspectives. In particular, the American idealistic view of decentralized
democracy is subject to critical scrutiny focusing upon its theoretical
limits, its practical constraints, and its remaining rhetorical power as a
political principle. Also, an argument is mounted against the structuralist
view that urban social movements are only political, wholly conceived in
the political structure. In contrast, I suggest that urban society has the
capacity to shift outside conventional limits, even if this capacity is
sometimes narrowly interpreted by the courts.

Dimensions of Local Autonomy

Local autonomy can be described, as has been seen in the previous
chapters, in many ways using many different perspectives. Here, the
focus of this book was on two related and interdependent principles,
initiative and immunity. The former referred to the capacity of local
governments to initiate their own policies, consistent with their interests
as bureaucratic organizations, conceived according to Weberian imperatives (see Clark and Dear 1984, chap. 3) and/or as representatives of local
residents' interests. On the other hand, immunity referred to the capacity
of local governments to act free from the interference of higher-tier state
agencies, such as review boards, judges, and the like. While deriving
from Bentham, these principles describe a basic characterization of the
dimensions of local autonomy in contemporary North America. Thus, for
example, local autonomy can be interpreted in Boston, Toronto,
Denver, and Chicago using this language, covering many different geographical settings and even two countries.[6] Bentham's logic has been a
useful way of conceptualizing local powers for judges and legal theorists
alike. For example, Frug (1980) used these concept to analyse U.S. city
powers over some two hundred years, and local public finance theorists
imply these kinds of powers when they analyze the functions and performance of local governments, whether in America or in Western
Europe (see Bennett 1980).

In terms of theory building, these twin concepts of initiative and
immunity have two virtues. For a start, their combination and pairing of
correlates and opposites allows us to envision a whole range of possible
local government powers and institutional capacities. These dimensions,
or ideal types, also provide a set of tools for describing contemporary
local government powers. Second, with these concepts we were able to
start from a common language which could order and structure the
various case studies noted in the four preceding chapters. Since it was a
readily identifiable language in American judicial decision making, we
were able to avoid the problems of translating one formal system of

classification into another. Thus, a symbolic template was used to order, arrange, and compare the various disputes. In this manner, their commonalities were emphasized rather than their dissimilarities.

Based on the discussion of Quine's (1953) two dogmas of empiricism in chapter 8, it is clear that initiative and immunity are best described as analytical statements so abstract and general that they have only an indirect and passing relationship with specific events. Thus, while these two principles can be used to classify different circumstances crudely, it is inevitable that there will be exceptions, problems of classification at their margins, and especially indeterminacies. It is not always clear what ideal type best describes a particular situation or if there is an ideal type relevant for the circumstances. For example, in the Boston case the construction unions had such a restricted interpretation of local initiative that their ideal type of local government might have been best described as simply being an administrative arm of Massachusetts and national governments. In contrast, the U.S. Supreme Court's expansive interpretation of initiative might place the City of Boston closer to "an inherent right of self-government" model of local government, more typically associated with writers like McBain (1916) than Dillon (1911).

Over the course of this book it must, nevertheless, have become apparent that there are two general types of local autonomy that dominate the American scene. On the one hand is Dillon's rule, narrowly restricting local initiative to state-enumerated powers and denying local immunity, and in combination describing a very restricted vision of local autonomy. On the other hand, there are competing interpretations like home rule, which allows for local initiative according to local matters or some other empirical rule of relevant local circumstances. This latter model describes a more expansive vision of local autonomy and, strangely enough, is more flexible than Dillon's rule. Yet even here, with an implied higher resolution of specificity, ambiguities abound. In some states, such as Illinois, judges have interpreted home rule by using the logic of Dillon's rule. In other states, such as Colorado, judges have gone out of their way to maintain a distinction between these two types of local autonomy. But even in Colorado, the judicial distinctions have obviously been unstable and circumstantial and have led on a number of occasions to complete reversals in the interpretation of past cases as well as the relevance and applicability of previous rules of thumb. "Local matters" was shown to be particularly unstable in this regard, although I would contend that this is the fate for any synthetic or empirical rule.[7]

Home rule is a difficult concept to operationalize. It has as many interpretations as circumstances, and it requires circumstances to have a substantive meaning. Thus, there is an inevitable circularity in the judicial application of general principles such as home rule to specific circumstances. While the applicability of a principle to a situation is based upon a kind of empirical recognition rule, recognition is only possible through past applications of the principle. It is not surprising, then, that principles can be at once tools of decision making and devices for legitimating judicial decision making. Judges simultaneously make a crude judgment as to the applicability of a principle to a situation and then justify their decision by appealing to the relevance of the circumstances vis-à-vis their interpretation of the principle.[8] Much of the public debate over the proper dimensions of local autonomy in states like Illinois and Colorado began from a dimly recognized appreciation of this kind of circularity in judicial decision making. Attempts to legislate specific powers of local government, however, will only serve to constrain local initiative as circumstances change over time.

State-level legislation which would detail the proper dimensions of local governments' powers is similarly fraught with ambiguities and indeterminacies. General legislation treats specific local governments according to their general group affiliation or empirical similarity with some other city.[9] Consequently, any one local government has only those powers granted its class, which may or may not be finely detailed enough to be relevant for many different possible circumstances. Since legislation is almost always broadly conceived, the courts have enormous discretion to interpret legislation according to circumstances. And, even if finely detailed, courts will still be needed to sort out others' contending interpretations, conflicts between different statutes, and the relevance of different circumstances to different statutes. One way or another, adjudication will be necessary, and with adjudication goes political power and a large measure of judicial independence.

Notice that I have been emphasizing the indeterminacy of general principles and general legislation as well as the specificity of circumstances. Herein lies a paradox. At one level, the indeterminacy of general principles like local autonomy implies a significant degree of institutional fragility. The judicial system is continually challenged to resolve disputes using general principles applied "judiciously" to specific circumstances. Indeterminacy is their enemy. It questions their capacity to arrive at reasonable decisions and limits the generality of their findings. Thus, a city like Des Plaines (chap. 7) can legitimately query the veracity of court decisions regarding the allocation of jurisdictional powers using similar logic and statutes as the courts. And, the courts may find it difficult to stop cities like Des Plaines from mounting challenges to their decisions, time after time. Not only are institutions like the judiciary vulnerable to open challenge because of indeterminacy, their appeals to general principles as justifications for their decisions are likely to go unappreciated. After all, it is precisely the indeterminacy of these principles that generates the disputes in the first place.

From institutional fragility it is but a short step to political vulnerability. Thus, one side of the paradox is that institutions are not and should not be assumed to be monolithic or impervious to outside challenge. Quite the contrary it is reasonable to suppose that the judiciary is very vulnerable to concerted political action, even if the channels of influence are vague and undefined. In these circumstances, the judiciary needs all of its rhetorical and argumentative techniques to sustain its position.

Yet this very possibility suggests the other side of the paradox. Just as the judiciary is fragile and vulnerable, it is very powerful. As the final creator of determinacy, its social position appears almost invincible. Not only is this functional role of incredible significance in contemporary American society, the generality of abstract social principles provides the courts with a tremendous range of discretion, even legitimacy. Consequently, courts make meaning as they define the dimensions of local autonomy. By doing so, the courts structure political discourse and the terms of dispute. Moreover, the courts have the power to reinterpret others' arguments in terms of their own. Consequently, the language of dispute becomes the courts' language, and the courts can then alter the dimensions of any dispute. Thus, I would contend that our social language is not inadequate or too narrow for expressing our ideals. Rather, it is the very openness of social language that provides the courts with such discretionary powers. It is judicial decision making that purposely limits language, structures dominant interpretations, and narrows governments' policy options. The paradox is that for all its fragility, the judiciary appears as an ominous institution. It is the ultimate decision maker in social conflicts and creates and re-creates its own power.[10]

The paradox of the power of indeterminacy is obviously a product of initial arguments made in chapter 1 of this book; that is, it depends upon the existence of moral pluralism and moral relativism. Pluralism provides the heterogeneity of social interpretation, a variety of interpretations of supposedly common values. General principles are invested with various and different meanings, all specific to the interests of different social groups in particular circumstances. General principles are, like all points of social consensus, virtually empty (see Rae et al. 1981 for example on the emptiness of the principle of equality). Relativism, on the other hand, refers to the hierarchical order of values—the relative significance we attribute to different interpretations of common principles and the order of those different principles. Here, indeterminacy exists simply because of the relativism of social life.[11] No absolute value is assumed to transcend any other, and no one truth can be established which would deny all others. Here the argument is obviously theoretical and moral; it is based on chapters 2 and 3 of this book and finds favor with other writers such as Geertz (1983) and Goodman (1984).

One final implication of this mode of theorizing should also be noted. If arguments are relative and if judicial decision making has the capacity to structure social discourse, can we imagine any limits to local autonomy? At one level, the answer is obviously no. The structure of interests, argument, and decision making all intersect at specific places to create local autonomy. No absolute limit could be imagined except perhaps as a rhetorical device. Thus, for example, if political discourse were limited to classical liberalism, we could imagine the courts or some other party invoking the protection of minorities as a limit on local autonomy (see chap. 6). Yet even here there is a choice of discourse; we need not confine social interaction to liberal principles, unless the courts force social discourse according to liberalism. Once forced into this pattern, however, the limits to local autonomy can be readily (abstractly) identified, if not practically adjudicated (once again see chap. 6). But this implies a qualification to the answer that there are no limts on local autonomy. The answer will obviously depend upon the terms of social discourse, the language of social association, and the underlying conception of social life.

Democratic Idealism and Community Integrity

Perhaps the most common argument for local autonomy is that decentralized decision making is a necessary condition for a vigorous and meaningful democracy. Two parts to this argument can be identified; the first deals with interests, the second deals with scale. In terms of interests, it is sometimes asserted that a proper measure of local autonomy enables people to act collectively in terms of their interests. Thus, there may be a closer relationship between citizens and government at the local level. This argument will look familiar to the reader since it appeals to similar principles that structure local public-finance models. Specifically, the decentralized nature of community and government is assumed to have a positive effect in facilitating the relationship between citizens' needs and their governments' response. Consequently, the second part of the argument concerning the scale of government is very much related to the first part. It is assumed that smaller governments speed voters' expressions of their needs and the responsiveness of local government. The Tiebout (1956) model obviously depends on these assumptions as many American writers, following de Tocqueville's lead, have proclaimed the virtues of a decentralized system of government (see, for example, the argument made by Nozick [1974] in favor of homogeneous community preference communities).

Liberals and many radicals hold to these propositions. As was noted earlier (chap. 2), a case could easily be made for local autonomy along the lines of American liberalism which would invoke de Tocqueville, Tiebout, and even Jefferson. Local autonomy is a value ingrained in American consciousness, albeit a value that is too often asserted without question. We find radicals making similar arguments, if not exactly in the same language, then at least with similar notions in mind. Thus, for example, Mansbridge (1980) promoted the virtues of town meetings and local democracy for its socialization effects as much as its possible socialism. Similarly, Castells (1983, 1984) has promoted the concept of peoples' everyday lives as the beginning point for radical action. The argument here is again quite familiar; it takes seriously parallel liberal notions, most often associated with writers such as Dahl (1956), which would promote the virtues of local democratic institutions. Indeed, as was argued in chapter 6, the radical vision can be subsumed by one side of the liberal principle-counterprinciple conundrum.

Notice that local autonomy as local democracy is an idealistic claim. As idealism, it is a value that depends upon our assumptions, choices, and moral commitments. In this regard Nozick (1981, p. 555) noted that idealism implies that values are created by us, as opposed to being received from god or some other higher-order form of life. Thus, it is entirely appropriate for community activists to promote the virtues of local autonomy, even though their conception has close ties with the dominant form of liberal ideology. And just because radicals promote local autonomy no one could suppose that Castells would invoke the liberal counterprinciple of centralization (the protection of individuals' rights or interests from the local community). After all, for Castells local autonomy is a means to an end; it facilitates community cohesion and social action leading to the social transformation of society at the local and national levels. Thus, the object of local autonomy in these circumstances is quite different in substance from liberal ideology, even if they appear similar in a procedural sense.[12]

However, I would contend that there remain difficulties with this kind of local autonomy argument, affecting both the liberal and radical visions of community life. Most broadly, these difficulties stem from their common society-centered mode of theorizing. That is, these kinds of liberal and radical arguments for local autonomy begin with local preferences and then derive community goals. Consequently, the legal arrangement of local government powers should follow from these preferences, whether radical or liberal in origin. Moreover, the legal structure should necessarily reflect social values, being a neutral image of the popular will. This style of argument is yet another version of the original position that so bedevils contemporary liberal thought. For it to make any sense, we have to assume that preferences exist separately from institutional structure, especially the dominant language of social discourse.

Granted, these implications are entirely consistent with liberal theory and a liberal would likely proclaim them to be part of a larger idealistic argument for the proper relationship between civil society and its institutions, like law.[13] For the social activist, however, these implied conditions should indicate that there are good reasons to pause at this juncture. While it is obvious enough that social radicals who argue the case for decentralization are not likely to agree totally with liberal local autonomy, if there are two contending classes in a local area, there are going to be two contending interpretations of local autonomy. If, as is most likely, local government has no immunity, then any such conflicts will be likely resolved by the judiciary.[14] And if the issue is then interpreted in liberal terms, that of protecting minorities from the community, then the social radical will be doubly disenfranchised. Not only will the courts deny the relevance of radicals' substantive goals for local autonomy, the issue of interpretation will be resolved according to the logic and language of a contending political ideology.

This argument concerning the political nature of interpretation depends upon a previous claim, substantiated in the four case studies of this book, that judges have tremendous discretion in choosing what to adjudicate, and how to adjudicate. Their social position is crucial in this regard. It is surely a simple matter for the courts to assert their interpretation of a dispute and enforce a decision which would ignore others' substantive interests. Judges are not, and cannot be, neutral. They may be convinced of the virtues of liberalism, perhaps they may have common interests with other elites, or perhaps they may fear the consequence of setting a precedent. All these reasons and others can be and were advanced at one time or another to understand the motivations of the judiciary in the preceding chapters. Thus, it is entirely reasonable to interpret the judiciary as another superpowerful political interest group.

I would argue, however, that there is a more insidious problem. If judges are so powerful, then the whole structure of local government may be so arranged that radical claims for local democracy are deadened. By that I mean to suggest that while a radical ideal may fit within an existing arrangement of local powers, its potential may be so circumscribed by the judiciary that radical action within this framework is a fruitless exercise in social activism. As was suggested in chapter 6, radical claims for local autonomy may simply reflect a limited arena for social action within the dominant mode of social discourse. Its limits would then be the limits of the dominant mode of political discourse, rather than any inherent limits of the radical vision of local autonomy.

It is easy to be defeatist about the whole enterprise of local social planning and activism, and I don't mean to suggest that local activism need be a blind alley. Many good things have come out of such local activism. However, we should not be carried away with the potential of local autonomy simply because a sphere of local initiative may appear available in specific circumstances. It must be acknowledged that local government powers are institutionally structured, by legal principles which are selectively applied by the judiciary. We should not be induced by society-centered reasoning to believe that our own interpretation of structures is somehow independent of the structures themselves. As Geertz (1983, p. 218, note) argued, social sentiments and ideals do not exist independent of law; in point of fact, social ideals will be more than likely derived from the dominant institutional structure, of which law is a fundamental part. The risks with radical local autonomy, local democratic strategies are twofold—they may be methodologically naive, being derived from society-centered modes of analysis, and/or they may mistake a partial dimension of liberal ideology for an arena of radical political action.

Of course, this argument should not be taken as suggesting that liberal ideology or judicial decision making is a seamless web of self-justifying and internally consistent logic. Much of the evidence presented in the preceding chapters suggested just the opposite; judicial decision making often seems contradictory and inconsistent, to paraphrase Tooke (1933). Reasons for this incoherence range from the internal indeterminacies of liberalism, the limits of empiricism, and the inability of judges to respond adequately to specific circumstances. Despite these inconsistencies and contradictions, a social reformer wishing to exploit local autonomy does have some options to exploit the indeterminacy of liberalism. For instance, while Huntington (1981) complained that the liberal ideal of equality was radically (and in his terms, incorrectly) reinterpreted during the 1960s, the ultimate adjudicators of correct interpretations need not have been moved by radical claims of a different substantive meaning to the concept of equality. Thus, it should be acknowledged that the judicial system has the power of determinacy in these circumstances, which may even go against conventional interpretations. The extent to which a radical reinterpretation of local autonomy can exploit this potential will obviously help the cause.

Huntington's claim ignored the fact that equality has always had many different interpretations.[15] So we should not be surprised if the courts are skilled at deflecting radical claims by all kinds of rhetorical methods. However, his second argument that democratic forces were "out of control" during this period seems to have more potential. While a radical reinterpretation of a common principle like local autonomy may easily founder upon judicial indifference, even outright dismissal, a radical social movement which stood outside the dominant language of social discourse would be harder to contend with, especially if motivated by a kind of idealism which challenged the whole logic of the current social structure. Huntington was fearful of radical interpretation of common principles and its implied social goals. But more troublesome would be the level of social mobilization behind a radical interpretation of society itself. By questioning the dominant institutions of society, radicals also question the dominant interpretations of social life manufactured by those institutions.

Why do social activists put such store in local autonomy? Why do they believe decentralized political systems to be better than centralized systems? One answer would invoke the history of American social thought as a common legacy which many social theorists have inherited. Thus, we can trace the writings of Jefferson and de Tocqueville, as examples, through to the present day in the language of theorists such as Castells and Mansbridge. This intellectual heritage is especially American, certainly less European although based upon intellectual roots going at least as far back as John Locke. The historical legacy argument would be sure to provide insight into current local government theories as the comparison between de Tocqueville and Tiebout demonstrated in chapter 8. I have less criticism of this concept than other justifications of decentralization. In part, the intellectual argument is moral and idealistic, rather than empirical and pragmatic. And, while it is possible to criticize de Tocqueville for his naturalism and organic conception of human association, we can only mount a serious critique from another contending interpretation of the "proper" mode of social association. One would have to assert one truth to do serious damage to de Tocqueville's idealism, and even then it would merely founder upon the shoals of relativism.

More problematic, though, are arguments for local autonomy which depend upon empirical notions of scale, efficiency, and size. For many theorists, liberal and radical, local autonomy is a matter of practical necessity. National political life is thought to be too complex, too large, even impersonal. Local autonomy, on the other hand, is thought to be more consistent with people's everyday lives. Yet, this argument is more difficult to justify than often supposed. For a start, it depends upon one interpretation of reality. Like the legal doctrine of local matters, it asserts a determinant and straightforward interpretation of empirical reality. However, there are many contending interpretations of local virtues of local powers, some of which raise serious questions about the efficacy of decentralized government. For instance, blacks segregated in ghettos would surely welcome the chance to participate on a broader spatial scale than their local community. In contrast to middle-class whites, blacks could reasonably interpret local self-determination as a prison that denies wider societal responsibility for their local problems. Furthermore, local autonomy may reasonably be interpreted as a means of excluding blacks from white enclaves.[16]

The virtues of decentralization are hollow once we introduce specific circumstances. And again, like the doctrine of local matters, decentralization is an unstable empirical category. What is a virtue in one situation need not be a virtue in another situation. Thus, for example, local responsibility for zoning could encourage local development opportunities, while local zoning ordinances may be used in other circumstances to maintain racial homogeneity. As a general rule, decentralization is obviously based on quite important liberal and radical principles. Yet as a general rule, it is virtually indeterminant in practice. Circumstances give it meaning, while principles are so removed from circumstances that there can be no principled check on one interpretation over another. This is, after all, Quine's (1953) argument regarding the underdeterminacy of analytical propositions which was developed in chapter 8. The empirical argument for decentralization is problematic at best; at worst it is yet another avenue for the judiciary to exert their power and dominance in social discourse.

The Structuration of Urban Life

A counterargument to liberal-cum-radical idealizations of local democracy would contend that localities structure personalities. That is, local autonomy is the fundamental mode of socialization affecting the lives, behavior, and modes of expression of local residents. Essentially, the structuralist critique of liberalism when taken to its ultimate conclusion contends that local circumstances can create local personalities. The reader might recall that I suggested in chapter 2 that liberal visions of community fail to account for the conditioning aspects of social life and that social life is a principal feature of human existence. And I have also argued throughout this book that liberal analytical devices such as original positions are fundamentally compromised by their ignorance of the material structure of social reality. Indeed, in chapter 2 it was suggested that devices like original positions presuppose the existence of complete personalities capable of making emotional decisions, even though it is not at all clear how it is possible to have personalities without society. This is very much Sandel's (1983) position as well, where he noted that liberal theory assumes an unemcumbered self—no social relations, no commitments, no obligations, and no social identity. The counterargument and critique is that contexts create personalities, and social structure is the ultimate basis of social decisions, the implication being that the structure of law can determine social action.

Surely, few would doubt that law both enables and sustains individual behavior. Similarly, few would doubt that the legal structure of local powers will likely engender a particular geography of individual be- havior, albeit simply recorded as an empirical phenomenon. Thus for example, it is easy enough to imagine that the existence of a sphere of local initiative related to zoning will enable local government to exclude other undesirable residents. It is also plausible that local powers are designed to create that kind of behavior. For instance a state government may wish to localize racial tensions by channeling these tensions to the local level. We could interpret the Boston resident employment prefer- ence policy as social behavior within the context of the law, where the legal system allowed for local initiative in terms of local hiring practices.

But the strongest claim of structuralism is more than the idea that institutions enable, channel, and sustain individual behavior. Like Chief Justice Warren Burger, a structuralist would assert that localities create people, in a particular social sense. As was noted in chapter 8, Chief Justice Burger has sought to protect religious communities' claims for the integrity of their own values, suggesting that they will only survive if they are allowed to socialize their children (see Burger's decision in *Wisconsin v. Yoder*).

Here, local autonomy is an instrument of domination, creating and re-creating communities of like-minded people by excluding outside influences. There are a number of ways that a structuralist might defend such a proposition. Most obviously, it would be argued that homo- geneous communities have a tremendous capacity for socialization. Sys- tematically structured education, a narrow interpretation of community life, and a structured language of social relations could all be constructed to create a closely integrated vision of proper local social relations. If this discourse was narrow enough, we could imagine that idealism and roman- ticism would similarly reflect the dominant mode of social intercourse. Moreover, in a rigid, hierarchically ordered social structure, discourse itself would be controlled by one or two institutions, thereby mandating legitimate and illegitimate social action. Again, there is a good deal of evidence for this kind of possibility in the cases discussed in previous chapters.

A second argument a structuralist might introduce to sustain that position concerns language and consciousness. Olsson (1976) has sug- gested that language is like a prison. According to him and others, language limits human development and the appreciation of what is possible, what social relations could be like.[17] In one passage he described language as a seamless ceiling, limiting his consciousness and future. One implication of this argument is that language is a structure which narrowly restricts human consciousness. Thus, we can only imagine and talk in a language inherited from society, which is itself structured according to social norms. If this analogy is taken further and applied to local conditions, the implication is that our consciousness is bound by circumstances. The more power a locality has to structure social life, the more likely that human relations will be stamped by their circumstances. It is no wonder liberals on the U.S. Supreme Court so vigorously opposed Burger in *Yoder* and have fought a rearguard action in other cases like *Mount Ephraim* to maintain plurality and individual freedom. Liberals take the structuralists seriously. That is why they have fought to maintain the liberal principle-counterprinciple dichotomy. The implication is, of course, that local autonomy is a threat to individual freedom.

If circumstances are so powerful and if the imperatives of community association so drastically socialize people that it is impossible to obtain an external vantage point on local principles, it is no wonder that liberals use devices such as original positions. While they assume a fully fledged person, liberals like Rawls go to great lengths to remove the confounding influences of contexts. In doing so, it is hoped that individuals will be able to arrive at integrated general principles which would then guide social life in all its complexity and diversity. To do so requires some heroic assumptions about the integrity of individuals separated from their social life. But also to maintain these principles once structure is introduced would require judges to be located in a similar position, that is, separate from the conditioning effects of material life. Liberals return to this kind of reasoning time after time because they do not trust people once community relations are introduced. Obviously it is a pessimistic view of individuals' motivations, and it implies that individuals are quite fragile in the face of social pressures.

How seriously should we take the structuralist argument? As a description of the structuring powers of the judiciary, the structuralists' argument seems to have a number of virtues. One of the lessons of the disputes over local autonomy reviewed in the previous chapters was that it is only through the introduction of circumstances, contexts, that we can interpret general principles. And it is quite clear that circumstances can create principles—there is a necessary circularity in any principled analysis of society. Similarly, the power of judges to create determinant interpretations of contending principles is formidable. There can be little doubt that the meaning of local autonomy, for example, is socially conceived and manufactured by our institutions.

While it would be repetitious to go back over the earlier discussion of structuralism in chapter 2, it should be remembered that any claim that individuals have a unique and separate vantage point outside society must be viewed with a good deal of skepticism. To make such a claim would involve assuming some kind of natural man or metaphysical consciousness conceived in some other place. For those of us schooled in post-Enlightenment social sciences, none of these suppositions seems entirely tenable. Most of us would be unwilling to locate the origin of social consciousness in an unknown third party. The virtue of structuralism is that it takes society seriously.

I would also argue, however, that the structuralist argument is incomplete. Specifically, it fails to provide an adequate understanding of how individuals make decisions. Like liberalism, structuralism has no real theory of human consciousness, even though it is often used as a critical weapon against liberalism on this same point. As was noted above, liberalism eschews context for a featureless original position in deriving general principles. In doing so, it also denies the social dimensions of personality, indeed maybe personality itself (Sandel 1983). In contrast, structuralism uses context to drive individual decisions. Here, people are the standard-bearers of social structure, reflecting their social position and thus acting according to their role. No individual consciousness is required to make this model work. All that is required is that people be true to their position. Even if they are not, institutions would presumably force them back to their correct behavior. Here, structuralism assumes an absorbent personality instead of an unencumbered self. Individuals are assumed to absorb local circumstances, the directives of institutions, and the local language of social intercourse. At the extreme, a structuralist society would be dominated by local personalities.

The difficulty with this concept of social consciousness is its one-dimensionality. It does not allow for revision, emancipation, even social change. Consequently, pluralism itself would be denied except that which was built into the structure itself. Moreover, the implication of this presumption is that even the structures of society would be hidden from view. After all, there would be no separate consciousness which could identify structure. Accordingly, people would act as if their world was natural, normal, and unstructured.[18] Indeed, they would believe what they were told.

While some social theorists do suppose that this model fairly describes current circumstances and that people are duped by social structure to believe their roles, this model makes impossible demands on our imagination. For a start, all social conflict should be understood, according to this model, to be part of a larger structure which both creates conflict and controls the dimensions of conflict. It is quite plausible that some conflict is so managed, especially by the courts, as we have seen in the previous chapters. However, it is difficult to believe that all conflict is so managed that "pluralism" is just another face of the totalitarian thought-state envisioned by George Orwell.

Moreover, this kind of structuralist model would make impossible demands on the state and the judiciary. For instance, someone or something would have to orchestrate this world. Like Richards's superjudge Cardozo or Dworkin's Hercules, superordinary judges would be needed to maintain the wheels of socialization, the integrity of community consciousness, and the subversion of the intellect. But how could that be? How could such a group exist outside society but nevertheless be reproduced over time? And why should they be the only ones with a superimaginative consciousness? Going on the evidence introduced in the previous chapters, it is clear that few judges would be capable of fulfilling such a role. In all circumstances, they are beset by ambiguities and indeterminacies. Their decisions seem all too human, prone to exaggeration, ignorance, and plain indeterminacy. Their interpretations of rules, of order, and of local powers (structures) are so often unstable and subject to the vagaries of circumstances. Even social science experts would seem ill-equipped to fulfill such a demanding role. Only someone unfamiliar with the practice of judicial decision making would propose judges for such a role.

At this extreme, the structuralist theory of local autonomy appears quite implausible. It presumes the existence of a Machiavellian elite, controlling, manipulating, and conspiring to rule social consciousness in terms of a hidden agenda. Moreover, it depends upon an assumption that human consciousness is so permeable and absorbent that it simply follows the lead of internally consistent rules and orders. The rules and orders, structures in a more general sense, have to be unambiguous and thoroughly determined, otherwise how could social life be so ordered? Based on the evidence presented in the previous chapters of this book, it is difficult to believe that structures are so consistent and determinant. And it has been my contention throughout that social life has many dimensions, many interpretations, and few if any infallible rules. Structuralism supposes a complete world, yet cannot help us in identifying the hidden structures that so determine social life. All we are left with are images, like Chief Justice Warren Burger fighting for the rights of communities to socialize their citizens.

If we step back from this extreme view, though, I would contend that the structuralist model can be fairly used to interpret institutional powers and the conditioning importance of circumstances. A less stringent model of structuralism would allow for indeterminacies, a fractured, and multifaceted human consciousness, and pluralism in one form or another. Similarly, a less stringent structuralism would allow for idealism and principled dissent. But, even so, this kind of structuralism would not find favor with structuralists. What I have described is an emerging new kind of social theory, one based on context and practical knowledge.[19]

Circumstances, Contexts, and Places

Throughout this book, the significance of circumstances, contexts, and places has been emphasized and reemphasized. These three analogous terms indicate the various positional facets of my argument, simultaneously indicating the specificity of the situations in which the judiciary has had to adjudicate between contending visions of local autonomy. Specificity has a great deal to do with position, that is, the vantage points from which claims are made for the veracity of one or more interpretations of events. Notice that position is implied, often explicitly acknowledged, in contending interpretation and decision making. Thus, there can be no circumstantial neutrality, whether we talk about the litigants of a dispute or the courts themselves.

Position and perspective are intimately related in my vision of social interaction. The latter flows from the former, as circumstances define interests, and structure arguments. This spatial conception of social discourse also means social heterogeneity. Heterogeneity was evidenced in the various interpretations of common principles, as in chapter 6, where the meaning of decentralized democracy was dealt with in detail, and in the clash of contending principles, as in chapter 8, where we dealt with local "matters" and statewide concerns. Continuing the spatial analogy about social heterogeneity, there can be no one map of social discourse; there are both different maps and different streams of argument. The judicial system does not so much merge contending maps of social discourse as impose one map over others. This may come about by judges taking sides in a dispute and thus using one map to deny another, as in chapter 5, where the courts alternated between the contending parties in the dispute over Boston's resident-preference policy, or where judges impose their own map, as in chapter 7, where the Illinois Supreme Court ignored statutory rules by holding to a very narrow interpretation of local initiative powers.

My argument has some similarities with Williams's (1979) critique of A. J. Ayer. Williams argued that Ayer's (1956) verification thesis, which required so-called token sentences to have the same factual content if they were to mean the same, was quite implausible. He noted that Ayer sought to claim the existence of neutral sentences, like neutral principles (since they are collections of ordered words, sentences, or phrases), independent of what Williams termed "perspective." Or, put another way, neutral sentences ought to have an eternal content, independent of time, place, and person. As was seen in this book, Ayer's claim is impossible because of the specificity of people's contexts. For Williams, position constitutes perception and interpretation. Thus, to the extent there are different positions, there will be different interpretations of common sentences and principles. Accordingly, the earlier argument made in chapter 1 regarding the distinctiveness of feminist, minority, and middle-class interpretations of concepts such as local autonomy has many parallels with Williams's position.

Another similar argument has been made by Pred (1984), regarding the specificity of geographical position. He suggested a modified structuralist (structuration) thesis to the effect that individuals are constituted as social beings in particular time-space settings. Logically, then, people can have no neutral vantage point, for they are stamped by circumstances and derive their interests out of their social-spatial positions. This argument, like Williams's is an effective counter to those who suggest that the spatial is somehow separate from the social (see Saunders 1981). In point of fact, the social and the spatial are one and the same thing. It is impossible to imagine the social separate from the spatial and vice versa (see Williams 1979 and Giddens 1981). Based upon the analysis of local autonomy presented in this book, it is quite obvious that I would willingly associate Williams's and Pred's arguments with my own. After all, much of chapter 2 was spent arguing that individuals are conceived as isolated, discrete individuals only in a very particular mode of social discourse—liberalism. Similarly, my critique of Rawls and others who use original positions to start off their social analyses had many parallels with the arguments of Williams and Pred.

Even so, despite these associations, I do not mean to suggest that Williams would totally agree with Pred, and neither would I. Structuralism has its own problems, many of which were detailed in the preceding section of this chapter. And generally, I would suggest that structural theories are too cumbersome to deal adequately with our institutions of social determination. Like so many other theorists of modern society, structuralists assume a ready-made world which simultaneously envelops individual life and places a ceiling on social emancipation. The irony is that even geography is narrowly interpreted as a stage for social discourse and as a prison denying social change. In this respect an adequate theory of how social life intersects and transforms the social and spatial dimensions of life is quite lacking.

What is needed is a social theory which takes structure and agency seriously. By structure I mean, of course, the social arrangement of discourse embodied in our various institutions. This structure is intimately geographical, from the specificity of situations through to the interpretation of institutions like local government. On the other hand, one of the lessons of this book was surely that structure has a variety of meanings and that it is through social conflict that society (as individuals, groups, and institutions) comes to determinant interpretations. As a consequence of this conception of social life, we should not assume a ready-made world, a complete and fully determined structure. Through social discourse over the "proper" interpretation of structure, society makes and remakes itself.

Limits of Judicial Power

At this juncture, it is reasonable to ask whether or not society can reach agreement on desirable social goals and objectives given the specificity of social position. Put another way, must determinacy always be imposed by institutions such as the judiciary? In terms of the preceding discussion, much of the analysis of disputes over the meaning of local autonomy was framed with reference to the judiciary because I wished to understand the institutional process of social determinacy, and so it may appear to the reader that determinacy can only come from one source. While I remain pessimistic about the capacity of social action to restructure circumstances outside the current institutional framework of American society, it would be misleading to dismiss this possibility altogether. We must recognize again that one of the lessons of the Boston jobs dispute was that community groups can be successful in their drive for social goals. Whatever the character of local initiative powers and the judicial interpretation of the terms of disputes, community action remains an important avenue for those who wish to remake society.

Another argument could be made in favor of social as opposed to institutional determinacy which is less empirical and more theoretical. To hold to the view that social position means that there can never be any social determinacy would surely go against my previous argument and, if taken to extreme, would imply a phenomenological conception of interpretation. That is, if social position counts so much in determining interpretation, then we could easily imagine that social position could be so defined that everyone would have a unique position—thus a unique interpretation. Yet it must be quite apparent that the model of social heterogeneity proposed in this book is more collectively than individually based. For instance, much of chapter 2 was devoted to an analysis of why the private sphere of liberal philosophy is only one part of a more ordered and inclusive social experience. Thus, to claim an individually centered model of interpretation would return to the fallacies of liberal theory and beg the question of how the private is conceived in the social arena.

The problem of creating determinacy out of social heterogeneity has two dimensions, one which could be characterized as being more technical than social and another more social than technical. Taking the *technical* issue first, one might ask whether or not it is possible to translate one interpretation of a situation into the terms of another. After all, if the basis of a contending interpretation could be immediately understood, its moral claim and the position of those making the claim, then it would be reasonable to suppose that the conditions for determinacy exist, even if the social will may not. But this is precisely the problem that has been dealt with throughout the book. It is not only the lack of political will that forestalls determinacy; translation between social-cum-spatial positions is problematic at best. The technical dimension is more important than one might originally suppose and exists despite the fact that Americans use a common language, even common political terminology, when it comes to matters of local autonomy.

Reasons for the indeterminacy of translation vary, but are all related to the contextual nature of social life. Fish (1980, pp. 282–83), for example, has noted that the meaning of any set of words, technical or common language, depends on the circumstances in which those words appear. And this was very much my argument in the previous chapters regarding the meaning of local autonomy. It should be easy enough by now to remember the variety of meanings attached to local matters in Colorado over the past eighty years as circumstances changed.[20] But, of course, there is another aspect to this issue: circumstances themselves have no independent status and are given texture by social position. Thus, as circumstances change the meaning of words, so, too, does our position change our interpretation of the circumstances and their relevance for interpreting words. A good example of this kind of conception can be seen in the Boston jobs dispute—the relevance of local economic circumstances, local autonomy, and racial discrimination for the unions, community, and judges.

Material interests obviously play a role in structuring interpretations, and so it could be suggested that self-interest promotes disagreements over the meaning of language. But while there are obviously many instances of strategic juggling of meaning, it is impossible to claim that there is one true, objective interpretation of meaning. Appeals to such truths are, in my terms, simply rhetoric. These appeals may be powerful, even convincing, but nevertheless based upon a moral claim not a truth claim. Such appeals ask us to set aside our own interpretations in favor of others, an entirely reasonable exhortation but not evidence of the existence of a determinant truth. To claim the existence of one truth goes against the whole thrust of this book and would fail, I believe, because it depends upon a ready-made world (to quote Goodman 1978 once again). Indeed, this objection is just like Williams's argument against Ayer; facts and language have no independent status separate from the position of the interpreter.

Quine (1960) has also suggested that translation is an indeterminant process, despite the existence of what he termed "translation manuals." According to Quine, the problem of translation is not that there are too few points of intersection between languages (and here we might substitute for languages, social positions and/or contexts), but rather that there are too many possibilities, too many possible translations to be able to reach determinacy. That is, local autonomy can mean many things to many people. And since circumstances have no independent status from social agents, there will be a myriad of meanings and translations. The problem for Quine was that there seems to be no way of choosing between apparently equally valid interpretations except by appealing to a moral order as opposed to a factual order. I would contend that this describes quite well the circumstances faced by judges and contending agents in the previous case studies. Conflicts over local autonomy arise because of the inability of contending parties to arrive at determinant interpretations; judicial reasoning is highly contentious because judges cannot reduce or translate contending interpretations in terms of one another.

Clearly Quine's argument is particularly appropriate for different languages and different circumstances. We could reasonably imagine circumstances and languages which have more in common, as we could imagine social systems which are more homogeneous than heterogeneous. Similarly, we could imagine that education and experience provide tools for improving our capacity to shift positions as we attempt to translate others' interpretations into our own. But there is a limit to this kind of imagination. Social-spatial homogenization would remove the problem of indeterminacy, but then we would not have a society in the usual sense of the word. Such homogeneity would make one truth, one interpretation, but leave us with no social texture (Hacking 1975). On the other hand, for experience and education to be able to arrive at a determinant truth, one must suppose that there exists a truth to be found—it must exist prior to the design of education since, by itself, education without a purpose would have no relevance. But if education is to be used to find the truth, then all we have is a dead end!

I would claim, then, that the indeterminacy of translation is a quite real problem, as the indeterminacy of any social value is similarly a real problem. Not only do position and context conspire to maintain different interpretations of common terms, there is no truthlike fact that could be invoked to integrate and adjudicate between interpretations. Thus, translation is not only a technical problem, as Quine (1960) suggested, it is fundamentally the product of social relativism. In this regard, I only partially agree with Hacking's (1982) argument that translation is a nonproblem. While he recognized the truth-seeking basis of Quine's notion to be ultimately compromised, he nevertheless ignored the other side of relativism—circumstances and places. It is just not possible to take a shortcut to the problem of social will by asserting that translation is a trivial or nonexistent problem.

Despite problems of translation and communication, social discourse is an everyday event. Moreover, in the terms of the preceding discussion of society, social agency requires translation between positions and between interpretations. There would not be a society if translation of some form or another did not occur. Indeed, people would not understand their own position, let alone others', if some form of communication were not possible. After all, in a world of relative claims, the relative dimension is only conceived through social discourse. What I would suggest is that society has many social ways of dealing with indeterminacy which, although not conceived to tell truths in the positivist sense, are socially accepted customary practices of dispute resolution. Compared with legal modes of manufacturing determinacy, these customary practices are only different in form, not type. Legal modes represent instances where customary practices break down, and/or where parties to a dispute have lost faith in the capacity of these practices to deliver a fair resolution. What, then, are these customary social practices?

The most convenient social practice which language theorists believe can establish a bridging-point between interpretations is the so-called principle of charity. Lukes (1982), in reviewing this notion, noted that this principle supposes people lend credibility to others' statements and beliefs by assuming others' statements and beliefs to be coherent and consistent (nonarbitrary).[21] From there on, comparisons between statements under like circumstances should establish a bridgehead. Note, however, that this method again depends on the existence of a determinant truth since statements are not relative to one another, rather relevant to an independent event; this is a positivist notion, through and through. A less truthlike principle is the principle of humanity, which holds that we must first assume others' views and interpretations to be similar to our own.[22] This establishes an optimistic basis for communication and intelligibility. From that point, this principle is not really capable of describing translations. It remains very much a pragmatic device for establishing contact.

The problem with both principles is that, despite their language, they are hardly social devices, but rather individually-based observations of others given the existence of a coherent world of comparable values and beliefs. Again, we have to assume a ready-made world, and again individuals have a separate status from social structure. Implied is a further assumption that language and beliefs are innate. As was noted in chapter 2, this kind of social theorizing seems implausible at best.

The alternative is to assume social interests, social positions, and a continual play of communication. Instead of assuming individually-centered devices of translation, I wish to emphasize the social basis of communication. In particular, I would argue that social discourse in a world of moral heterogeneity is facilitated by four moral sentiments: reciprocity, altruism, collectivity, and justice. These sentiments, four among many others, have no independent status, like positivists' truth statements and depend on circumstances, contexts, and places for specificity. Moreover, I do not assume that there is a particular hierarchy of value to these four sentiments; rather their relative significance depends upon circumstances, contexts, and places. Thus, it is best to understand these sentiments as strategies, that is, devices for social discourse which depend on social relations rather than isolated individual will. Their virtue is their social character; they are invoked, made, and remade by and for social interaction.

As generally understood, reciprocity refers to mutual interaction and exchange. It is not simply a discrete market exchange; it is a relational concept which requires mutual interaction and affection. As a mode of reaching social determinacy, reciprocity supposes that competing claims and interpretations can be resolved, if not reconciled, through mutual regard for one another. This does not mean that all people will get what they want or that there need be a "balance" between partners. Rather reciprocity is a strategy based upon mutual regard for one anothers' claims; sacrifices may be made in order to maintain mutual affection. Similarly, altruism can also be a basis for social discourse. It goes beyond individual ego and requires a measure of social generosity: a regard for others which is more than part of a reciprocal relationship. There is no doubt that both sentiments are part of contemporary life and cannot be reduced to a utilitarian calculus of benefit versus cost.

Collectivity and justice refer to more communitarian values of social association and regard for others' circumstances. They are paired because they seem more related together than with reciprocity or altruism although there are links between all four moral sentiments. Collectivity can be reasonably interpreted as a claim for the social good as opposed to individual advancement. It finds expression in other notions like community, patriotism, nationalism, and like claims for the integrity of higher-order social association. Notice as well that collectivity is an integrative value which argues for the subordination of individuals' interests to a larger whole. Justice is a more powerful claim, at least in contemporary society, but similarly depends on due regard for others' positions.

None of these sentiments depend upon a complete understanding of others' values and their interpretations. No factlike determination is required in, for example, reciprocity or altruism. All four sentiments do depend on some measure of social regard for others which goes beyond liberalism and structuralism. They all make claims upon our emotional character. In these ways, determinacy is fundamentally social, a process which cannot be simply solved by some technical device. Indeed, technical solutions are bound to fail because of their lack of social texture.

While I have only sketched the elements of social determinacy, I hope the essentials are clear. To go further along these lines will require another project. At the present, a final word needs to be said concerning the future of judicial determinacy in America, an issue which is, nevertheless, closely related to social determinacy.

As was argued in this book, the legal apparatus gains considerable power from its discretion as statute interpreter and statute maker. Rules, laws, and statutes are the life of law, but also the power of the courts as interpretation is required to bring about determinacy. But notice that I have also argued that the courts need not be the only agents of determinacy. Other institutions, even individuals, can perform this role, and do so on occasion. In addition, it is hard to believe that the courts are so powerful just because the legal profession is so large. Granted, lawyers have had considerable influence in democratic politics, but this has not always been the case (apart from outstanding individuals). To suppose that the power of the judiciary is a product of the significance of the legal profession may be simply to mistake association for causality. Indeed, it is more plausible to relate the rise of the legal profession to the changing status of the courts then the other way around.

While the courts have a tremendous bureaucratic-cum-institutional inertia which will protect them from radical shifts in public opinion and challenges from other institutions, it would be too much to suppose that there are no limits on the judiciary's power in American society. I would suggest that the courts will continue to dominate the process of social determinacy as long as other institutions, like the legislature, find themselves unable to cope adequately with competing claims and values. Enough has been written about legislative decision making to realize that the open texture of many statutes is quite deliberate.[23] Textual openness builds coalitions of interest groups and minimizes the risk of creating ardent critics. Determinacy resides in the courts in these circumstances and depends on the capacity of those affected to effect real outcomes. But, of course, the process of influencing decisions in these circumstances is more problematic and encourages the employment of smart lawyers, the design of strategic arguments, and the recognition of judges' biases—it is game playing on a grand scale.

All these issues are important. Legislative incapacity is a problem which has been recognized by many writers, both liberal (Lowi 1979) and conservative (Huntington 1981). Similarly, judicial activism has been severely criticized (see Berger 1977). I would contend, however, that as much as these issues are important, the really big problem lies deeper in American social structure. While this problem remains more a hypothesis for future research than a full-fledged argument, the elements of the argument seem quite straightforward. Essentially, the problem is the failure of customary social practices to deliver determinacy. And, this failure is a product of the fragmentation of moral sentiments, reciprocity, altruism, collectivity, and justice. Social relations are, in my view, being continually challenged by material life, inequality, and social alienation. And, in this sense, the failure of moral sentiments to provide the glue for social determinacy is a reflection upon American society.

Notes

Chapter 1   Introduction

1. When combined with empirical description, logical positivism claims to provide an objective representation of the world, natural and social. Yet, as MacIntyre (1981, p. 76) noted, this is surely a most pernicious claim since it also supposes that the facts of the world stand independent of observers' positions—spatial, political, and theoretical. Surely a fact can only be recognized as a fact through some pre-existing lens. While there is, of course, some measure of interaction between theories and observations, the recognition of facts requires a systematic reference point.

2. As Berlin (1978, p. vii) commented, logical positivism is a field of inquiry "in which new discoveries and techniques superseded the old ones—this was [sic] a field of exact knowledge in which genuine progress occurred." Many philosophers of knowledge are willing to grant logical positivists their due in terms of the natural sciences although, even here, in recent times some considerable doubts have been raised concerning the usefulness of logical positivism (see Wigner 1982).

3. Gregory (1978) based his attack on positivism in social science, and in geography more specifically, on the implausibility of this incremental theory of knowledge. Two of his more important arguments were: first, this premise supposes that intellectual knowledge is somehow independent of social interests and thus above the realm of ordinary language. Second, and more political, this premise also displays a measure of intellectual elitism and snobbery which is at once undemocratic and naive.

4. See also Bhaskar 1979 for a critical analysis of the claims made by logical positivists for the superiority of natural reason in the social sciences. While naturalism as a form of social inquiry peaked in England with John Locke, it remains a forceful academic theology in American social theory today (for more details see Clark 1982).

5. Despite its importance in social science, the supposed virtues of logical positivism have been largely discredited in philosophy. For instance, Nozick (1981, p. 630) dismissed logical positivism with a mere wave of the hand by saying "logical positivism is in decline, its verifiability theory of meaning now repudiated," even though he also recognized that "its spirit lives on in our culture." See also Putnam 1981, chap. 6, on logical positivism as a "cocktail party philosophy."

6. It is difficult, nonetheless, to define rationality in a way that would satisfy all social theorists. There is the rationality of logical deduction, and then there is the rationality of doing the best one can under specific circumstances. Those who hold to the first kind of rationality are unlikely to find favor with the second kind. There

are many kinds of rationality and arguments over the virtues of rationality. For two recent but rather different approaches, see Habermas 1984 and Elster 1983.

7. Similar points have been made by Morris (1982) in his treatment of adjudication and the relevance of general rules in terms of particular circumstances. He suggested that it is only possible to understnad disputes through the particularities of social relations and context. Thus, general rules may only create havoc with fair adjudication.

8. The kind of pluralism I have in mind is not liberal pluralism, where belief in one central value, specifically individual freedom, allows for a variety of lower-order beliefs, like freedom of expression. Rather, I follow Berlin 1978 in assuming pluralism to be a methodological stance based upon a belief in the heterogeneity of social interpretations and a belief in the indeterminacy of facts.

9. Relativism has been roundly criticized by many social philosophers. Williams (1972), for example, criticized a vulgar form which is more functionalist than moral for being, paradoxically, nonrelative. That is, some relativists assert that as circumstances change, so too does the correctness of different social practices. Williams had in mind anthropologists' notions that different societies have different beliefs which are so functionally correlated that one cannot be imposed on another. I would suggest in contrast, that relativism exists as a matter of course since we have no access to an external world with which to compare our descriptions. Put another way, we perceive the world through various filters which are necessarily socially conceived. While interpretations can be compared, contrasted, ordered, and debated, they can be hardly sorted by reference to so-called factual statements like truth. Similarly, I agree with Barnes and Bloor (1982, p. 23), who argued that "all beliefs are on a par with one another with respect to the causes of their credibility."

10. The term "manufactured" is used to denote the man-made (or should I say person-made) quality of social discourse. Goodman (1978) used a similar term, "fabrication," to capture much the same idea; modes of reference, social discourse, and social symbols are made or socially conceived not found in nature.

11. See, for example, Burger's argument in Schad v. Mt. Ephraim (1981), wherein he suggested that the community is a social unit capable of deciding its residents' proper social behavior. Chesler (1983) observed that Burger's vision of the community is quite conservative, especially as regards his choice of community standards. Note that Mt. Ephraim is a New Jersey community composed principally of New York city workers. In these terms, community is a moral conception as much as a functional reality.

12. See also Peterson 1981 for a brief discussion of the capitalist state in a structuralist context. Clark and Dear (1984, chap. 2) provide a more extensive review of this literature.

13. What are important and trivial issues will obviously depend on the circumstances. Consequently, there must be a sphere of local initiative wide enough to accommodate changing circumstances. Otherwise, local governments would be locked into increasingly insensitive and arbitrary definitions of local power. As we shall see in later chapters, this is precisely the problem in many disputes over local autonomy.

14. In this context, it is instructive to compare Castells 1984 with Saunders 1981, since the latter author goes to some length to extend the earlier arguments of Castells 1977 by suggesting that urban sociology is nothing more than sociology in a physical urban setting. The irony, of course, is that just as Castells's earlier views are being integrated into mainstream sociology, he has shifted his own

position in his latest book closer to those whom he might have criticized some ten years ago.

15. We need only consider the South African government's policies against black nationalists to realize that political units such as autonomous homelands can be reasonably interpreted as coercive geographical structures dressed, rhetorically speaking, in a spatial ideology. While few would equate American racial discrimination with South African policies, it is, nevertheless, a forceful analogy which brings to the fore black Americans' resentment of white American suburban enclaves.

16. See again, Chief Justice Warren Burger's views on community integrity in Schad v. Mt. Ephraim (1981).

17. By the term "romantic" I mean to suggest that de Tocqueville sought to represent New England life as an experiment in social organization that aimed to achieve a way of life more in keeping with nature than European materialism.

Chapter 2   Public and Private Space

1. For a general analysis of this kind of argument in the contemporary context, see Perin 1977 on zoning, land use, and ideology in America. Not everyone is optimistic about the likelihood of positive socialization based upon community association. For instance, Glazer (1981) was quite pessimistic about the chances of overcoming racial prejudice and residential segregation, despite federal efforts to desegregate urban schools.

2. Pred (1984) put it well in the phrase—"the social becomes the spatial, and the spatial becomes the social." It is probably not fair to label Pred a structuralist since he has argued for a revised kind of structuralism that might be termed "structuration." Like Giddens (1981), Pred argued that structuralism does not adequately allow for human agency, although he retained a social definition of individuality that makes structuralism different from liberalism and even some forms of Marxism. See Gregory 1978, for a review of the related literature in geography, and the book by Harvey (1982), which retains the more conventional Marxian view of urban economic systems, compared with his more recent work (Harvey 1984).

3. I would characterize Duncan and Ley (1982) as liberals in this context, although they do profess to have a socially oriented view that emphasizes social context. A more fundamentalist critique of structuralism is to be found in Couclelis and Golledge 1983, where they raise individuals to the status of unique importance.

4. Chouinard and Fincher (1983) have attempted to put the structuralist-cum-Marxist case, although not with as much success as one might have hoped. Their version of structuralism seems very mechanical compared with Pred's (1984) structuration theory.

5. Here, I have much sympathy with Berlin's (1978) fascination with the construction of categories of social classification, much more than the empirical measures associated with such categories. While I would readily admit to the usefulness of empirical research, I would also argue that the categories we use in empirical research are socially constructed. Thus, a major research task must be to understand how empirical categories are so structured.

6. In these terms, Mansbridge's study has much in common with the work of philosophers like Nozick (1974) in that her study aimed at establishing the possibility of community cohesion, based on social values (what Nozick might call preferences). Of course, there are crucial differences between them, especially as

regards the relevance of underlying economic variables and questions of social power.

7. It should be acknowledged, however, that the Reagan administration substantially cut many social programs that had been introduced by Nixon under the rubric of the new federalism. For instance, there are virtually no funds now available for school desegregation and only limited enforcement of federal regulations regarding the use of federal funds by institutions that practice racial discrimination (for example, private colleges).

8. See Hanson 1982 for a general review of American urban policy since 1970 and the various administrations' attempts to decentralize program implementation.

9. In fact, there has been a great deal of research on defining the optimal spatial scale for providing public goods like health-care, welfare, etc. For an earlier treatment see Smith 1977 and for more recent analyses see McLafferty 1982 and compare with Kirby 1983. Recent developments in this research tradition have begun to question the whole institutional basis behind this mode of analysis (Dear 1981).

10. This pro-growth argument was especially important to President Carter's Commission on an Agenda for the Eighties (1980). Despite the fact that the urban policy panel was selected by President Carter, its recommendations were so conservative that Carter formally disavowed its recommendations. Indeed, the urban panel's report was very close to Reagan's urban policy, at least ideologically, and provided a rationale for the 1982 President's National Urban Policy Report (U.S. Department of Housing and Urban Development 1982; see Clark 1983a for an extended review and critical analysis).

11. The basic principle of contemporary public policy research is that disagreements can be resolved by appeal to facts. Implied, however, is an assumption that facts exist to be discovered and have an objective quality separate from the interests and socio-spatial position of researchers. My argument in this book is that this assumption is entirely misleading and obscures the larger, more problematic issue—moral pluralism.

12. Fosler and Berger (1982) provided a useful overview of the evolution of public-private partnerships and a series of case studies in Baltimore, Chicago, and four other large U.S. cities. Among the key elements of public-private partnerships are leadership, cooperation, and a "positive civic culture that encourages citizen participation rooted in a practical concern for the community as a whole" (p. 10). In a number of cities these imperatives of civic cooperation have been institutionalized in organizations like private industry councils, private assemblies of selected business leaders and highly placed government officials. As described in these terms, public-private partnerships could as easily be described as yet another form of corporatism; see Schmitter and Lehmbruch 1979 for a general overview of this mode of bureaucratic organization, which has become very popular in Europe.

13. It is assumed in liberal models of society that individuals' interests are only subjectively conceived and perhaps only dimly recognized by those involved. Thus, one important thread of philosophical liberalism is essentially utilitarian. For an overview of this connection, see Sen and Williams's 1982 introduction to their edited volume of essays on utilitarianism.

14. For a review of various theories of the state and their spatial implications, see Johnston's (1982) brief review. Elsewhere, it has been argued that liberal

theories of the state hardly take seriously the capitalist mode of production and are so abstract as to be quite irrelevant to contemporary American material circumstances (Clark and Dear 1984). However, as ideology, as a normative vision of society, the liberal theory of the state is a fundamental datum point for contemporary analysis.

15. Many rights theorists depend upon a logic wherein universal rights facilitate individual actions, leaving undetermined what outcomes should result at the individual and/or aggregate level. Perry's (1982) analysis of the role of the courts in this context is especially revealing. He suggested that the state cannot be trusted to observe individuals' preferences so it is up to the courts to ensure that peoples' rights are protected in such a way as to allow for "moral growth." As he recognized, this kind of argument is procedural, not substantive (p. 3).

16. To say that individuals decide on their best interests is probably an overstatement, since liberal theory does not articulate how people make decisions about their interests. Indeed, this is a crucial issue to be resolved because in the absence of such an articulation liberal theory simply ignores local circumstances (Sandel 1983).

17. In this regard, the Kaldor-Hicks compensation principle seems entirely liberal in conception and implementation. See Arrow 1983 for a broad view of compensation theory and welfare theory in general.

18. Clark and Dear (1984) argued that the crisis of the American state is very much related to the failure of the state to provide for the exercise of these options at the local, state, and even national levels. For instance, racial discrimination and segregation is such a pervasive aspect of urban life that options like exit, voice, and loyalty are fundamentally compromised (see Orfield 1978 on urban segregation and its implications for school desegregation).

19. Essentially, liberal theory seeks to outlaw intercommunity imperialism and limit the domination of all communities by higher-tier state organizations (Nozick 1974).

20. Pierre Bourdieu (1983, p. 5) made an analogous, albeit critical, point when discussing the nature of philosophical reasoning. He noted that philosophers "never ask what are the necessary social conditions for that particular way of performing the activity of thinking which defines the thinker." And in terms of practice, Bourdieu argued that "the incapacity of both philosophy and social science to comprehend practice . . . lies in the fact that, just as in Kant, reason locates the principle of its judgments not in itself but in the nature of its objects, so the scholarly thinking of practice includes within practice the scholarly relation to practice." Thus, inquiry is structurally conceived.

21. Compare Tuck 1979 on natural rights theories with Kennedy 1976 on the form of legal discourse as related to social structure. See also Atiyah 1981 for a more social, if not structuralist, vision of law in terms of social relationships.

22. A good example of this point is to be found in the interpretation and adjudication of the employment-at-will doctrine. MacNeil's (1981) survey of contract theory pointed to significant changes in this doctrine which have occurred as a result of changing political and economic circumstances. He also argued for a theoretical revision of contract theory which would be both more relational and contextual.

23. See Sen 1982 on the problem of rights and agency; he attempted to go beyond liberal-utilitarianism by reconsidering the role of social circumstances and position in making choices. Sen's (1983) recent writings have emphasized that

separating the logic of choice from its outcomes cannot be defended; thus the Paretian liberal is impossible. Without doubt, Sen draws a great deal of inspiration from Berlin.

24. Thrift (1983a) made a similar point when reviewing recent developments in structuralism and urban theory.

25. Denial of the relevance of positivists' empirical rule is one of the central arguments of this chapter. Basically, facts cannot stand independent of values, theories, and perspectives; facts have no external existence.

26. The implication of this argument is that words have an innate meaning distinct from interpretation and ascription. Ultimately, for this idea to have any credibility we have to assume words have a physiological origin and that meaning is organically derived. Both of these propositions seem difficult to accept, especially since words like local autonomy have so many different interpretations that depend upon context and position.

27. See Berlin's (1978) argument against the independent status of knowledge—independent, that is, from the conditions of action and decision. His argument, like mine, is contextual and circumstantial since knowledge can only be valued in terms of its capacity to effect outcomes. And outcomes can only be derived from circumstantial positions. Fish (1980) made a similar argument stressing that the value of added information depends on prior conditions—moral and material.

28. Compare Rorty 1982 with Oakeshott 1962.

Chapter 3   Making Law and Interpreting Law

1. Of the massive literature on the courts in American life, the books by Horowitz (1978) on social policy and especially juvenile justice, Orfield (1978) on racial segregation and education, and Baer (1983) on equality and the Fourteenth Amendment are but a small indication of the extent of judicial involvement in contemporary American life. In contrast, for an English perspective on the role of law in modern society, see Atiyah 1983. Lord Scarman, in a review of Atiyah's book (*Times Literary Supplement*, 10 February 1984) noted that the English tradition has been quite different in that the judiciary has resisted attempts to become involved in rights issues.

2. See especially Berger's (1977) argument against judicial activism and the reinterpretation of the Fourteenth Amendment.

3. For a critical assessment of the rhetorical consequences of the rule of law, see the Introduction by Wolff (1971) to his book of the same title. His perspective was formed in the Vietnam War era, and promoted a radical-anarchistic vision of community association. Thus, he was not sympathetic to claims of judicial privilege. See also Ronald Dworkin's essay in the same volume, where he began to sketch an alternative to Hart's (1961) positivist theory of law.

4. There is a conventional distinction in the literature between the interpretation of law and the making of law through radical reinterpretation. The issue is supposed to be a distinction between applying principles and making principles and between applying customary interpretations and introducing new (radical) interpretations. Practically, however, it is very hard to draw a distinction since the judgment of whether an interpretation is customary or radical typically depends on the observer's perspective; see Ely 1980.

5. Unger (1983) provided a critical analysis of legal formalism and its relation to contemporary legal scholarship while Kennedy (1976) provided a more doctrinal analysis. Both authors have been criticized by Ackerman (1984) for being

simply realist, as if the problems of legal formalism have long since been recognized and the real issue is one of moving forward, beyond the rhetoric of law-as-politics. Unger proposed a new critical legal studies movement while Ackerman proposed a constructive movement.

6. Since a fundamental characteristic of capitalism is its wage-labor market, one could argue that this description is an essential underlying characteristic of American capitalism from which other social factors derive. Harvey's (1982) analysis of capitalism is quite similar, especially as regards the significance of property rights.

7. See Hart 1961, pp. 89–91, for a description of his two kinds of rules, a distinction between social obligations and remedies.

8. MacNeil (1981) provided a good discussion of the differences between unilateral and bilateral powers as evidenced in employment contract theory and exchange.

9. This argument depends upon a previous argument made in Clark and Dear 1984, chap. 1, which sought to represent the state as a relatively autonomous social agent.

10. Many people have argued that the courts are the handmaiden of the ruling elite (see Wolff 1971 for just one example). One does not have to be a Marxist to recognize the conservatism of the current court. This issue is of real concern to scholars of various persuasions including Ely (1980).

11. Here I find myself in sympathy with Murdoch's (1983) argument regarding the incompleteness of structure(s), their internal inconsistencies, and partial natures re other competing structures.

12. Compare this description of judges to Devlin's (1979, p. 23) argument that judges are ordinary (if not average) citizens. By ordinary he meant, I believe, highly educated, professional men, not working classes of society. His description would be amusing if it were not so obviously firmly held by the judicial establishment.

13. In this regard, Choper's (1980) argument is not too different from Edmund Burke's in that Burke was most concerned to restrain majoritarian tyranny (as he called it). For a recent review of Burke, see Freeman 1980.

14. The changes in racial attitudes and practices, especially in the South over this period have been nothing short of remarkable. Indeed, there is some irony in the fact that southern schools are thought by some to be now more progressive and racially balanced than their northern counterparts. The Warren Court and the administrations of Johnson and Nixon deserve a great deal of credit for these changes, all of which were based on a fundamental reinterpretation of the civil rights amendments.

15. Posner's (1977) textbook on the neoclassical economics of law is a good place to start for the inquiring researcher.

16. I have applied this argument to national urban policy and the relevance of Reagan's claims that national efficiency should not be comprised by urban policies (Clark 1983a).

17. It is striking that just as Ely (1980) was proclaiming the virtues of participation, the planning profession was voicing dissatisfaction with the realities of citizen participation. Paradoxically, citizen participation can further insulate bureaucracies from open challenge by providing them with a public defense. For instance it might be argued that participation routinizes political disputes, deflects major grievances, and serves to legitimate public institutions—this despite the fact that those involved may be quite sensitive to the potential for co-option.

18. See also Hart 1961, pp. 120–23, where he observed that all rules are, to some extent, open-textured.

19. Again, Hart (1961) followed Austin's conception of words being open-textured and pliable so that meanings are ascribed to words depending on the situation at hand.

20. Here, I follow the state-centered logic of Clark and Dear 1984 and Nordlinger 1981, in which institutions are interpreted as goal-oriented social actors working to ensure their reproduction and power.

21. In the introduction to the special issue of the *Ohio State University Law Journal*, James Meeks (1981) noted the cyclical nature of arguments over the legitimacy of judicial review. I suspect these types of arguments occur and reoccur because of the problematic nature of the judicial role. While I don't find much to agree with in Perry's (1982) defense of judicial review, I do think that he was right to suggest that radical commentators on this debate are "dead wrong" to dismiss the issue as hopelessly muddled and incoherent (see, for instance, Brest 1981). Radicals may be right about the muddled nature of the debate, but this reflects a fundamental structural problem with American democracy which should be recognized as such by radical theorists.

22. In a lecture given at the University of Chicago Law School in February 1984, Raoul Berger went so far as to suggest that original facts can be discovered in, for example, the resolutions of the Founding Fathers of the American Constitution. He used metaphors like exploration to evoke an image of legal inquiry that can find truth in historical documents. He undercut his whole presentation at the end by quoting from Confucius. First he gave the quote and then, as if the words did not contain enough information, indicated what he thought they meant in the current context. Either originalism was not enough even for Berger, or he believed that the Founding Fathers are still alive for him in a way which you and I cannot understand, while Confucius is dead for all of us.

23. Huntington (1981, pp. 2–3) described how he listened to a 1969 Harvard commencement speaker reinterpret American ideals in terms of current practices while nevertheless maintaining and affirming these ideals. Here, student radicals took issue with the dominant meaning of common symbols and language and turned the language inside-out. Few if any radicals disavowed the principle itself, even though it is, practically speaking, empty.

24. See Morris 1982 on the dilemmas of applying precedent to different cases.

25. Tushnet (1983) went over similar issues in his critique of the concept of interpretative neutrality. He noted that neutral interpretivism requires that social institutions and practices be stable and determinant, but, of course, this is just the problem. While we can attempt to contain history through precedent and originalism, it is an impossible task in general.

26. Dworkin 1978 has a good treatment, as does Ely 1980.

Chapter 4   Models of Local Autonomy

1. According to Hardin (1983), the term *consequentialist* describes moral theories that are concerned with the ends of an agent's actions. Thus, process-based theories are not consequentialist, while substantive ends theories are. Anscombe (1958) is credited with first use of the term.

2. Bentham has been a target of criticism by Foucault in recent times, especially for his plan for the Panopticon. Foucault takes Bentham's model prison to be representative of a disciplinary technology—a mechanical domination of others through functionally designed architecture (see Dreyfus and Rabinow

1983, pp. 184–204 for an extended discussion). While Foucault's criticisms are no doubt well-founded, it would be a mistake to dismiss Bentham's contribution to understanding legal structures just because of this issue. Whatever the implied structures of power in his model his theory of discourse provides a useful starting point for analysis.

3. This discussion of Illinois is the basis of a deeper discussion of local autonomy in the state; see chap. 7.

4. Arthur Maass (1959) and his colleagues were interested in extending the notion of separate powers to the geographical arena. Maass suggested that this aspect of the Founding Fathers' image of America has been largely ignored in the academic literature compared with studies of administrative divisions of power. See Clark 1981*a* for a recent treatment of this issue.

5. For an exception to this practice, see T. N. Clark's (1974) attempt to integrate local democratic politics with the federal hierarchy of government structure in the U.S.

6. Nozick's (1981) notion of choice has been subject to a great deal of criticism. For an earlier argument compare the positions taken by Nozick (1974) and MacPherson (1973).

7. Some readers might find it strange that I believe Rawls's theory of justice to be procedural rather than substantive, even though he is famous for his principle that we must help the worst-off in society. I would suggest that this principle derives from a procedural device introduced prior to society and does not have an independent status as a moral right.

8. See also Berlin 1969 for a set of conditions for choice which are contextual as opposed to procedural. I have used these conditions elsewhere to evaluate the efficacy of national urban policy; see Clark 1983*b*.

9. Notice, though, that utopian visions of society need not replicate the map of existing class positions somehow transformed to a higher plane. Utopianism is often based upon altruism and may seek a radical departure from the structures of existing social life; see Davis 1981 for an extended treatment.

10. Power need not be a zero-sum concept. Volition is an important aspect which refers to agency rather than the distribution of influence as if it were just a commodity to be divided among contending parties; see Parsons 1969.

11. I have some doubt about the stability of these categories, since they are just two among a number of other functional descriptions of state activity. Hidden from view is, I suspect, a theory of the state which depends upon an exchange or transactions model of social behavior; see Clark and Dear 1984 for a discussion of other functionalist models of state behavior and the next chapter for an extended treatment of this dispute.

12. Surely a most obvious and traditional democratic model of government functions. Such a functionalist description has been very popular in the academic literature; see Archer 1981 for a treatment of this literature in economics and geography.

13. Yarmolinsky, Liebman, and Schelling 1981 is a testament to the overwhelming influence of the federal and state governments on local policies, particularly with regard to racial segregation and schools.

14. For more details see the case study on local matters in Colorado reported in chap. 8.

15. Ideal types are valuable for two reasons. First, they guide interpretation by identifying the boundaries of such concepts as local autonomy. Second, ideal types are a useful analytical device. But I don't suppose that this typology

describes all options; there will be many different combinations of initiative and immunity set within these dimensions.

16. Tiebout's (1956) model is the basis of most economic models of urban public finance and urban structure in general. Its roots are in Samuelson's (1954) notion of pure economic theory and neoclassical positivism. Bennett's (1980) whole approach to the geography of public finance depends upon its assumptions. The Tiebout model is the heart of mainstream urban public finance.

17. Notice that where I refer to the OMB in subsequent chapters, I will always mean the Ontario Municipal Board, not the U.S. Office of Management and Budget.

18. The capacity of state governments to grant local powers means that state government has tremendous residual powers over local governments. It is a most paternalistic type of arrangement, which requires local government continually to ask for power.

19. These simple contrasts are a quite powerful critique of the Tiebout model just in terms of its claims to realism. This issue will be further explored in chap. 7.

20. O'Malley 1980 provides both a critical assessment of local powers in Illinois and a proposal for the courts to use what he termed a balancing test for adjudication. This proposal is suspect on a number of grounds, most especially the neutrality imputed to the courts and the possibility of identifying true facts which would then create a balance. Like other techniques reviewed in chap. 3, balance is yet another rhetorical device.

21. While much of this chapter deals with the legal autonomy of local government, equally importnt is the issue of fiscal autonomy. For a recent but extensive treatment of this issue in the context of President Reagan's new federalism, see T. N. Clark 1983.

Chapter 5   The Politics of Local Jobs

1. Executive orders do not require debate or approval in the Boston City Council. These orders are administrative actions.

2. Neil Pierce, writing in the *Public Administration Times*, 15 April 1983, suggested that the Boston jobs policy would become particularly popular in large central cities with significant minority populations. And, indeed, cities like Chicago and Philadelphia have experimented with this kind of policy since the election of new city mayors.

3. See, for example, the editorial by *The Boston Globe*, 4 August 1979, supporting the policy and the activities of the Boston Jobs Coalition.

4. Compare Mayor White's pronouncements in March 1983 in community newspapers such as the *Dorchester Argus Citizen*, claiming victory for his policy with his cautious support of the Boston Jobs Coalition's policy in September 1979, as reported in *The Boston Globe*.

5. Much of the historical record of this dispute is culled from a series of interviews with Charles Turner, Paul Kingston, and union representatives during May 1983. Many people were involved over the course of ten years of struggle, and I don't wish to imply that the people mentioned by name in this chapter were the only important actors. On the contrary, their views and opinions should be understood as being representative of many others.

6. Rowan and Rubin (1972) documented the experience of other similar plans in Washington, D.C., and Indianapolis. The federal government was actively involved in many cities during the late 1960s and early 1970s, fostering minority

access to construction unions. Most plans were voluntary and were organized on a tripartite basis, unions, contractors, and community groups.

7. A comment made in a private letter to the Kennedy School of Government, Harvard University. Note that even as far back as 1972, Rowan and Rubin commented that while the Washington Plan had increased black participation in skilled construction employment, "it has not, as yet, assured that negroes will become a permanent part of the work force through union membership" (p. 110).

8. Like the previous plans for minority participation in construction unions, the City of Boston's 1975 policy was voluntary. The city acted as a broker between various community groups, fostering cooperation and discussion rather than enforcing legal requirements. This kind of role has lately been labeled public-private partnerships. See the prospectus of the Boston Private Industry Council, Inc., 110 Tremont St., Boston, Mass., 02108, for a detailed guide to this kind of role in Boston and Fosler and Berger 1982 for a review of other cities' experience.

9. Hanten (1981, pp. 223–26) provides a brief overview of the Boston court-ordered busing crisis and a general review of similar actions in other large U.S. cities during this period. Orfield's (1978) study of court-ordered busing is probably the best in-depth treatment of the issue.

10. There are, in fact, many such statutes that are hardly ever recognized, let alone enforced at both the state and federal levels. Calabresi (1982) noted that the existence of such statutes stems from a departure from common law traditions to a more regulatory conception of lawmaking based upon legislative design. One consequence, though, has been a proliferation of statutes that have relatively short administrative lives but are, nevertheless, kept in place. Calabresi (1982) has called for a return to the common law tradition to avoid what he termed "choking on statutes."

11. Even though the mayor's office was involved in negotiations with the BJC, it was never clear to the mayor's officials that the mayor would actually agree to all elements of the BJC's proposals. For Charles Turner, this negotiation phase was quite frustrating because it was always ambiguous what the final role of the mayor would be.

12. These two policies in combination gave the compliance office new powers and a degree of public credibility, which had been seriously lacking. For many working in this office, the policies were a chance to deliver jobs to those in need in a manner not previously thought possible.

13. Previously, I reviewed the evidence and doctrine regarding the geography of the Commerce Clause and noted that it has been a major tool in integrating, economically speaking, the spatial economy (Clark 1981b). To an extent, I overemphasized the importance of this clause implicitly following a logic not too different from Kingston's. But see also a recent paper by Easterbrook (1983) along these same lines.

14. Kingston implied in his argument that Dillon's (1911) rule applied in the interpretation of Boston's powers vis-à-vis the Commonwealth of Massachusetts.

15. Quotations from Tribe's argument are based on the text of his presentation which is on file at the Harvard Law School.

16. The U.S. Justice Department moved in recent times to quell the spread of this kind of policy. As reported in *The Wall Street Journal*, 6 March 1984, the department has joined a group of contractors in challenging the right of Dade County (Florida) to set aside a certain portion of construction contracts for minority businesses. Boston has used similar policy for a number of years and has linked it to the jobs policy.

17. Not all such policies have met with success. The Pittsburgh City Council passed a plant-closing ordinance in 1983 using its home rule charter, requiring notification of plant closings within its jurisdiction. While popular with the general public, it was ruled unconstitutional by the Court of Common Pleas on the grounds that it violated the Commerce Clause (among other clauses of the U.S. Constitution). The circumstances in Pittsburgh were much worse than Boston, and other cities and states have passed similar legislation. Yet, in this case, the court held to a conservative and absolute reading of the clause. See for a note on this case *The New York Times*, 21 August 1983. McKenzie (1984) has provided a more scholarly review of much the same issue, but from a conservative economists' perspective. *The New York Times*, 4 March 1984, p. F15 reviewed this book as a contribution to the "corporate bookshelf." Compare McKenzie to the more radical argument by Bluestone and Harrison (1982).

Chapter 6   The Structure of Land-Use Adjudication

1. This is not to say that there has been no other tradition in the theory and practice of community life. Kanter (1972) provided a sociological account of communes and utopias stressing their commitment to family and social association. Thomas (1983) has given an historical perspective on the writings of the alternative tradition, including the works of Henry George and Edward Bellamy. And, for an account of contemporary neighborhood life, see Crenson 1983. All these theorists though, write with reference to the liberal tradition, even if in opposition.

2. While Canada has a quite different history, found in its institutions and landscape, it is nevertheless very much a part of the American economic system. See Mercer 1979 on the similarities and differences between the two countries in the urban context.

3. As expressed through the Ontario Municipal Board (OMB) the province has responsibility for local government actions.

4. The Canadian judicial system is nominally based on English common law, although Quebec maintains the French continental system. In Ontario however, statute interpretation has become a very important aspect of judicial activity, a factor entirely consistent with the American experience.

5. Indeed, Nozick (1974) is quite deliberately normative in his assessment of the logic of decentralized democracy. A purely technical approach to the functions of local government is more consistent with an apparatuslike model of local autonomy than a moral conception of the proper arrangement of society. See again chap. 4 on the rationale for different models of local autonomy.

6. See T. N. Clark 1983 on the fiscal dimensions of local autonomy and Clark and Dear 1984, chap. 7, on fiscal autonomy in Massachusetts.

7. Notice that I retain the importance of ideology as a moral statement of proper social structure because I believe it to be an essential aspect of social life. In contrast to more economically oriented theorists, I suppose that reality has no independent theoretical status apart from how we interpret it in specific circumstances. Thus, I cannot agree with Sheppard (1981), who suggested that ideology merely screens our appreciation of the reality of geographical and social stratification.

8. This discussion of liberal formalism is based on Unger 1983 and his notion of liberal legal discourse.

9. Mind you, knowing the formal arrangement of powers does not mean that we will be able to provide an unambiguous link between structures and outcomes.

The problem with formalism is its indeterminacy; this is true for legal interpretation and social theory in general. See Quine 1953 and compare with my earlier work in Clark and Dear 1984.

10. Discussion of the structure, history, and character of Ontario local government is based on Gertler 1981.

11. See Mercer and Goldberg 1983 and Mercer 1982 for more details on Canadian urban finance compared to the U.S.

12. Objections to local zoning ordinances reach OMB through either of two channels. First, the OMB approves any zoning bylaw or bylaw that repeals a zoning bylaw, unless the municipality has a master plan in effect and no person files a notice of objection; Planning Act, Ont. Rev. Stat., chap. 349, sec. 35 (9, 10, 25), 1970. Second, if the local council refuses to consider or enact an amendment proposed to the council, the applicant may appeal to the OMB; Planning Act, Ont. Rev. Stat., chap. 349, sec. 35 (22), 1970.

13. Where any person requests the council to initiate an amendment to the official plan and the council (a) refuses to propose the amendment or (b) fails to propose the amendment within thirty days from receipt of request, such person may request the minister to refer the proposal to the municipal board; Planning Act, Ont. Rev. Stat., chap. 349, sec. 17 (3), 1970. The minister "may refuse the request or refer to the Municipal Board"; Planning Act, Ont. Rev. Stat., chap. 349, sec. 17 (4), 1970.

14. I do not intend that these cases should be taken as illustrating the entire set of possible questions of adjudication and jurisdiction. Rather they are "hard cases," instances where conventional rules, precedent, and accepted practice do not provide an adequate guide to their resolution. As Dworkin (1978) suggested, hard cases reflect upon the coherence of the whole and thus are internal tests of the structure of theory. Notice that Unger (1983) refers to hard cases when he analyzes "exemplary" cases.

15. Planning Act, Ont. Rev. Stat., chap. 349, sec. 35 (22), 1970.

16. Planning Act, Ont. Rev. Stat., chap. 349, sec. 14 (2), 1970.

17. Fish also made this point where "facts can only be known by persons, and persons are always situated in some institutional context relative and do not have a form independent of the structure of interest within which they emerge into noticeability" (1982a, p. 497).

18. Fish (1980) argued that "interpretive communities" are socially conceived associations that define what constitutes scholarship, critical enquiry, and even adjudication (as in this instance). The rules of creating interpretations need not be explicitly stated, for their logic comes from the acceptance of certain social conventions and, ultimately, a world view, both of which are clearly a product of social position. The crudest conception of this image would be of judges who come from distinct class backgrounds, schools, and training. But interpretative communities are more than simple instrumental products of social structuration; there are many "interpretative communities," all vying for dominance. Social thought is a process, an organized social function.

Chapter 7   The Tensions of Urban Public Service Provision

1. See the various Census of Government of the U.S. Department of Commerce for more details of the sources of revenue of the Sanitary District, as well as the pattern of expenditures over the relevant period of time.

2. For details on how government policy affects the form and structure of urban areas, see Pollakowski 1973 on property taxes and land values and Stone

1978 for an institutional perspective. While economic theorists like Pollakowski probably believe the impact of government policy to be unintended or at least not self-serving, radical theorists believe that public sector impact is deliberate and structured.

3. An unnamed source interviewed in Chicago in early 1984.

4. Compare Clark and Dear 1984 and Nordlinger 1981 on state-centered theories with Johnston 1979 on society-centered theories of local government. Not all society-centered theories need be liberal, as not all state-centered theories need be radical. Which perspective is used depends, I believe, on more general methodological issues, such as how we should evaluate the role of institutions in society. Throughout this book the state-centered mode of enquiry is emphasized and is based on the argument in chap. 1 regarding heterogeneity and indeterminacy.

5. For a recent critique of this position from a liberal legal theorist, see Ackerman 1984. Critical legal theorists have also attacked this conception with extraordinary vigor; see Kennedy 1981. Both Kennedy and Ackerman find economic positivism a real threat to the moral integrity of legal adjudication. Ackerman believed Kennedy to be simply re-expressing the old realist position, but Unger (1983) has attempted to distance himself and Kennedy from this position. See also Posner 1985 and Tribe 1985 for contending blueprints for the revision of American legal practice, couservative and liberal revisionist, respectively.

6. For a detailed review of the public-choice literature, see Mueller 1979. Notice that Sen and Williams (1982) have been very critical of this perspective from the relativist philosophical position.

7. It would be misleading to suggest that this is a failure of public-choice models. Few attempts have been made to analyze the origins of preferences; it is enough for public-choice theorists to assume preferences exist even if only dimly perceived by individuals. Sen (1983) has been more critical than most regarding the shallow moral basis of neoclassical public choice models. Similarly, Arrow (1983) has recognized that not all choice models need be so bare of normative and moral characteristics.

8. For a standard treatment of Hotelling's "problem," see Lloyd and Dicken's 1977 textbook on location theory.

9. I assume efficiency means least cost in this context; see Buchanan's 1969 seminal treatment of neoclassical public-choice theory and its basis is conventional interpretations of efficiency and optimality. As was noted previously (chap. 3), however, efficiency can have many different images; indeed, it is as empty as local autonomy (compare Buchanan 1969 with Dworkin 1980a).

10. That is, local governments are assumed to have one basic objective function, one related to maximizing return on their efforts. This model is very similar to Downs's 1957 economic theory of bureaucracy.

11. Indeed, it should be recognized that Bennett's 1980 objective is to provide a positivist rationale for normative ideals regarding the proper design of our local government institutions. Unlike some theorists of local public finance, he does not assume the positive and normative to be totally divorced from one another.

12. Tiebout's model does not allow for social motives, like association for interaction and moral support. The limit on jurisdictional fragmentation is, for Tiebout, ultimately efficiency. But if so, this also means that choice is itself conditional, even irrelevant in some cases. This issue has not been explored in the literature, despite its undemocratic implications.

13. Ackerman (1984) noted that the Chicago school's claims for the virtues of

wealth maximization and pareto optimality are naive. As a single decision variable, this criterion begs other relevant issues like the relative equality of people. We can easily imagine circumstances where the pareto rule would bring about conditions which were not desirable (see Ackerman for details). Despite their belief in this principle, the Chicago school's objective function is not at all as consensual as they would suppose.

14. See also Lord Devlin's (1979) claim about the virtues of ordinary men. A close reading of his definition would seem to suggest that an ordinary man has a university degree (preferably from Oxford or Cambridge), has a professional job, and lives in Hampstead Heath. A similar observation could no doubt be made about what an equivalent ordinary American man would look like!

15. Clark 1983a was based on a critique and reconceptualization of current conservative policy options that would maximize national growth as represented in variables such as the gross national product, without regard to the urban and social impact of such policies. But, even here, it is not particularly clear what national wealth means in these circumstances, apart from the most crude idea of maximizing U.S. power in the world today.

16. See Arrow 1983 for an analysis of welfare economics that attempts to take seriously the implications of distribution and the relevance of compensation rules. The Kaldor-Hicks criterion seems all well and good in theory; its practical relevance seems, nevertheless, very doubtful.

17. This section is based on Gertler 1981.

18. See Yates 1977 on the institutional incapacity of U.S. local governments, especially as regards their powers and dependence upon higher tiers of government. The irony of municipal fragmentation is that its origins lie with state-level legislation, as the powerlessness of local governments similarly depends upon state-level policies.

Chapter 8   The Doctrine of Local Matters

1. Instability of doctrine need not be considered a bad thing, or even something which can be practically avoided. However, in terms of the doctrine of local matters considered here, instability of doctrine questions the whole integrity of judicial decision making because of the claims of the judiciary for substantive neutrality through the application of principles to disputes. Instability of adjudication questions the very possibility of such neutrality claims.

2. De Tocqueville was not predisposed in favor of American democracy. Coming from France and the ruling elite, he held an image of mass democracy based on recent French history. Taub and Taub 1974 provides a useful overview of de Tocqueville's background and motivations.

3. This kind of liberalism is still very much alive in American political culture, even today. Nozick's (1974) theory of liberalism is replete with arguments and ideals which could as easily be traced to Locke and de Tocqueville. Similarly, the whole natural rights thesis, depends upon a Lockean liberal conception of the ultimate centrality of the individual in society. For an historical review of the origins of the rights thesis, see Tuck 1979.

4. In this manner, de Tocqueville's model of government has many elements in common with Nozick 1974—a model of local association based upon consent and residency. From there on, higher tiers of the state are derived, not imposed. In this regard, the model implied is closest to type 2, decentralized liberalism, as noted in chap. 4.

5. Compare de Tocqueville with Warner 1968, especially as regards the latter's

critical assessment of liberalism and private interests (see also chap. 2 for more details).

6. The idea of local institutions as natural laboratories of socialization and experiment is pervasive through past and recent writers on American democracy. At the most abstract level, this idea provides a rationale for federalism and the spatial separation of powers (see the volume edited by A. Maass [1959] for an expansive version). Most concretely, it provides a practical rationale for local public goods, especially education (see Finch and Nagel 1984 on the doctrine and Johnson 1979 on the economics of local school districts in Connecticut and Wisconsin, respectively).

7. De Tocqueville was not overly optimistic regarding the likely future coherence of American democracy. He recognized that there were internal factors, like the power of other "less educated" regions to force revisions in the New England model, as well as external factors, like the continuing emigration of European working classes to America (see, again, Taub and Taub 1974).

8. Implied here is an expansive definition of local initiative and a narrow definition of state-level initiative. It would be like applying Dillon's rule to the state-level as opposed to local governments. Or, put another way, it would be like inverting the apparatus model of local government (see chap. 4) so that the state was the apparatus, not local governments.

9. Compare Tiebout 1956 and Samuelson 1954 on this issue.

10. Notice that Clark 1983a was based on Berlin's (1969) contextually-based model of the conditions of choice wherein circumstances make choice, as much as choice defined the proper circumstances for choicelike actions.

11. By modern, I simply mean that form of liberalism concerned with maintaining the rights of individuals against encroaching society. Gewirth 1978 probably best typifies this kind of approach.

12. See, for example, Hart 1961 on the positive theory of law, and a recent defense by Raz (1979) against Dworkin (1972).

13. Indeed, I would suggest that a major theme in the judicial literature is the rationalization of judgment and experience in terms of the virtues of consistency and coherence. What writers such as Richards (1981) seek is a routine procedural model of experience which somehow makes judgment a noncontroversial aspect of *good* adjudication. The idea is to transform the exceptional issue into routine practice.

14. For Quine 1953, there will be many, many interpretations of empirical observations which would reasonably fit theoretical expectations. The problem then becomes ruling out the many competitors. Here, however, some other rule is needed which would make determinant the indeterminant.

15. See Richard Rorty 1982 on the theory of pragmatism. Notice that Quine's conclusion was quite appropriate for his interpretative position, being from the American university (Harvard) which was the intellectual home of pragmatism. This theme of philosophical inquiry is almost exclusively found in the U.S.

16. I would suggest, in fact, that the sentiment behind home rule in Colorado is very strong when compared, for example, with Illinois. In the former state, it has a strong image in judicial decision making, so much so that it seems to have the status of presumption. In the latter state, as we saw in the previous chapter, home rule was hardly taken seriously by the courts.

17. In terms of the logic of chap. 4, I would locate the Colorado situation closer to type 3 than type 4, that is, closer to that kind of local government which is the result of representative democracy than simply Dillon's rule.

18. See Fish 1982b on Austin and Derrida.

Chapter 9   Local Autonomy in Contemporary Society

1. In point of fact, Geertz (1983, p. 184–85) suggested that law is just like any other language or symbol system—conceived in society and structured by institutions. He argued that law is neither a wholly autonomous self-contained system of rules, nor the exclusive domain of the ruling classes (p.214). Thus, we need not raise law above everyday discourse nor assail it as something uniquely evil.

2. Nelson Goodman (1978, 1984) also suggested that claims for such exclusive determincy are the closest we come to "the fundamental lie."

3. Tooke argued that rules derive from principles in some logical and determinant fashion. Tooke's analysis is just like those of contemporary theorists who hold to the positivist theory of law (see Raz 1979 for a series of essays on this theme).

4. By "reasonable," I only mean coherent and perhaps convincing. Both standards of reasonableness depend upon the reader's own interpretation of my argument, so I am willing to accept that some readers found my interpretation unreasonable.

5. Specifically, Geertz (1983, p. 215) suggested law "is local knowledge; local not just as to place, time, class, and variety of issue, but as to accent—vernacular characterizations of what happens connected to vernacular imaginings of what can."

6. Much of my analysis, though, was based on the liberal interpretation of these terms and its representation in the various disputes over local autonomy. Liberalism is just not an idealogy that can be picked up or set aside at will; it is also a method of social analysis. Thus, while Canadians might not identify themselves as liberals in an American sense, their institutional arrangements imply a formal commitment to liberalism's central propositions.

7. I would also suggest, however, that there can be no one-to-one determinant correspondence between princple and circumstances. Quine (1953) identified, perhaps unwillingly, a fundamental limit to positivism—a limit which shows no sign of being overcome. It is likely that Quine finds this disturbing and unfortunate (see Romanos 1983 for a critical and sympathetic reading of Quine's work), while Goodman (1984) has taken Quine's analysis to heart.

8. Compare this description of judicial decision making to Devlin's (1979) model of reasoned and authoritative decision making.

9. In many states, the legislature is barred from passing rules which would be applicable to one local government unit. Broad categories such as population size are the most common mode of classifying urban areas (see Dear and Clark 1981 for a related discussion of the Massachusetts case).

10. Geertz (1983, p. 217) also suggested that the courts depend upon muddle as much as order for their power. And, in the terms of my discussion, this kind of social disorder is very much part of the claims of the judiciary for its legitimacy. To my mind at least, Geertz did not give adequate recognition to this issue, what I have described throughout the book as social heterogeneity.

11. Again, it should be emphasized that my conception of relativism should not be confused with nihilism. Like Barnes and Bloor (1982), I suppose that all moral claims have an equal claim to credibility. How these claims are then ordered depends upon how we decide to order them; as Wittgenstein (1953, para. 241) suggested, truth is designed by us, not found in nature.

12. Castells's (1984) argument is quite similar to Suttles's (1972) in that both depend upon communitarian notions of social life, as opposed to the atomism of liberalism.

13. See, for example, Taylor's (1982) reconceptualization of the liberal theory of community in contrast to Nozick 1974.

14. Of the few recent instances where a society has sought to restructure itself along socialist lines, and provide for significant local autonomy, the Portuguese example deserves special mention. Their new constitution deliberately carves out a sphere of local initiative which is considered consistent with local interests. Localities have autonomy to the extent to which their actions are consistent with national goals. Deviations away from national goals are, however, considered illegal and can be appealed to higher tiers of the state. In such a pluralist-socialist state it is easy to imagine that there is considerable conflict, local and national, over the meanings of local initiative and national goals-determinacy would need to be imposed, even here (Blaustein and Flanz 1977).

15. Westen (1982) suggested, like Rae et al. (1981), that the notion of equality is so empty to be capable of many different interpretations, depending upon the circumstances. See also Greenawalt's (1983) critique and the replies by Westen (1983a, b). This is, I believe, a relatively simple claim, being quite consistent with the tenor of this book.

16. See, for example, the short-lived move to citywide school busing which sought to cross school district boundaries and reintegrate the schools of children left behind (overwhelmingly black).

17. I would suggest that theorists like Habermas (1984) have a very similar idea in mind when discussing the limits of communication. In my view, Habermas maintains that language has a very specific structure which systematically excludes multiple interpretations. Language is then an instrument of domination. While I would agree that rhetoric is a very useful strategy, as has been shown previously; I would, nevertheless, contend that language is indeterminant by itself. Domination comes from those who would deny the open texture of social principles.

18. On this point compare Goodman 1978 with Derrida 1982. The former writer believes structures to be shallow, partial, and incomplete. Derrida, on the other hand, believes structures to be deep, determinant, and coherent.

19. See Thrift's (1983b) editorial on contextualism and Murdoch's (1983) argument concerning the rumble jumble of everyday life.

20. Fish (1982b) provides another example of the importance of context by referring to a most commonplace phrase in academic circles "with the compliments of the author." Fish was quite taken with this phrase, but probably exhausts the example within the first few pages.

21. Lukes (1982, pp. 262–63) noted that this concept originates with Davidson (1980) wherein, according to Lukes, "one should be maximally charitable in assigning truth conditions across the indicative sentences of the language which are held true by those being interpreted."

22. Lukes (1982, p. 264) attributed this principle to Grandy (1973); it minimizes the possibility of unintelligibility and is more a pragmatic device than a formal statement.

23. On the conservative side, see Choper 1980 for an argument about the failures of contemporary politics. More radically, I have argued elsewhere that consumption politics has replaced moral claims as the basis of governmental legitimacy—local, state level, and national (Clark and Dear 1984, chap. 8).

Cases Cited

Baldwin v. Seelig, 294 US 511 (1935)

Borough of Scarborough and Minister of Housing for Ontario et al., 67 DLR 3d 387 (Ont. Div. Ct. 1976)

Cadillac Development Corp. Ltd. et al. and City of Toronto, 39 DLR 3d 188 (Ont. 1973)

Canon City v. Merris, 137 Colo. 169, 323 P2d 614 (1958)

City of Aurora v. Martin, 181 Colo. 72, 507 P2d 868 (1973)

City and County of Denver v. Hallett, 34 Colo. 393, 83 P. 1066 (1905)

City and County of Denver v. Henry, 95 Colo. 582, 38 P2d 895 (1934)

City and County of Denver v. Sweet, 138 Colo. 41, 329 P2d 441 (1958)

City and County of Denver v. Tiben, 77 Colo. 212, 235 P. 777 (1925)

City of Des Plaines v. Metropolitan San. Dist., 124 Ill. App 2d 301 (1970)

City of Des Plaines v. Metropolitan Sanitary Dist., 48 Ill. 2d 11, 268 NE2d 428 (1971)

City of Des Plaines v. Metropolitan San. Dist., 16 Ill. App 3d 23 (1973)

City of Des Plaines v. Metropolitan S.D. of G. Chicago, 59 Ill. 2d 29, 319 NE2d 9 (1974)

City of Philadelphia v. New Jersey, 437 US 617 (1978)

Commonwealth v. Hana, 195 Mass. 262, 81 NE 149 (1907)

Davis v. City and County of Denver, 140 Colo. 30, 342 P2d 674 (1959)

Decatur Park Dist. v. Becker, 368 Ill. 442, 14 NE2d 490 (1938)

Delong v. City and County of Denver, Colo. 576 P2d 1308 (1978)

Exxon Corp. v. Governor of Maryland, 98 S. Ct. 2207 (1978)

Fishel v. City and County of Denver, 106 Colo. 576, 108 P2d 236 (1940)

Heft v. Zoning Board of Appeals of Peoria County, 31 Ill. 2d 266, 201 NE2d 364 (1964)

Hicklin v. Orbeck, 98 S. Ct. 2482 (1978)

Hills v. Gautreaux, 425 US 284 (1976)

H. P. Hood & Sons Ltd. v. DuMond, 336 US 525 (1949)

Hughes v. Alexandria Scrap Corp., 426 US 794 (1976)

Hunter v. City of Pittsburgh, 207 US 161 (1907)

Local 24, Teamsters v. Oliver, 362 US 605 (1959)

Mauff v. People, 52 Colo. 562, 123 P. 101 (1912)

Metro. San. Dist. of Chicago v. City of Des Plaines, 63 Ill. 2d 256, 347 NE2d 716 (1976)

Milheim v. Moffatt Tunnel Improvement District, 211 P. 649 (1922)

Munn v. Illinois, 94 US 113 (1877)

National League of Cities v. Usery, 426 US 833 (1976)

North Carolina v. Califano, 98 S. Ct. 1597 (1978)

Paul v. Virginia, 75 US (8 Wall.) 168 (1869)

People v. Graham, 107 Colo. 202, 110 P2d 256 (1941)

Pierce v. City and County of Denver, 193 Colo. 347, 565 P2d 1337 (1977)

Pike v. Bruce Church, Inc., 397 US 137 (1970)

Ray v. City and County of Denver, 109 Colo. 74, 121 P2d 886 (1942)

Reeves Inc. v. Stake, 447 US 429, 65 L.Ed2d 244 (1980)

Ronda Realty Corp. v. Lawton, 414 Ill. 313, 111 NE2nd 310 (1953)

Salla v. County of Monroe, 423 NYS2d 878 (1979)

Schad et al. v. Borough of Mount Ephraim, 452 US 61 (1981)

Southern Pacific Co. v. Arizona, 325 US 761 (1945)

Toomer v. Witsell, 334 US 385 (1948)

209 Lake Shore Drive Bldg. Corp. v. City of Chicago, 3 Ill. App. 3d 46, 278
   NE2nd 216 (1971)

United States v. Butler, 297 US 1 (1936)

United States v. City of Chicago, 411 F. Supp. 218, ND Ill. (1976)

Vela v. People, 174 Colo. 465, 484 P2d 1204 (1971)

Village of Schiller Park v. City of Chicago, 26 Ill. 2d 278, 186 NE2d 343
   (1962)

White v. Mass. Council of Constr. Employers, 103 S. Ct. 1042 (1983)

Wisconsin v. Yoder et al., 406 US 205 (1972)

Woolverton v. City and County of Denver, 146 Colo. 247, 361 P2d 982 (1961)

Bibliography

Ackerman, B. A. 1984. *Reconstructing American law*. Cambridge, Mass.: Harvard University Press.

Adler, G. M. 1971. *Land planning by administrative regulation: The policies of the Ontario Municipal Board*. Toronto: University of Toronto Press.

Althusser, L. 1971. *Lenin and philosophy and other essays*. New York: Monthly Review Press.

Anscombe, G. 1958. Modern moral philosophy. *Philosophy* 33:1–19.

Archer, J. C. 1981. Public choice paradigms in political geography. In *Political studies from spatial perspectives*, ed. A. Burnett and P. J. Taylor. New York: J. Wiley.

Aristotle. 1982. *The politics*, trans. T. A. Sinclair. New York: Penguin Books.

Arrow, K. 1953. *Social choice and individual values*. New Haven, Conn.: Yale University Press.

————.1981. Introduction: the social choice perspective. *Hofstra Law Review* 9:1373–80.

————. 1983. *The collected papers of Kenneth Arrow*, Vol 1: *Social choice and justice*. Cambridge, Mass.: Harvard University Press.

Atiyah, P. S. 1981. *Promises, morals and law*. Oxford: Clarendon Press.

————. 1983. *Law and modern society*. Oxford: Oxford University Press.

Auld, D. A. L. 1977. Fiscal dimensions of provincial-local government relations in Ontario. In *Issues and alternatives, 1977: Intergovernmental relations*. Toronto: Ontario Economic Council.

Austin, J. L. 1975. *How to do things with words*. 3d ed. Cambridge, Mass.: Harvard University Press.

Ayer, A. J. 1956. *The problem of knowledge*. Harmondsworth: Penguin Books.

Baer, J. A. 1983. *Equality under the constitution: Reclaiming the Fourteenth Amendment*. Ithaca, N.Y.: Cornell University Press.

Barnes, B., and D. Bloor 1982. Relativism, rationalism, and the sociology of knowledge. In *Rationality and relativism*, ed. M. Hollis and S. Lukes. Cambridge, Mass.: MIT Press.

Barry, B., and R. Hardin, eds. 1982. *Rational man and irrational society?* Beverly Hills, Calif.: Sage Publications.

Bennett, R. J. 1980. *The goegraphy of public finance*. London: Methuen.

Bentham, J. 1970. *Of laws in general*, ed. H. L. A. Hart. London: University of London, Athlone Press.

Berger, R. 1977. *Government by judiciary: The transformation of the Fourteenth Amendment*. Cambridge, Mass.: Harvard University Press.

Berlin, I. 1969. *Four essays on liberty*. Oxford: Oxford University Press.

231

――――. 1978. *Concepts and categories*, ed. H. Hardy with an introduction by B. Williams. Harmondsworth: Penguin.

――――. 1982. *Against the current*. Harmondsworth: Penguin.

Bernstein, R. J. 1983. *Beyond objectivism and relativism*. Philadelphia: University of Pennsylvania Press.

Bhaskar, R. 1979. *The possibility of naturalism: A philosophical critique of the contemporary human sciences*. Atlantic Highlands, N. J.: Humanities Press.

Blaustein, A. P., and G. H. Flanz. 1977. *Constitutions of the countries of the world: Portugal 1974–1977*. Dobbs Ferry, N.Y.: Oceana Publications.

Bluestone, B., and B. Harrison. 1982. *The deindustrialization of America*. New York: Basic Books.

Bourdieu, P. 1983. The philosophical institution. In *Philosophy in France today*, ed. A. Montefiore. Cambridge: Cambridge University Press.

Bowles, S., D. M. Gordon, and T. E. Weisskopf. 1983. *Beyond "The Waste Land": A democratic alternative to economic decline*. New York: Anchor Press.

Brest, P. 1980. The misconceived quest for the original understanding. *Boston University Law Review* 60:204–38.

――――. 1981. The fundamental rights controversy: The essential contradictions of normative constitutional scholarship. *Yale Law Journal* 90:1063–1109.

――――. 1982. Interpretation and interest. *Stanford Law Review* 34:765–73.

Buchanan, J. M. 1969. *Cost and choice: An inquiry in economic theory*. Chicago: University of Chicago Press.

Burns, M. 1983. The exclusion of women from influential men's clubs: The inner sanctum and the myth of full equality. *Harvard Civil Rights–Civil Liberties Law Review* 18:321–407.

Calabresi, G. 1982. *A common law for the age of statutes*. Cambridge, Mass.: Harvard University Press.

Calabresi, G., and A. D. Melamed. 1972. Property rules, liability rules, and inalienability: One view of the cathedral. *Harvard Law Review* 85:1089–1128.

Castells, M. 1977. *The urban question*. Cambridge, Mass.: MIT Press.

――――. 1978. *City, class and power*, trans. E. Lebas. London: Macmillan.

――――. 1983. Crisis, planning, and the quality of life: Managing the new historical relationships between space and society. *Environment and Planning D: Society and Space* 1:3–21.

――――. 1984. *The city and the grass roots*. London: Ed. Arnold.

Cavell, S. 1979. *The claim of reason*. Oxford: Oxford University Press.

Chesler, R. D. 1983. Imagery of community, ideology of authority: The moral reasoning of Chief Justice Burger. *Harvard Civil Rights–Civil Liberties Law Review* 18:457–82.

Choper, J. H. 1980. *Judicial review and the national political process*. Chicago: University of Chicago Press.

Chouinard, V., and R. Fincher. 1983. A critique of "Structural Marxism and human geography." *Annals, Association of American Geographers* 73:137–45.

Clark, G. L. 1979. Predicting the regional impact of full employment policy in Canada: A Box-Jenkins approach. *Economic Geography* 55:213–26.

――――. 1981a. Democracy and the capitalist state: Towards a critique of the Tiebout hypothesis. In *Political studies from spatial perspectives*, ed. A. D. Burnett and P. J. Taylor. New York: J. Wiley & Sons.

――――. 1981b. Law, the state, and the spatial integration of the United States. *Environment and Planning A* 13:1197–1232.

――――. 1982. Rights, property, and community. *Economic Geography* 59: 120–38.

————. 1983*a*. *Interregional migration: National policy and social justice*. Totowa, N.J.: Rowman & Allanheld.

————. 1983*b*. Spatial labor markets and the distribution of transaction costs. *Environment and Planning D: Society and Space* 1:305–22.

————. 1984. A theory of local autonomy. *Annals, Association of American Geographers* 74:195–208.

Clark, G. L., and M. Dear. 1984. *State apparatus: Structures and language of legitimacy*. London: George Allen & Unwin.

Clark, T. N. 1974. Community autonomy in the national system: Federalism, localism, and decentralization. *Social Science Information* 12:101–28.

————. 1983. Local fiscal dynamics under old and new federalisms. *Urban Affairs Quarterly* 19:55–74.

Coase, R. 1960. The problem of social cost. *Journal of Law and Economics* 3:1–44.

Coleman, J. 1980. Efficiency, utility, and wealth maximization. *Hofstra Law Review* 8:509–52.

Commission on an Agenda for the Eighties. 1980. *Urban America in the eighties*. Washington, D.C.: Government Printing Office.

Cornelius, J. 1972. *Constitution-making in Illinois, 1818–1970*. Urbana: University of Illinois Press.

Cornford, F. Mac. 1941. *The republic of Plato*. Oxford: Clarendon Press.

Couclelis, H., and R. Golledge. 1983. Analytic research, positivism, and behavioral geography. *Annals, Association of American Geographers* 73:331–39.

Crenson, M. A. 1983. *Neighborhood politics*. Cambridge, Mass.: Harvard University Press.

Dahl, R. A. 1956. *A preface to democratic theory*. Chicago: University of Chicago Press.

————. 1982. *Dilemmas of pluralist democracy: Autonomy vs. control*. New Haven, Conn.: Yale University Press.

Davidson, D. 1980. *Essays on actions and events*. Oxford: Clarendon Press.

Davis, J. C. 1981. *Utopia and the ideal society: A study of English utopian writing, 1516–1700*. Cambridge: Cambridge University Press.

Dear, M. 1981. The public city. In *Residential mobility and public policy*, ed. W. A. V. Clark and E. Moore. Beverly Hills, Calif.: Sage Publications.

Dear, M., and G. L. Clark, 1981. Dimensions of local state autonomy. *Environment and Planning A* 13:1277–94.

Derrida, J. 1982. *Margins of philosophy*, trans. with additional notes by A. Bass. Chicago: University of Chicago Press.

Devlin, P. 1979. *The judge*. Chicago: University of Chicago Press.

Dillon, J. 1911. *Commentaries on the law of municipal corporations* 5th ed. Boston, Mass.: Little, Brown & Co.

Downs, A. 1957. *An economic theory of democracy*. New York: Harper & Row.

Dreyfus, H., and P. Rabinow. 1983. *Michel Foucault: Beyond structuralism and hermeneuties*, with an Afterword by M. Foucault. 2d ed. Chicago: University of Chicago Press.

Dummett, M. 1978. *Truth and other enigmas*. Cambridge, Mass.: Harvard University Press.

Duncan, J., and D. Ley. 1982. Structural marxism and human geography: A critical assessment. *Annals, Association of American Geographers* 72:30–59.

Dworkin, R. 1971. Philosophy and the critique of law. In *The rule of law*, ed. R. P. Wolff. New York: Simon & Schuster.

————. 1972. Social rules and legal theory. *Yale Law Journal* 81:855–90.

————. 1978. *Taking rights seriously*. Cambridge, Mass.: Harvard University Press.

————. 1980*a*. Is wealth a value? *Journal of Legal Studies* 9:191–242.

————. 1980*b*. Why efficiency? *Hofstra Law Review* 8:563–90.

————. 1982. Law as interpretation. *Texas Law Review*. 60:527–50.

Easterbrook, F. H. 1983. Antitrust and the economics of federalism. *Journal of Law and Economics* 26:23–50.

Eldridge, J. E. T., ed. 1971. *Max Weber: The interpretation of social reality*. New York: Schocken Books.

Elster, J. 1983. *Sour grapes: Studies in the subversion of rationality*. Cambridge: Cambridge University Press.

Ely, J. H. 1980. *Democracy and distrust: A theory of judicial review*. Cambridge, Mass.: Harvard University Press.

The Federalist Papers. Introduction by C. Rossiter. New York: Mentor, 1961.

Finch, M., and T. Nagel. 1984. Education policy and labor relations in Connecticut. Mimeo, Harvard Law School, Cambridge, Mass.

Fincher, R. 1983. The inconsistency of eclecticism. *Environment and Planning A*. 15:607–22.

Fish, S. 1980. *Is there a text in this class? The authority of interpretive communities*. Cambridge, Mass.: Harvard University Press.

————. 1982*a*. Interpretation and the pluralist vision. *Texas Law Review* 60:495–506.

————. 1982*b*. With the compliments of the author: Reflections on Austin and Derrida. *Critical Inquiry* 8:693–721.

————. 1983. Fish vs. Fiss. Mimeo. Department of English, Johns Hopkins University, Baltimore, Md.

Fiss, O. 1982. Objectivity and interpretation. *Stanford Law Review* 34:739–63.

Fosler, R. S., and R. A. Berger, eds. 1982. *Public-private partnership in American cities*. Lexington, Mass.: D. C. Heath.

Foucault, M. 1977. *Language, counter-memory, and practice*. Ithaca, N.Y.: Cornell University Press.

Freeman, M. 1980. *Edmund Burke and the critique of political radicalism*. Chicago: University of Chicago Press.

Fried, C. 1983. Liberalism, community, and the objectivity of values. *Harvard Law Review* 96:960–68.

Friedmann, J. 1979. *The good society*. Cambridge, Mass.: MIT Press.

Frug, G. E. 1980. The city as a legal concept. *Harvard Law Review* 93:1057–1154.

Geertz, C. 1983. *Local knowledge: Further essays in interpretive anthropology*. New York: Basic Books.

Gertler, M. 1981. Local autonomy and land policy in Canada and Ontario. Mimeo. Ph.D. Program in Urban Planning, Harvard University, Cambridge, Mass.

Gewirth, A. 1978. *Reason and morality*. Chicago: University of Chicago Press.

Giddens, A. 1981. *A contemporary critique of historical materialism*. Berkeley: University of California Press.

Glazer, N. 1981. Race and the suburbs. In *Race and schooling in the city*, ed. A. Yarmolinsky, L. Liebman, and C. Schelling. Cambridge, Mass.: Harvard University Press.

Goodman, N. 1978. *Ways of worldmaking*. Cambridge, Mass.: Hackett Publishing.

————. 1982. *Fact, fiction, and forecast*. 4th ed. Cambridge, Mass.: Harvard University Press.

————. 1984. *Of mind and other matters*. Cambridge, Mass.: Harvard University Press.

Gould, W. P. 1977. *Black workers in white unions*. Ithaca, N.Y.: Cornell University Press.

Grandy, R. 1973. Reference, meaning and belief. *Journal of Philosophy* 70: 439–52.

Greenawalt, K. 1983. How empty is the idea of equality? *Columbia Law Review* 83:1167–85.

Gregory, D. 1978. *Science, ideology, and human geography*. London: Hutchinson.

Guterbock, T. M. 1980. *Machine politics in transition: Party and community in Chicago*. Chicago: University of Chicago Press.

Gutmann, A. 1980. *Liberal equality*. Cambridge: Cambridge University Press.

Habermas, J. 1979.*Communication and the evolution of society*. Boston, Mass.: Beacon Press.

————. 1984. *The theory of communicative action*, vol. 1: *Reason and the rationalization of society*, trans. T. McCarthy. Boston, Mass.: Beacon Press.

Hacking, I. 1975. *Why does language matter to philosophy?* Cambridge: Cambridge University Press.

————. 1982. Language, truth, and reason. In *Rationality and relativism*, ed. M. Hollis and S. Lukes. Cambridge, Mass.: MIT Press.

Hanson, R. 1982. *The evolution of national urban policy, 1970–80: Lessons from the past*. Washington, D.C.: National Academy Press.

Hanten, L. 1981. Bilingual education and school desegregation. In *Race and schooling in the city*, ed. A. Yarmolinsky, L. Liebman, and C. Schelling. Cambridge, Mass.: Harvard University Press.

Harcourt, G. C. 1972. *Some Cambridge controversies in the theory of capital*. Cambridge: Cambridge University Press.

Hardin, R. 1983. Morality within the limits of reason. Mimeo. Department of Philosophy, University of Chicago.

Hart, H. L. A. 1961. *The concept of law*. Oxford: Clarendon Press.

————. 1982. *Essays on Bentham*. Oxford: Oxford University Press.

Harvey, D. 1982. *The limits to capital*. Oxford: Basil Blackwell.

————. 1984. On the history and present condition of geography: An historical materialist manifesto. *The Professional Geographer* 36:1–10.

Hayden, D. 1976. *Seven American utopias: The architecture of communitarian socialism, 1790–1975*. Cambridge, Mass.: MIT Press.

————. 1981. *The grand domestic revolution: A history of feminist designs for American homes, neighborhoods, and cities*. Cambridge, Mass.: MIT Press.

Hirschman, A. 1970. *Exit, voice, and loyalty*. Cambridge, Mass.: Harvard University Press.

Hobbes, Thomas. *Leviathan*, ed. M. Oakeshott. London: Macmillan, 1962.

Hohfeld, W. 1913, 1917. Some fundamental legal conceptions as applied in judicial reasoning. *Yale Law Journal* 23:16–59, 26:710–66.

Horowitz, D. 1978. *The courts and social policy*. Washington D.C.: Brookings Institution.

Horwitz, M. 1975. The rise of legal formalism. *American Journal of Legal History*. 19:251–64.

————. 1977. *The transformation of American law, 1789–1860*. Cambridge, Mass.: Harvard University Press.

Huntington, S. 1981. *American politics: the promise of disharmony*. Cambridge, Mass.: Harvard University Press.

Inman, R. P. 1979. The fiscal performance of local governments: An interpretative review. In *Current issues of urban economics*, ed. P. Mieszkowski and M. Straszheim. Baltimore, Md.: Johns Hopkins University Press.

Johnson, M. 1979. Community income, intergovernmental grants, and local school district fiscal behavior. In *Fiscal federalism and grants-in-aid*, ed. P. Mieszkowski and W. Oakland. Washington, D.C.: Urban Institute.

Johnston, R. J. 1979. *Political, electoral, and spatial systems*. Oxford: Clarendon Press.

————. 1982. *Geography and the state*. London: Macmillan.

Kanter, R. M. 1972. *Committment and community: Communes and utopias in sociological perspective*. Cambridge, Mass.: Harvard University Press.

Keat, R., and J. Urry. 1982. *Social theory as science*. 2d ed. London: Routledge & Kegan Paul.

Kennedy, D. 1976. Form and substance in private law adjudication. *Harvard Law Review* 89:1685–778.

————. 1979. The structure of Blackstone's commentaries. *Buffalo Law Review* 29:205–381.

————. 1981. Cost-benefit analysis of entitlement problems: A critique. *Stanford Law Review* 33:387–94.

King, M. 1982. *Chains of change*. Cambridge, Mass.: MIT Press.

Kirby, A. 1983. Neglected factors in public services research: A comment on "Urban structure and geographical access to public services." *Annals, Association of American Geographers* 73:289–95.

Klemme, H. C. 1964. The powers of home rule cities in Colorado. *University of Colorado Law Review* 36:321–63.

Krouse, R. W. 1983. Classical images of democracy in America: Madison and Tocqueville. In *Democratic theory and practice*, ed. G. Duncan. Cambridge: Cambridge University Press.

Ladd, H. F. 1977. An economic evaluation of state limitations on local taxing and spending powers. Discussion paper D77–19. City and Regional Planning Program, Harvard University, Cambridge, Mass.

Lea, A. C. 1979. Welfare theory, public goods, and public facility location. *Geographical Analysis* 11:217–39.

Lewis, J. W. 1971. *Constitution of the State of Illinois and United States*. Springfield: State of Illinois.

Lloyd, P., and P. Dicken. 1977. *Location and space*. 2d ed. New York: Harper & Row.

Lowi, T. 1979. *The end of liberalism*. 2d ed. New York: W. W. Norton.

Lukes, S. 1982. Relativism in its place. In *Rationality and relativism*, ed. M. Hollis and S. Lukes. Cambridge, Mass.: MIT Press.

Maass, A. 1959. Division of powers: An areal analysis. In *Area and power: A theory of local government*, ed. A. Maass, Glencoe, Ill.: Free Press.

McBain, M. L. 1916. The doctrine of an inherent right of local self-government. *Columbia Law Review* 16:190–299.

MacIntyre, A. 1981. *After virtue*. Notre Dame, Ind.: University of Notre Dame Press.

MacKay, A. F. 1980. *Arrow's theorem: The paradox of social choice*. New Haven, Conn.: Yale University Press.

MacNeil, I. 1981. *The new social contract*. New Haven, Conn.: Yale University Press.

MacPherson, C. B. 1973. *Democratic theory*. Oxford: Oxford University Press.

McPherson, M. 1982. Mill's moral theory and the problem of preference change. *Ethics* 92:252–73.

McKenzie, R. B. 1981. The case for plant closures. *The Public Interest* 15:119–34.

———. 1984. *Fugitive industry: The economics and politics of deindustrialization.* Cambridge, Mass.: Ballinger.

McLafferty, S. 1982. Urban structure and geographical access to public services. *Annals, Association of American Geographers* 72:347–54.

Mandelker, D. R., and D. C. Netsch. 1977. *State and local government in a federal system: Cases and materials.* Indianapolis, Ind.: Bobbs-Merrill Co.

Mansbridge, J. J. 1980. *Beyond adversary democracy.* New York: Basic Books.

Marx, K. 1843. *On the jewish question.*

Manuel, F. E., and F. P. Manuel. 1979. *Utopian thought in the western world.* Cambridge, Mass.: Harvard University Press.

Meeks, J. E. 1981. Foreword. *Ohio State University Law Journal* 42:1–2.

Mercer, J. 1979. On continentalism, distinctiveness, and comparative urban geography: Canadian and American cities. *Canadian Geographer* 23:119–39.

———. 1982. Comparing the reform of metropolitan fragmentation, fiscal dependency and political culture in Canada and the United States. Mimeo. Metropolitan Studies Program, Syracuse University, Syracuse, N.Y.

Mercer, J., and M. Goldberg. 1983. The fiscal condition of American and Canadian cities. Mimeo. Department of Geography, Syracuse University, Syracuse, N.Y.

Michelman, F. I. 1977. Political markets and community self-determination: Competing judicial models of local government legitimacy. *Indiana Law Journal* 53:145–206.

Michelman, F., and T. Sandalow. 1970. *Materials on government in urban areas: Cases, comments, questions.* St. Paul, Minn.: West Publishing Co.

Miliband, R. 1969. *The state and capitalist society.* London: Quartet.

Miller, D. 1983. The competitive model of democracy. In *Democratic theory and practice*, ed. G. Duncan. Cambridge: Cambridge University Press.

Miller, R. 1983. The Hoover in the garden: Middle-class women and suburbanization, 1850–1920. *Environment and Planning D: Society and Space* 1:73–87.

Mills, C. W. 1957. *The power elite.* Oxford: Oxford University Press.

Morris, N. 1982. *Madness and the criminal law.* Chicago: University of Chicago Press.

Mueller, D. 1979. *Public choice.* Cambridge: Cambridge University Press.

Murdoch, I. 1983. *The philosopher's pupil.* London: Chatto & Windus.

Murphy, W. 1964. *Elements of judicial strategy.* Chicago: University of Chicago Press.

Nordlinger, E. 1981. *On the autonomy of the democratic state.* Cambridge, Mass.: Harvard University Press.

Nozick, R. 1974. *Anarchy, state, and utopia.* New York: Basic Books.

———. 1981. *Philosophical explanations.* Cambridge, Mass.: Harvard University Press.

Oakeshott, M. 1962. *Rationalism in politics.* London: Methuen.

Oates, W. E. 1979. Lump-sum intergovernmental grants have price effects. In *Fiscal federalism and grants-in-aid*, ed. P. Mieszkowski and W. H. Oakland. Washington, D.C.: Urban Institute.

———. 1981. On local finance and the Tiebout model. *American Economic Review* 71(2):93–98.

Ohio State Law Journal. 1981. Symposium: judicial review versus democracy. 42(1).

Olson, M. 1965. *The logic of collective action*. Cambridge, Mass.: Harvard University Press.

Olsson, G. 1976. *Birds in eggs, eggs in bird?* London: Pion.

O'Malley, T. M. 1980. A balancing analysis: The construction of Illinois home rule powers—*County of Cook v. John Sexton Contractors Company*. *Loyola University Law Journal* 11:543–75.

Ontario Economic Council. 1973. *Subject to approval: A review of municipal planning in Ontario*. Toronto.

Ontario Ministry of Housing. 1980*a*. *A Guide to the Planning Act*. Toronto: Local Planning Policy Branch, Programs Section.

————. 1980*b*. *A planner's reference to legislation in Ontario*. Toronto: Local Planning Policy Branch, Programs Section.

Ontario Municipal Board. 1980. *Seventy-fifth annual report of the Ontario Municipal Board*. Toronto.

Orfield, G. 1978. *Must we bus? Segregated schools and national policy*. Washington, D.C.: Brookings Institution.

Papageogiou, G. J. 1978. Political aspects of social justice and physical planning in an abstract city. *Geographical Analysis* 10:373–85.

Paris, C. 1983. Whatever happened to urban sociology? Critical reflections on *Social theory and the urban question*. *Environment and Planning D: Society and Space* 1:217–25.

Parry, G. 1982. Tradition, community, and self-determination. *British Journal of Political Science* 12:399–419.

Parsons, T. 1969. *Politics and social structure*. New York: Free Press.

Pateman, C. 1983. Feminism and democracy. In *Democratic theory and practice*, ed. G. Duncan. Cambridge: Cambridge University Press.

Perin, C. 1977. *Everything in its place*. Princeton, N.J.: Princeton University Press.

Perry, M. J. 1982. *The constitution, the courts, and human rights*. New Haven, Conn.: Yale University Press.

Peterson, P. 1981. *City limits*. Chicago: University of Chicago Press.

Plant, R. 1978. Community: concept, conception, and ideology. *Politics and Society* 8:79–107.

Pocock, J. G. A. 1975. *The machiavellian moment: Florentine political thought and the Atlantic republican tradition*. Princeton, N.J.: Princeton University Press.

Pollakowski, H. 1973. The effects of property taxes and local public spending on property values: A comment and further results. *Journal of Political Economy* 81:994–1003.

Posner, R. A. 1977. *Economic analysis of law*. Boston, Mass.: Little, Brown.

————. 1980. The value of wealth: A comment on Dworkin and Kronman. *Journal of Legal Studies* 8:243–52.

————. 1981*a*. A reply to some recent criticisms of the efficiency theory of the common law. *Hofstra Law Review* 9:775–94.

————. 1981*b*. *The economics of justice*. Cambridge, Mass.: Harvard University Press.

————. 1985. *The federal courts: Crisis and reform*. Cambridge, Mass.: Harvard University Press.

Poulantzas, N. 1978. *State, power, socialism*. London: New Left Books.

Pred, A. 1984. Place as historically contingent process: Structuration and the time-geography of becoming places. *Annals, Association of American Geographers* 74:279–97.

Putnam, H. 1981. *Reason, truth, and history*. Cambridge: Cambridge University Press.

———. 1983*a*. *Philosophical papers*, vol. 3: *Realism and reason*. Cambridge: Cambridge University Press.

———. 1983*b*. Is the causal structure of the physical itself something physical? Mimeo. Department of Philosophy, Harvard University, Cambridge, Mass.

Quine, W. 1953. *From a logical point of view*. Cambridge, Mass.: Harvard University Press.

———. 1960. *Word and object*. Cambridge, Mass.: MIT Press.

Rae, D., et al. 1981. *Equalities*. Cambridge, Mass.: Harvard University Press.

Rawls, J. 1971. *A theory of justice*. Cambridge, Mass: Harvard University Press.

Raz, J. 1979. *The authority of law: Essays on law and morality*. Oxford: Clarendon Press.

Richards, D. A. J. 1979. The theory of adjudication and the task of great judges. *Cardozo Law Review* 1:171–218.

———. 1981. Rights, utility, and crime. *Crime and justice: An annual review of research* 3:247–94.

Romanos, G. D. 1983. *Quine and analytical philosophy: The language of language*. Cambridge, Mass.: MIT Press.

Rorty, R. 1982. *Consequences of pragmatism*. Minneapolis: University of Minnesota Press.

Rose, C. M. ed. 1953. *Colorado revised statutes*, vol 1. Chicago: Callaghan & Co.

Rosen, S. 1969. *Nihilism: a philosophical essay*. New Haven, Conn.: Yale University Press.

Rowan, R. L., and L. Rubin 1972. *Opening the skilled construction trades to blacks: A study of the Washington and Indianapolis plans for minority employment*. Philadelphia: Industrial Research Unit, University of Pennsylvania.

Ryan, M. 1982. *Marxism and deconstruction: A critical articulation*. Baltimore, Md.: Johns Hopkins University Press.

Sack, R. 1983. Human territoriality: A theory. *Annals, Association of American Geographers* 73:55–74.

Sager, L. G. 1969. Tight little islands: Exclusionary zoning, equal protection, and the indigent. *Stanford Law Review* 21:767–800.

Said, E. W. 1983*a*. *The world, the text, and the critic*. Cambridge, Mass.: Harvard University Press.

———. 1983*b*. Opponents, audiences, constituencies, and community. In *The politics of interpretation*, ed. W. J. T. Mitchell. Chicago: University of Chicago Press.

Samuelson, P. 1954. The pure theory of public expenditures. *Review of Economics and Statistics* 36:387–98.

Sandalow, T. 1964. The limits of municipal power under home rule: A role for the courts. *Minnesota Law Review* 48:643–721.

Sandel, M. J. 1982. *Liberalism and the limits of justice*. Cambridge: Cambridge University Press.

———. 1983. The procedural republic and the unencumbered self. Mimeo. Department of Government, Harvard University, Cambridge, Mass.

Saunders, P. 1980. *Urban politics*. Harmondsworth: Penguin Books.

———. 1981. *Social theory and the urban question*. London: Hutchinson.

————. 1983. On the shoulders of which giant? The case for Weberian political analysis. In *Social process and the city*. Urban studies yearbook 1, ed. P. Williams. Sydney: George Allen & Unwin.

Scanlon, T. M. 1976. Nozick on rights, liberty, and property. *Philosophy and Public Affairs* 6:3–25.

Schmitter, P., and G. Lehmbruch, eds. 1979. *Trends toward corporatist intermediation*. Beverly Hills, Calif.: Sage Publications.

Scott, A. J. 1983. Editorial. *Environment and Planning D: Society and Space* 1:119–20.

Scott, F. R., and W. R. Lederman. 1972. A memorandum concerning housing, urban development, and the Constitution of Canada. *Plan Canada* 12:33–44.

Select Committee on the Ontario Municipal Board. 1972. *Report of the Select Committee on the Ontario Municipal Board*. Toronto: Legislature of Ontario.

Sen, A. 1982. Rights and agency. *Philosophy and Public Affairs* 11:3–39.

————. 1983. Liberty and social choice. *Journal of Philosophy* 80:5–29.

Sen, A., and B. Williams, eds. 1982. *Utilitarianism and beyond*. Cambridge: Cambridge University Press.

Sheppard, E. 1981. Comment on altruism and individualism in analysing the law. *Environment and Planning A* 13:1230–32.

Simeon, R. 1977. Current constitutional issues. In *Issues and alternatives, 1977: Intergovernmental relations*. Toronto: Ontario Economic Council.

Simmons, A. J. 1979. *Moral principles and political obligations*. Princeton, N.J.: Princeton University Press.

Smith, D. M. 1977. *Human geography: A welfare approach*. London: Ed. Arnold.

Stokey, E., and R. Zeckhauser. 1978. *A primer for policy analysis*. New York: W. W. Norton.

Stone, M. E. 1978. Housing, mortgage lending, and the contradictions of capitalism. In *Marxism and the metropolis*, ed. W. Tabb and L. Sawyers. New York: Oxford University Press.

Suttles, G. 1972. *The social construction of communities*. Chicago: University of Chicago Press.

Taub, R., and D. Taub, eds. 1974. *American society in Tocqueville's time and today*. Chicago: Rand-McNally.

Taylor, M. 1982. *Community, anarchy, and liberty*. Cambridge: Cambrdige University Press.

Thomas, J. L. 1983. *Alternative America: Henry George, Edward Bellamy, Henry Demarest Lloyd, and the adversary tradition*. Cambridge, Mass.: Harvard University Press.

Thompson, E. P. 1975. *Whigs and hunters: The origin of the Black Act*. New York: Pantheon.

Thrall, G. I. 1979. Public goods and the derivation of land value assessment schedules within a spatial equilibrium setting. *Geographical Analysis* 11:21–35.

Thrift, N. 1983*a*. On the determination of social action in space and time. *Environment and Planning D: Society and space* 1:23–58.

————. 1983*b*. Editorial: The politics of context. *Environment and Planning D: Society and Space* 1:371–76.

De Tocqueville, A. 1969. *Democracy in America*, trans. G. Lawrence and ed. J. P. Mayer. New York: Anchor Books.

Tiebout, C. M. 1956. A pure theory of local expeditures. *Journal of Political Economy* 64:416–24.

Tooke, C. W. 1933. Construction and operation of municipal powers. *Temple Law Quarterly* 7:267–89.

Tribe, L. H. 1980. The puzzling persistence of process-based constitutional theories. *Yale Law Journal* 89:1063–80.

———. 1985. *Constitutional choices.* Cambridge, Mass.: Harvard University Press.

Tuck, R. 1979. *Natural rights theories: Their origins and development.* Cambridge: Cambridge University Press.

Tushnet, M. 1980. Darkness on the edge of town: The contributions of John Hart Ely to constitutional theory. *Yale Law Journal* 80:1037–62.

———. 1983. Following the rules laid down: A critique of interpretivism and neutral principles. *Harvard Law Review* 96:871–927.

Unger, R. M. 1975. *Knowledge and politics.* New York: Free Press.

———. 1983. The critical legal studies movement. *Harvard Law Review* 96:561–675.

U.S. Department of Housing and Urban Development. 1982. *The President's national urban policy report.* Washington, D.C.: Government Printing Office.

Vanlandingham, K. 1975. Constitutional municipal home rule since the AMA (NLC) model. *William and Mary Law Review* 17:1–34.

Walzer, M. 1983. Philosophy and democracy. In *What should political theory be now?* ed. J. S. Nelson. Albany, N.Y.: State University of New York Press.

Warner, S. B. 1968. *The private city: Philadelphia in three periods of its growth.* Philadelphia: University of Pennsylvania Press.

Warwick, D. P. 1981. The ethics of administrative discretion. In *Public duties: The moral obligations of government officials*, ed. J. L. Fleishman, L. Liebman, and M. H. Moore, Cambridge, Mass.: Harvard University Press.

Westen, P. 1982. The empty idea of equality. *Harvard Law Review* 95:537–96.

———. 1983*a*. To lure the tarantula from its hole: A response. *Columbia Law Review* 83:1186–1208.

———. 1983*b*. The meaning of equality in law, science, math, and morals: A reply. *Michigan Law Review* 81:604–63.

Whiteman, J. 1983. Deconstructing the Tiebout hypothesis. *Environment and Planning D: Society and Space* 1:339–53.

Wigner, E. 1982. The limitations of the validity of present-day physics. In *Mind in nature*, ed. R. Q. Elvee. New York: Harper & Row.

Williams, B. 1972. *Morality: An introduction to ethics.* New York: Harper & Row.

———. 1979. Another time, another place, another person. In *Perceptions and identity*, ed. G. F. MacDonald. Ithaca, N.Y.: Cornell University Press.

———. 1981. *Moral luck.* Cambridge: Cambridge University Press.

Wittgenstein, L. 1953. *Philosophical investigations*, trans. G. Anscombe. London: Macmillan.

Wolch, J. 1979. Residential location and the provision of human services: Some directions for geographic research. *The Professional Geographer* 31:271–77.

Wolff, R. P., ed. 1971. *The rule of law.* New York: Simon & Schuster.

Wood, R. 1970. Intergovernmental relationships in an urbanizing America. In *Towards a national urban policy*, ed. D. P. Moynihan. New York: Basic Books.

Yarmolinsky, A., L. Liebman, and C. Schelling, eds. 1981. *Race and schooling in the city.* Cambridge, Mass.: Harvard University Press.

Yates, D. 1977. *The ungovernable city: The politics of urban problems and policymaking.* Cambridge, Mass.: MIT Press.

Yinger, J. 1979. Prejudice and discrimination in the urban housing market. In *Current issues in urban economics*, ed. P. Mieszkowski and M. Straszheim. Baltimore, Md.: Johns Hopkins University Press.

———. 1981. Capitalization and the median voter. *American Economic Review* 71(2):99–103.

Young, G. 1977. Financing local government. In *Issues and alternatives 1977: Intergovernmental relations*. Toronto: Ontario Economic Council.

Index

243